CONTENTS

Contents

UNDERBELLY
TRUE CRIME STORIES

Published in Australia by
Floradale Productions Pty Ltd and Sly Ink Pty Ltd
November 1997
Reprinted Feb 1998, June 1999, Nov 1999, June 2000, June 2001, March 2002, Dec 2003
Aug 2005, April 2007, April 2008, August 2008

Distributed wholesale by
Gary Allen Pty Ltd,
9 Cooper Street,
Smithfield, NSW
Telephone 02-9725 2933

Underbelly
True Crime Stories

ISBN – 0 646 3392.4.9

Cover design by Chris Rule
Typesetting and layout by Write Impression Publishing

ŭ′nderbĕllў *n.* Under surface of animal thing, esp. as area vulnerable to attack. UNDER- 4 + BELLY[1]]

THE AUTHORS

John Silvester has been a crime reporter in
Melbourne since 1978. He worked for The
Sunday Times 'Insight' team in London in
1990, and has co-authored several crime
books. He is currently a senior reporter
for The Sunday Age.

Andrew Rule has been a journalist since
1975 and has worked in newspapers,
television and radio. He wrote *Cuckoo*,
the true story of the notorious 'Mr Stinky'
case, and has edited and published several
other books. He is a feature writer for
The Sunday Age.

CHAPTER 1

Who killed Jenny Tanner?
How police ignored a murder

*'Many suspect they know who really
pulled the trigger, and it frightens them'*

BONNIE Doon is a pair of road signs sandwiching a motel, store, service station and a few houses scattered beside the Maroondah Highway where it crosses the northern tip of Lake Eildon in Victoria's high country.

It would flatter this humdrum collection of buildings, imply some non-existent charm, to call it a hamlet. To all but a few locals who get their beer, bread and mail there, it's an irritating slow spot on the main road to the Mount Buller snowfields beyond Mansfield, twenty minutes drive further east.

In summer, the place hums with activity and outboard motors as visitors swarm in from the highway to fish and water-ski on the vast man-made lake, a tangle of drowned river valleys sprawled among the brooding mountains that stretch to the horizon. The rest of the year, the district drifts back to sleep.

Holiday houses and retirement retreats have crept into the valley, perching on blocks carved from properties whose titles date to the gold rushes.

But the bleak, granite-scarred ridges rising like battlements each side of the valley are as lonely today as they were when the diggers left five generations ago. Gold reefs run along hilltops, so the shafts the miners left behind are on the crest of the ridge.

Up here, where the only sound is wind whimpering through stunted gums that cling to the shale slopes, a wandering farmer or hunter might occasionally disturb kangaroos and rabbits.

But few know exactly where the old shafts are.

It's almost the perfect place to get rid of a body ...

That would mean going the long way, around a winding back track from Lake Eildon. Or taking a shortcut through farmland, which would mean getting a horse, tractor or four-wheel-drive to carry the bleeding burden uphill through steep back paddocks to its deep and lonesome grave.

In 1978, someone did. And, for nearly two decades, the mine kept its secret.

SIX years later, in 1984, there was another violent death in Bonnie Doon. A young wife and mother was found, shot dead, with her husband's rifle placed between her knees.

At first, the district wondered why one of its own would commit suicide. More than a decade later, some still talk about it, though mostly behind closed doors, and rarely to strangers.

But, later, the talk was not so much why she would commit suicide, but how the case could ever have been considered anything but murder. Many suspect they know who really pulled the trigger, and it frightens them.

It happened late in the spring, on a property called Springfield, which runs south from the highway towards the same ridge where there is an old mine known as the Jack of Clubs.

Around 7.30 pm on 14 November, a Wednesday night, Laurie Tanner drove out the front gate of the property, where he and his younger brothers had grown up, and which his family had farmed for generations. The 39-year-old shearer and fencing contractor, known more as a hard worker than a deep thinker, was going to Mansfield to clean a shop, a part-time job he shared with his second wife, Jennifer, known to her family as Jenny.

He left just after *Sale of the Century* ended on television, first kissing his 21-month-old son. As he was going, Jennifer asked him to buy bread, milk, the local paper and 'a surprise', meaning a chocolate bar. In the following months and years, this cheerful last-minute request might have struck investigators as unlikely to have been made by a woman supposedly about to kill herself.

After finishing the cleaning job, Tanner had other chores to do. As president of the Mansfield Show Society, he had to prepare for the annual show the following Saturday. He drove around the showgrounds to check a new arena fence.

Soon after 9 pm, he dropped in on friends, 'Curly' and Angie McCormack, to discuss other arrangements for the big day. When he arrived, Angie mentioned she had just been chatting to Jenny on the telephone. 'About babies,' she would later testify.

Laurie Tanner left just after 10 pm, he testified later. At home, he found his own little bit of hell.

He would later give police his stilted recollection of what happened: 'I ... walked in the back door, put the milk, bread, Courier (newspaper) and Cherry Ripes on the kitchen table.

'The TV was going, and I noticed through the loungeroom door, which was open, Jenny on the couch, covered in blood and the rifle between her legs.

'I didn't think there was anything I could do for her. I believed, from the way she looked, she was dead. I'm not sure exactly what I did, but I'm pretty sure I checked the baby and found that he was asleep in bed.

'I rang the ambulance and said there had been a death in the house ... I then rang Hughie Almond, my neighbor. I didn't say what was wrong. I just said that I needed help and could he come straight down.

'I met him at the back door and told him to prepare himself for a shock. I ushered him in, and he nearly collapsed when he saw her. He sat me down at the table and went into the lounge.

'When he came out he said he didn't think there was anything we could do. He asked who I'd called, and I said the ambulance.

Hughie then rang the Mansfield police.'

WHEN Senior Constables Bill Kerr and Don Frazer reached the farmhouse, a shaken Laurie Tanner and his neighbor were drinking whisky from a bottle the latter had fetched from his house across the highway.

The ambulance had arrived a little earlier, at 10.40pm, but apart from ensuring the woman was dead, there was nothing the driver, Gerard O'Donnell, could do until the policemen had finished their grim routine in the loungeroom.

At first glance it looked like a classic suicide, although Kerr was surprised the victim had chosen to use a rifle: he knew women almost invariably choose gentler exits, such as drug overdoses.

He was surprised, too, at the amount of blood, as if she had moved violently before dying. And he did not know why, given nothing had been touched, there was a blood-soaked towel to the left of the body – and, further away, a blood-stained cushion, looking as if something had been wiped on it.

The victim's left hand was wrapped around the rifle barrel, according to Kerr and Frazer's subsequent statements. This was puzzling, because she had bullet wounds to both hands, which seemed to indicate they had been in front of her forehead when the gun was fired.

There were other things that, in hindsight, didn't jell to Kerr. On the floor near the body was a half-drunk cup of coffee, and a plate with three biscuits on it. Nearby, a wet disposable nappy and a tin of nappy powder. There was no suicide note.

Kerr picked up the rifle. Underneath the trigger guard was a spent bullet case. He worked the bolt to open the breech; the ejector spat out another shell.

Two empty shells. Did that mean two shots? Laurie Tanner later said he often stored the rifle with an empty shell in the breech. An unusual habit that might explain the presence of two empty shells in the room ... that is, if only one shot had been fired by the victim. Or at her. In the magazine were two live hollow-point bullets, making it almost certain that the empty shells had also been hollow-points.

A hollow point gives a .22 cartridge extra hitting power because the slug spreads on impact. The odds against surviving one through the forehead at close range are long.

Even if she had survived, a pathologist surmised afterwards, the likelihood of being knocked senseless by the impact made it unlikely she could work the bolt with four separate movements to eject the spent shell and re-load a live round, let alone reverse the rifle and neatly shoot herself again. All these thoughts were to niggle Kerr during the next twelve years. But that was later. That night, as the minutes ticked towards midnight, there was work to be done.

He'd already done one job soon after arriving. That was to call the nearest Criminal Investigation Branch, at Alexandra, far enough away for the detective sergeant on the line to decide not to go to what he later said sounded like a simple suicide. Kerr described the scene, and asked if photographs should be taken before anything was disturbed.

The detective sergeant made a decision over the telephone that helped skew the investigation of Jenny Tanner's death from that moment. No photographs. No forensic tests. No fingerprinting. And no order to preserve the scene.

According to evidence Kerr was to give many years later, at a second inquest into Jenny Tanner's death in October, 1997, he telephoned the detective sergeant again that night, when he found the second empty shell.

He did this, he told a packed coroner's court, because he found it hard to believe that anyone could shoot themselves twice with a bolt-action rifle. He was surprised when the detective sergeant had again said there was no need to order photographs or forensic tests, or to preserve the scene. The detective sergeant said he still thought – based on Kerr's original description of the scene – that it was a suicide.

The word 'suicide' – repeated to each new person introduced to the case – settled over the tragedy like a shroud, obscuring the body of evidence. So when Dr Ross Gilham, called from Mansfield, arrived just after midnight formally to pronounce life extinct, he did exactly that, and no more. Some later wondered if the doctor took more than a cursory glance at the scene. He was known by locals more for his erratic behavior than his medical skill, and was later charged with injecting himself with drugs.

Judging from Dr Gilham's brief statement, he did not notice anything odd about the body – in fact, there was so much blood and matter covering the victim's head that he totally missed the forehead wound, and assumed she had placed the barrel in her mouth.

A reason for this might be that a policeman, the doctor claimed in his later statement, told him 'the rifle had been placed between the woman's legs with both hands holding the barrel … in her mouth.' By the time the doctor inspected the body, the weapon had been placed to one side. Curiously, the neighbor, Hugh Almond, did not recall seeing the rifle barrel in the woman's mouth.

When Kerr and Frazer drove off into the dark to face the worst job of the policeman's unhappy lot – the 'death knock' to break the news every parent dreads – they kept any twinges of doubt to themselves.

In two hours, a fatal shooting had become just another sad domestic incident, to be settled as discreetly as possible, for the benefit of all concerned. Almost all.

'JEN had never given us a moment's worry,' Kath Blake was to say often of the eldest of her four daughters. The one who, had she lived, would have turned 40 in 1997.

Les and Kath Blake lost more than their first-born the night the police brought the news; they lost peace of mind. Hardly a day goes past that they don't think about their 'Jen' … and wonder how she really died.

The Blakes are a close family. The girls grew up in the spotless white weatherboard house hidden behind huge elms in a picture postcard spot on the Delatite River flats, exactly twelve kilometres south of Mansfield. They moved the house from Dingley in the 1960s, after Les started managing the Mansfield sawmill.

After 30 years, they're 'nearly locals', they joke. They have been robbed of happiness, but not their sense of humor, nor a sense of proportion. This calm absence of bitterness makes them powerful witnesses.

Les Blake is tall, fit for his age, and still has some of the physical toughness of a man used to hard work. His wife is small, with inquiring eyes, a sharp mind and a strong character.

Of the two, Les seems more philosophical about their daughter's death. Nothing, he says gently, will fix things up. Not revenge, not even seeing the case reinvestigated, could lighten the loss.

'We have never rocked the boat much because of Jen's little boy,' he says carefully of the child, who lives with his father in Mansfield. 'We don't point the finger at anyone.'

His wife agrees. But she craves the truth about her girl's death. Les leans forward in his chair and says: 'Whatever you write, we've got that grandson there.' It's half warning, half plea.

Suddenly, he adds: 'But one day he's going to want to know what really happened to his mother.'

A snapshot of the boy and his dog is stuck to their refrigerator door. Above it a fridge magnet bears the words: 'A friend is someone who has the same enemies as you.'

Les and Kath Blake sit at the same timber table – underneath the same picture of the Sacred Heart on the wall – as the grim-faced policemen did the night they brought the news all those years ago, and relive it the thousandth time.

'They said,' Les recalls softly, they said, 'Jennifer's shot herself'.'

The Blakes didn't believe it then, and still don't. It would make their lives easier to accept suicide as an explanation, and let it rest, but time has hardened the belief they rarely put into words.

Their girl was murdered.

NOTHING the Blakes were told about Jennifer's death rang true to them. She had no reason to commit suicide, they insist.

Even if she had wanted to kill herself, she wouldn't use a gun. And if she did use a gun, she would not shoot herself twice in the head … through the hands. Apart from everything else, it seemed almost a physical impossibility.

'Jen hated guns,' says her mother. 'We always had a hatred of firearms, and instilled it in our children. When she was first married and Laurie used his rifle to kill a snake, instead of a shovel or something, she was so surprised she rang and told us. She didn't like the way he'd go to the back door and fire off shots to stop his dogs barking.

'She wasn't dexterous. She was very left-handed, and would have had great trouble trying to use a bolt-action rifle. And she didn't like blood. She nearly passed out once when she cut herself shaving her legs in the bathroom. Why would she shoot herself through the hands?'

Nothing in Jennifer's behavior indicated to her parents, sisters or friends that she was dangerously depressed. Later, a coroner would accept some vague evidence from her husband and from her doctor, Dr Geoffrey Patience, about her emotional state and her supposed difficulties with her child.

But Dr Patience readily conceded, both under cross-examination and privately afterwards, that his comments would have been different had he had any reason to question the apparently firm police assumption that it was a suicide. At no point did police tell him that there were two bullets found in her skull, something he hadn't known until twelve years later, when a 'Sunday Age' reporter told him. Had he known that, he said, he would have rejected outright any suggestion her death was suicide.

Some facts. The Saturday before her death, Jennifer Tanner went to a clearing sale with her mother and was delighted to buy an antique jug for herself, and two small tables for her son's room.

The following Monday, she went to Melbourne with her mother and sister, Clare, to do Christmas shopping. She wanted to buy a plug-in car 'fridge' for Laurie to use for his lunch when he was shearing.

She ordered furniture for her son's bedroom and bought him a pair of sandals. She called on her grandmother and asked her to come to Springfield for Christmas dinner.

She promised her grandmother she'd be back soon to finish her shopping, and that she 'couldn't wait' for her Christmas Club cheque to arrive. She was delighted to have saved $100 on the furniture, and said she'd put it towards a Christmas holiday at Cowes.

To the Blakes, all this was evidence of her commitment to family and future – as was an earlier visit to a Melbourne specialist to discuss if she could become pregnant again. It contrasted starkly with Laurie's recollections of his wife before her death.

He claimed that she had suffered from 'post-natal depression', but that her parents, sisters and friends didn't know about it because 'she covered it up pretty well'.

On the day she died, Jennifer hosted a playgroup of children and their mothers at home, and seemed normal and happy. The last person known to talk to her was Angela McCormack, whose husband had dialled the Tanners' number around 9 pm, looking for his friend Laurie, then handed over to his wife a few minutes later. Angela McCormack spoke to her for about 20 minutes, and later said she had sounded cheerful. Jenny Tanner had at least two other telephone calls that day. One, about 3.30 pm, had been to a close friend in Queensland, Rosslyn Smith, to tell her about the antique jug she'd bought.

Rosslyn was relieved that Jennifer was much happier than she had been when she had called three weeks earlier.

The second call came around 5 pm, according to evidence given later. It was Laurie's brother, Denis, then a police sergeant stationed in Melbourne. Sergeant Tanner spoke briefly to Jennifer, then to his brother. In his later statement to the inquest, he said he talked to Laurie about getting a horse broken in.

SOMEBODY knew Laurie Tanner's movements, and what vehicle he drove, judging by strange events in the weeks before his wife's death. One night Laurie and Jennifer arrived home after dinner at her parents' house to find Laurie's valuable kelpie working dog shot dead. The Blakes noted later that a detective came from Alexandra to make a report on the dog's death – but didn't turn up the night their daughter was killed.

The detective's line of inquiry about the dog was whether Laurie had 'an enemy'. Laurie could not think of any. There were two possible explanations: either he did have an unknown enemy, or someone wanted to make it look that way. Either way, it's easier to sneak up on farmhouses without barking dogs.

There was another night-time incident, one that prompted Jennifer to telephone her mother the morning after it happened.

The previous night, when Laurie would normally have been at an Apex meeting, a car had come up the drive. The Tanners were in bed. Laurie went to a window, and saw the car reversing quickly; with someone running behind it.

Jennifer told her mother it seemed the intruders had fled when they recognised Laurie's car and realised he was home.

THREE weeks before her best friend was killed, Rosslyn Smith took a call that she still recalls clearly thirteen years later.

About 11 am on 23 October, 1984, the telephone rang at her home at Sorrento Waters, on Queensland's Gold Coast. It was Jenny Tanner.

They had known each other since going to the convent together in Mansfield, they had taken holidays together before they married, and stayed in touch since.

Long-distance charges did not stop Jenny from calling often.

But, according to Rosslyn Smith's sworn statement later tendered to the inquest, this time it was no idle chat.

The previous night, when her husband was at one of his meetings, Jenny had gone out the back door to get firewood when she was surprised to find her brother-in-law, Denis, standing on the step. She hadn't heard a car arrive.

She invited him in, and asked what he was doing in Bonnie Doon. He said he'd had a fight with his wife, and had told her (his wife) he was going to the races, but that he wanted to 'go shooting'. He then asked for Laurie's rifle, according to Rosslyn Smith's statement.

'Jennifer said she went to the bedroom and obtained the rifle with bullets and gave it to Denis.'

He declined her offer of coffee, and went with her into the bedroom when she put the baby to bed, according to the statement.

'Once (the child) was in bed, Jennifer and Denis returned to the loungeroom where Denis asked Jennifer if she was leaving Laurie. She stated that she wasn't. She asked him where she had heard this, and he said, 'a friend'.'

Before he left, Jennifer told Rosslyn, Denis had asked her not to tell Laurie about the visit or the conversation. But she had immediately reported both to her husband when he got home.

When Laurie was asked at the first inquest a year later about the conversation with his wife, he said that Denis had walked across for a friendly chat and cup of coffee after delivering some building materials. (Denis had testified: 'I did not mention to the deceased that I had gone there to go shooting ... I did not look at any of Laurie's guns ... I didn't inquire into the deceased's private life.') Not in the witness box, nor in his original statement to police, did Laurie Tanner say Jennifer had told him about Denis handling the rifle and talking of marriage splits.

Laurie Tanner was not cross-examined about the puzzling difference between his story and Rosslyn Smith's. Despite the subsequent open finding, Rosslyn was relieved her ordeal had ended. She had been nervous about giving evidence. 'I had nightmares … for the whole eleven months until the inquest,' she was to confide years later.

THE oldest and youngest of the four Tanner brothers were opposites in temperament, and to look at. Laurie was thin, gangly and quiet. Denis wasn't. In the police force he earned the nickname 'Lard' and a reputation as a knockabout cop.

People who knew both regarded Denis as the dominant brother.

In an inversion of most sibling relationships, it was the younger brother who acted as a protector for the less worldly Laurie.

Laurie had been married before, and it had ended in divorce.

When he remarried the much younger Jennifer, according to evidence Denis was to give at the inquest, he borrowed money to buy out his parents and brothers so that he and Jennifer owned Springfield outright.

Denis used his part of the proceeds to take a third share of the neighboring property, Stanleys, with his parents. He regularly came up from Melbourne, and the two brothers and their father worked the properties together.

For all their outward stability, and Jennifer's determination to have another child, there was probably friction in the marriage, as in many others. But not enough friction, say her parents and close friends, that she would seriously contemplate leaving her husband. Let alone commit suicide.

WHEN Senior Constable Kerr typed what police cryptically call an '83', the formal notice of death to the coroner, he stopped at the space where the familiar words 'no suspicious circumstances' are usually inserted. He left it blank.

Two days later, in his opinion, his instinct was proved right. But some of his superiors disagreed.

The post-mortem examination was done on Friday morning at Shepparton, a 24-hour delay later criticised by the coroner.

Part-way through it, the pathologist, Dr Peter Dyte, stopped to call Mansfield police with what he obviously thought was interesting information. He was put through to a telephone to which Kerr had attached a tape recorder. He greeted Dr Dyte, then handed the handpiece to a Sergeant Neil Phipps, a big, bluff man who had once worked in the Homicide Squad.

Kerr kept the tape, along with several others he made in what became one man's attempt to investigate a death other police ignored.

The taped conversation reveals how key officers enthusiastically embraced the assumption of suicide, and dismissed more likely possibilities.

Dr Dyte, described by his colleagues as a shy and obliging man, opens hesitantly: 'I was just ringing up to confirm that you had no suspicions about this death.'

Sergeant Phipps, confidently: 'No, we haven't ... What, ah, seems to be the trouble?'

Dyte: 'I thought I'd just talk to you before we complete the post mortem, just to check, really. There's certainly two definite wounds in the forehead.'

When Phipps doesn't answer, he adds quickly: 'Which would be quite possible. She could still be alive after the first one.'

Phipps: 'You are satisfied she would have lived after the first one.'

Dyte, nervously: 'Well, I am saying it's possible.'

After finishing the autopsy, Dr Dyte immediately calls again to say he had found two bullets in the brain. Despite this, he nervously assents to Phipps's suggestion that 'there's a strong possibility she would be alive after the first bullet'.

The sergeant, trying to explain the hand wounds, theorises that the victim had pushed the trigger with her toe. There is no discussion of the possibility of foul play – or of tests to check for gun residue on either hands or feet. Decisions against that had already been made by Alexandra CIB, an attitude supported by other senior officers.

Instead, the sergeant asks if the body will be ready soon because 'the family' (meaning the Tanners) was anxious to make funeral arrangements.

Jennifer was buried next day, just 60 hours after her death. Her mother, a devout Catholic, resented the fact that Denis Tanner made all the arrangements and that her daughter was to have a Protestant service.

After the funeral, the mourners drove to the Blakes' house for a brief wake. Jennifer's sister Christine approached Laurie Tanner sympathetically to tell him the family had been to the undertaker's to view the body and 'say goodbye'.

Mrs Blake recalls that before Laurie could answer, Denis snapped: 'Laurie doesn't want to hear any of that,' and shepherded his older brother away. She also recalls that one of the four Tanner brothers shepherded their father, Fred Tanner, away from the Blakes. Mr Tanner senior had been a daily visitor to Springfield, often had lunch with Jennifer, and had been very close to her.

Meanwhile, the investigation proceeded entirely on the basis of what Dr Dyte called the 'possibility' of suicide. Five months later, on 30 April, 1985, Detective Sergeant Ian Welch took the trouble to drive from Alexandra to Shepparton to get Dr Dyte to 'clarify' his opinion that suicide was possible, and to make some additions to his report to reflect that.

Dr Dyte, who was suffering a terminal illness that ultimately prevented him attending the inquest, was characteristically helpful. But he later seemed to have misgivings about the way his report was being interpreted.

When Jennifer's sister, Miriam Blake, spoke to him just before the inquest opened in October, he told her the family had 'a good case' to argue that she had been murdered.

It seemed that the pleasant Dr Dyte had either changed his mind, or tended to agree with whoever he was talking to.

Dr Terry Schultz, a pathologist called at the first inquest, was not so flexible. He said, after reviewing Dr Dyte's post mortem findings, 'it's virtually impossible that it's suicide.'

When Dr Kevin Lee, one of the world's leading gunshot wound experts, was to study details of Jennifer Tanner's death years later. His conclusion was even blunter: 'It's a homicide until proven otherwise.'

BILL KERR was as surprised as almost everyone else when the pathologist found two bullets. He had been uneasy. Now, like a few other local police, he was suspicious. He ran through the 'suicide' scenario.

Jennifer Tanner had asked her husband to bring home milk, bread and chocolates, chatted on the telephone, changed her baby's nappy, made a cup of coffee and got some biscuits to settle down in front of the television ... then suddenly decided to shoot herself in the head. Twice. With a bolt-action rifle that had to be manually operated for each shot. Without leaving a note.

It sounded outrageously unlikely. But trying to prove otherwise was not easy. Already, the best chance of gathering evidence had gone, with the scene cleaned up, no photographs, no tests, the body buried.

One thing Kerr had was the rifle. But each time he requested forensic tests in the following weeks, it was ignored by his superiors. 'They kept saying it wasn't warranted.'

Bill Kerr remembers asking for certain people to be interviewed in Melbourne – and to have particular questions put to them.

But when they were interviewed, key questions were not asked, he claimed. Instead, they were allowed to make simple statements that avoided vital points.

He tried as much as a prudent country copper can in a big bureaucracy riddled with the usual bureaucratic ills: jealousies, inefficiency, apathy and maddeningly slow procedure. There are 'proper channels', but they are easily blocked.

Frustrated, he contacted Rosslyn Smith in Queensland on his own initiative – and discreetly arranged for Queensland police to interview her about what Jennifer had revealed to her. He got her statement in record time – then was 'rapped over the knuckles' for sending the request direct to Queensland instead of through the chain of command.

It was, Kerr later mused, 'like one bloke against the system'.

He started to keep his doubts to himself. A police station, like a schoolyard, can be hard on those at the bottom of the pecking order. He did not want to stir up more trouble than he already had.

Which is one reason, when he visited Les and Kath Blake a week after the funeral, that he did not tell them their daughter had been shot twice.

They didn't find that out for ten months, and then only because a friend was married to a policeman who persuaded Kerr to tell the Blakes all the facts.

Facts that should have turned her death into a homicide investigation. But, by then, it was far too late to unravel.

Even for the coroner at the first inquest.

THE day after the funeral, Laurie Tanner came to the Mansfield police station to make a formal statement. Denis came with him.

Kerr asked the Tanners into the mess room. He used a tape recorder to record the conversation. The recording was muffled, but Kerr remembered nonchalantly asking Denis Tanner where he'd been on the night Jennifer died.

Tanner, Kerr later testified on oath, said he had been at 'the trots', an answer at least one other policeman then stationed at Mansfield also heard about that week.

Kerr did not attach any great significance to Denis Tanner's alibi – until ten months later, just before the inquest was to start, when he read a deposition made by a Melbourne bookmaker, John Francis O'Hanlon, which appeared to give Tanner a different alibi.

O'Hanlon's deposition stated in vague terms that Tanner had spent the evening 'minding' a bingo night at the Carmelite Hall in Richardson Street, Middle Park, a job he sometimes did on the side. This technically breached police regulations.

The deposition was made on 16 October 1985, eleven months after the shooting and just two days before the inquest was to open.

It was witnessed by Senior Sergeant Peter Fleming, the police prosecutor who appeared at the inquest to assist the coroner.

O'Hanlon's deposition was vague about days, dates and times.

It read, in part: 'I have been asked to recall a bingo night at the Carmelite Hall in Richardson Street, Middle Park, in approximately the months of November or December last year (1984).

'In particular, I have been asked to recall the bingo evening that I said farewell to Mr and Mrs Keith Brown. I can't remember the date exactly, but it was after the Melbourne Cup ... I can't remember whether it was a Wednesday or a Friday night, but I can vaguely remember Denis Tanner standing at the back of the Browns ...

'We had been held up by a gunman previously, and Denis was there to assist the committee. I can't recall any conversation I had with Denis that night ...'

Then, half way through making the statement, O'Hanlon apparently became more certain of dates, faces and names. If Sergeant Fleming noticed this sudden improvement, he did not comment on it.

'After thinking about it (continued O'Hanlon's statement) I am pretty sure it would have been a Wednesday night, and it would have been the Wednesday week after the Melbourne Cup ... I can't remember whether Denis went to the bank with the committee or not, but he has on occasions escorted us with the takings to the bank.'

John 'Jack' Francis O'Hanlon is now dead. But his son, John, also a bookmaker, remembers Denis Tanner well from when the policeman was stationed at South Melbourne in the late 1970s and early 1980s.

'Denis did quite a lot of work with my father,' he told a journalist years later. 'Dad used to run functions and Denis used to help out on the door. He and other police often used to come around.'

THE legal firm of Mal Ryan, Jackson and Glen has been in Mansfield since last century, and in that time has acted in the routine legal affairs of generations of the Tanner family and their relatives. So when a date was finally announced for Jennifer Tanner's inquest, the firm naturally gave first offer of its services to Laurie Tanner.

The Tanners, however, had already made a decision. Mal Ryan, Jackson and Glen was told that Denis Tanner had already hired a well-known Melbourne barrister, Joe Gullaci, often instructed by the Police Association on behalf of its members.

Instead, the Blakes engaged Mal Ryan, Jackson and Glen. They instructed a solicitor, Rodney Ryan, that they wanted an open finding. They said they did not know who killed their daughter, only that she did not do it herself.

The fact the Blakes engaged a solicitor at all seemed to anger the Tanners. And when, in October 1985, the coroner, Hugh Adams, made an open finding, Laurie was 'furious', Kath Blake was to recall.

'I went to speak to him and say "That's good that we got an open finding," but he flounced out of the courtroom. My daughter Clare was outside the court and he walked straight past her.

'From then on he hardly had anything to do with us. He said later we'd 'shamed him' in the court, and that he didn't want our grandson to have anything to do with us again.'

It seemed, to the Blakes, a peculiar reaction by a grieving husband to the family of his dead wife.

'What we can't understand is why people don't think it was just someone off the road, a rabbit shooter or something, ' Les Blake was to say later. 'All we are saying is that it wasn't suicide. Someone shot Jen. The Blakes are law-abiding, God-fearing people. For them, the open finding was enough. It left the way clear for a day of reckoning. Some time, they believed, the truth would come out.

IT WAS almost eleven years after Jennifer Tanner's death that Bonnie Doon was jerked awake by what some called 'another' murder mystery. After seventeen years, the mineshaft in the hills behind Tanners' old place gave up its grisly secret.

On the afternoon of Thursday, 20 July 1995, two young men out shooting decided to tie a rope to a tree and climb down to explore the old Jack of Clubs mine.

Ten metres down, David Twomey and his mate Mick Bowen hit the mine's drive, running horizontally. They shone a torch – and saw something red half-hidden in debris. They looked closer. It was a red jumper. Inside it were bones. They took one, climbed out and rang the police.

The homicide detectives arrived next day. Under the debris they found a skeleton and faded feminine things: aqua panties, cream woollen socks, high-heeled ankle boots, vanity mirror, Timex watch, cheap jewellery. And a pair of silicone breast implants.

Within two days, pathologists were able to tell that the remains, judging from the masculine heaviness of the bones, were probably those of a transsexual.

From then, officially at least, the hunt was on. But it was not until an Auckland family read about the case two months later in a Melbourne gay and lesbian newspaper, 'The Star-Observer', that one part of the mystery was solved.

They feared it might be their transsexual prostitute 'sister', Adele, a Pitcairn Islander born Paul David Bailey in Auckland in 1955, and missing from St Kilda's streets since 1978. Dental records proved them right, but the mystery lingers. Despite thousands of pages of fresh statements gathered from dozens of witnesses by the police task force, leading to a new inquest being ordered in late 1997, two tantalising questions remain.

Who put Adele Bailey's body in the mineshaft? And did the same person kill Jennifer Tanner?

IN his summing up, the Coroner who presided at the first inquest, Hugh Adams, bluntly criticised the investigation of Jennifer Tanner's death, describing it as 'slanted' towards an assumption of suicide when the evidence could suggest otherwise. In making an open finding into the death, he said there was no evidence to show either Denis or Laurie Tanner were responsible. Unlike the Coroner, Sergeant Denis Tanner had no qualms about the investigations. 'As far as I am concerned it was a thorough investigation,' he told 'The Sunday Age'.

Below is an edited text of the Coroner's summing up of the first inquest into Jennifer Tanner's death, which was quashed in 1996 in readiness for a second inquest by Graeme Johnstone.

'MY INITIAL first comment would be (to ask) why the brief took so long, some seven months, to be completed ...?

This inquest has highlighted ... the lack of initial proper investigation. In my opinion, this brief should not have been passed in its initial state by the District Superintendent's Office, nor indeed accepted by the local coroner, because the investigations were all slanted towards a situation of self-inflicted injuries, and it was only when further investigations were conducted through this office, some eleven months unfortunately after the event, and what appeared on the surface to be a non-suspicious matter ... indeed may not have been so.

The initial investigating officer should have been alerted to the situation of possible non-self-inflicted injuries because of some unusual features ... evident at the scene.

The fact that there were two expended cartridge cases (and the) lack of any correspondence from the deceased to indicate an intention to take her own life.

But on this initial assessment ... the scene was allowed to be cleared and no autopsy performed until the 16th. Yet when the autopsy revealed two entry wounds, neither forensic nor ballistic tests were sought.

Now I am at a loss – having regard to the two injuries to the forehead and the fact the weapon was a manually loaded rifle ... (why) the Homicide Squad was not asked to assist from at least the day of the autopsy onwards. Simple tests by the Forensic Science

Laboratory officers would have shown whether the rifle was discharged by either the hands or the foot ...

Neither were ballistic tests done to determine if the recovered bullets were in fact fired from the rifle in question. The scene was not photographed with the body in situ and an incomplete set of photographs (was) taken at the autopsy.

A lot of unanswered questions could have been resolved and suspicion removed from certain persons if proper initial investigations and tests (had) been instituted by the police officers and the pathologist.

Now what evidence have we in support of self-infliction? The entry position of the two head wounds certainly is a common sight in respect to persons who take their own lives by the use of firearms.

The deceased was left-handed, the rifle was found at the scene on her left side. Her emotional state – now the evidence of Dr Patience shows the deceased had suffered depression after the birth of her son and this was combined with a shy and not very outgoing nature.

Now the evidence to be considered against self-inflicted injury ... There was no written correspondence found that would show a motive for the deceased taking her own life ... the question arises, who other than the deceased may have been responsible? The evidence indicates that Mr Laurie Tanner could not have been responsible for his wife's death ...

And likewise the same situation in respect to Mr Denis Tanner.

His movements on the night of the 14th have been investigated. His answers substantiated. I am satisfied that he was in no way responsible.

There is another possibility that certainly an unknown person inflicted the wounds.

However, there were no signs of a struggle ... And this person would have had to have known the location of the weapon and the magazine.

... Before a coroner can return a finding that a person has the intention to die by their own hand, and in fact did so, there must be clear and conclusive evidence to that fact.

And here in my opinion that is not so.

... Jennifer Ruth Tanner died ... from the effects of gunshot wounds to the head ... And on the evidence adduced I am unable to determine if the wounds were self-inflicted or otherwise.'

IF the body of Adele Bailey had not been found by a fluke the Tanner case would still have remained dormant, but when homicide detectives started to ask questions about the dead transsexual the answers made them look back at events long relegated to police history. Nearly twelve years after the original unsatisfactory inquiry into the death of the young mother a new generation of detectives called for the old files.

Late in 1996 the Attorney General moved to quash the original coronial open finding and order a new inquest. The court was told, more than ten years too late, that the Tanner case was murder.

In the hearing, the head of the task force, Detective Inspector Paul Newman, said there was 'significant evidence disproving an alibi offered by Denis Tanner.'

He said fresh forensic evidence gathered after Mrs Tanner's body was exhumed in July 1996 indicated she 'could not have caused her own death and the only likely cause of death was murder.'

Here was a senior investigator pointing the finger squarely at a fellow policeman. Ugly accusations until then alluded to only behind closed doors were now being made in open court.

In an earlier hearing in the Supreme Court, designed to stop 'The Sunday Age' newspaper publishing results of its own inquiry into the Tanner death, police were even more specific.

In a sworn affidavit, Detective Chief Inspector Rod Collins said that Detective Sergeant Denis Tanner was a suspect in the alleged murders of Jennifer Tanner, and a transsexual, Paul David Bailey, known as Adele Bailey.

Mr Collins swore that the death of Adele Bailey was being treated as a murder. 'Bailey's body was found in a mine shaft in Crown land adjacent to a rural property known as Springfield. At all times Springfield has been owned by the parents of a serving police officer (Detective Sergeant Denis Tanner) and Laurence Tanner.

'In 1984 the wife of Laurence Tanner (Jennifer Ruth Tanner) was found deceased in Springfield with two bullet wounds to the forehead.

'Following the discovery of Bailey's body in a mine shaft adjacent to Springfield in July 1995, the death of Jennifer Ruth Tanner is being investigated as a homicide. Detective Sergeant Tanner is a suspect in our investigations into the death of Jennifer Ruth Tanner and Bailey.

'Detective Sergeant Tanner was the second last person to arrest Bailey in 1978.'

Bailey went missing from St Kilda, where she worked as a prostitute in 1978. Sergeant Tanner worked in the St Kilda area in the 1970s.

Collins said in the affidavit: 'Detective Sergeant Tanner inquired of Jennifer Ruth Tanner where her husband (Laurie Tanner) kept the guns in the Springfield residence shortly before she died; the deceased (Jennifer Ruth Tanner) had informed an acquaintance that her brother-in-law (Detective Sergeant Tanner) had made sexual advances to her; the part of the Crown land where Bailey's body was discovered is unknown to even local residents and is virtually only accessible by four-wheel-drive through the Springfield property.'

The Tanner family later sold Springfield. The empty farmhouse was burnt to the ground shortly after police began investigating the Bailey murder in 1995.

The fire, which started in the house late at night, ended any chance of forensic experts examining the room where Jenny Tanner was shot. The fire was regarded as highly suspicious, as the house was empty at the time, which meant there was no use of cooking, heating or electrical appliances, most often the cause of accidental house fires.

The then Chief Commissioner, Mick Miller, a respected and forthright senior officer, was stunned to learn, twelve years later, of the original Tanner investigation. He said he should have been told of the Coroner's criticism of the slanted inquiry but that it appeared to have been kept from him. 'There are two options, either someone neglected to pass the information on, or it was deliberately suppressed,' he said.

CHAPTER 2

Cop vs cop
Vindicated on appeal

A scandal waiting to break

OF ALL the things a rogue cop can do, the lowest is to sell out someone else's investigation, to steal information and sell it to the enemy. It risks the lives of undercover operatives and informers for nothing but naked greed.

Those who will stoop to such treachery leave the protected trenches of the police brotherhood, but are never fully trusted by the criminals they are prepared to serve. They exist in a moral no-man's land, surviving on rat cunning, exploiting contacts on both sides of the fence and showing a ruthless desire to look after number one.

Many police are prepared to turn a blind eye to the bash artist or the officer who fakes evidence to get a conviction, but they have nothing but contempt for traitors willing to sell out 'The Job'.

In December 1988, the Drug Squad decided to target William John Hackett, known as a major amphetamines trafficker.

The operation was given the code name 'Mint' and put under the control of one of Victoria's most respected detectives, Sergeant Ron Iddles.

Two undercover police were introduced to the target as interstate drug buyers who could move large quantities of 'speed'. Melbourne was then the amphetamines capital of Australia, so it made sense that dealers would come to the source.

The two experienced detectives were well-tutored in their roles and, on 2 January 1989, they had their first bite. They bought a pound of amphetamines for $8000 from Hackett. On 18 January, they bought another three pounds for $24,000.

Although the police had the evidence to move on Hackett, Ron Iddles decided to let the job run, to scoop up as many members of the syndicate as could be identified. With two men on the inside, it looked as if it could be a big win.

The detectives knew their target was cunning and experienced but they also calculated that greed, and the cash they were spreading around, might well ultimately trap the heads of the network. Although Hackett was a wary criminal, the undercovers were confident.

But, on 26 February, Hackett told one of them that a policeman was demanding $28,000 from the drug syndicate and had a police tape implicating a key member of the amphetamine ring. The undercover was told that $5000 had already been paid.

This news put both police at great risk. They didn't know if the new information was real or just a try-on. If it was true, had they been sold out from within? If they had been identified as police, what would the heads of the syndicate do?

Investigators have been killed for less. Sydney undercover agent Mick Drury was shot at his home in 1984 while washing dishes. He had also been sold out by a brother officer. Police knew that no-one's safety was guaranteed.

However, Hackett said in a secretly-recorded conversation on 6 March that the allegedly corrupt policeman had been warned off from continuing the approach. On 22 March, the day before a deal to deliver two pounds of speed to the undercovers was to go down, a member of the syndicate, Terrence John Moon, was observed going into the McKinnon Hotel in Melbourne to meet another man.

To this day the identity of that man remains a mystery, even though police in five unmarked cars were watching him. They saw he walked with a limp. A former policeman with a shady reputation was known to have a leg injury around that time, but a distinctive gait was hardly foolproof identification. Moon left the hotel and went home, where a listening device had been hidden. He told his wife that he was about to be arrested and the two men he had been dealing with were undercover police. He said the house was probably bugged. Iddles listened, outraged that his job had been sold out.

At 10.30 that night, 'Mint' was terminated and Moon, Hackett and a woman were arrested. Hackett was found to have several firearms, proof that the leak was dangerous, and potentially fatal, for the undercover police. Moon, Hackett and the woman were later convicted.

On 30 March, Hackett was granted bail on a $50,000 surety. A former policeman was in court and provided the surety. Detective Inspector Dave Foley confronted the former policeman and later gave sworn evidence of the conversation.

FOLEY: 'I've been told you passed on an offer on to Moon … What do you know about that?'

FORMER POLICEMAN: 'I don't know what you're talking about, Dave.'

FOLEY: 'Come on. Moon told me you passed the information on to him.'

FORMER POLICEMAN: 'What can I say?'

FOLEY: 'I want the name of the policeman or policemen who asked you to pass on the information about the tapes for money.'

FORMER POLICEMAN: 'Dave, you know me. You know what it's like. I can't tell you who they are; it would be worth my life.'

FOLEY: 'Did you pass the information, the message from the police officers to Moon. I mean, the offer of tapes for money?'

FORMER POLICEMAN: 'Yes, I did, but that's all I can tell you. I can't say anything else.'

FOLEY: 'You should know us, we won't rest until we find out who the crooked police officers are.'

FORMER POLICEMAN: 'You'll never find out, Dave. Moon doesn't even know who they were.'

DENIS Tanner joined the police force on 22 October, 1973, and graduated on 15 March, 1974, in 22nd position of 24 recruits. He began his active service in the records section at Russell Street, then worked at South Melbourne, Shepparton and St Kilda before transferring to the CIB in March, 1979.

He was promoted to senior detective and worked in some of the heavy squads, including the major crime squad. A former colleague remembers Tanner as 'a real good detective'.

'He was a real tough bastard who loved to lock up crooks. I never saw him flinch once. Some coppers talk tough but lack a bit when it's really willing. Denis was not like that. He was hard as nails.'

In September 1988, the position of detective sergeant at Benalla was advertised in the 'Police Gazette'. Tanner was the successful candidate. Another policeman appealed against the decision, but the Police Service Board dismissed the appeal and, on 7 December, Tanner transferred to the posting, which was in the area where he had been brought up.

For Tanner, it was completing the circle. He had worked in the city but he had decided it was time to return to the country he knew. His wife, a policewoman, resigned her position at Altona when she could not get a country posting with him.

He believed that, with his city experience and his country upbringing, he would prove to be an efficient and respected detective who could make a difference in Benalla. The Police Service Board was later to say that he 'took up his position with interest and enthusiasm whilst displaying marked initiatives to improve the working conditions at the division'.

While Tanner was settling in, Ron Iddles, another hard-nosed detective with a reputation for not taking a backward step, was stewing. Universally respected, Iddles was not prepared to walk away from his drug operation without trying to find out who sold him out.

It was an open secret at the time in police circles that a lot of Drug Squad jobs were being leaked to criminals. There was a traitor in the camp.

Soon, through a variety of sources, he came to believe that a member of a squad stationed in the same building as the Drug Squad had become aware of the operation and passed on the information to Tanner who, in turn, used the former policeman as a go-between to warn the targets.

It was a scandal waiting to break. Iddles was determined that this would not be swept under the carpet.

Tanner and Iddles were old mates. Both were raised in the country and were big, tough, no-nonsense types. They joined the job together and were in the same academy class, graduating on the same day. They both wanted to catch crooks and did detective training school together. Iddles finished dux of the course, but Tanner struggled through at the tail, passing with a mark of 75.25 per cent when the cut-off point was 75.

In April 1990, two senior officers, Detective Superintendent Neil Comrie, later to be chief commissioner, and veteran corruption investigator Chief Inspector Tony Warren of the Internal Investigations Department, were assigned the job of finding out how the job leaked.

It was not long before Denis Tanner knew he was in the frame. The detective suspected of initially finding out about the job and passing the information to Tanner was interviewed as a suspect.

The Police Service Board was later to find the detective 'emerged in the judgment of the board as a member with unexplained knowledge of some aspects of Operation Mint'.

The detective was interviewed by Chief Inspector Warren on 18 October 1989. Within six weeks the suspect resigned from the force.

On 16 January 1990, the then Deputy Commissioner (administration), Brendan Crimmins, dropped a bombshell. He wrote to Tanner and effectively accused him of being a crook.

'An investigation has been conducted into the corrupt leak of information from the Drug Squad, in respect to an operation into the large scale manufacture and trafficking of amphetamines,' he wrote.

'The maintenance of efficiency of the force requires the regional commander always has confidence in his personnel and that I, too, have the same confidence in them. As the result of this investigation, these degrees of confidence are not present and in the interests of the maintenance of the efficiency of the force, you are appointed to Force Reserve as of 17th January, 1990, under the provisions of Regulations 901, Police Regulations, 1979.'

Denis Tanner was nothing if not a fighter. He was not prepared to cop the transfer. If he did nothing he knew his professional reputation would never recover. His credibility would be shattered and he would be branded a leak for ever more. He appealed to the Police Service Board, where the case was fought in a marathon hearing of twenty days before County Court Judge Walsh, a former police commander, Eric Sutton, and a respected veteran policeman, Fred Leslie, in 1990.

REPUTATIONS were made and lost at the bitterly-fought hearing. Police turned on police, officers who had been friends for years gave sworn evidence that illustrated alarmingly different recollections of conversations.

The board issued subpoenas to certain people it believed could shed light on the mystery, but they could not be found. Meanwhile, Denis Tanner argued strongly that he had been accused and punished on the basis of guilt by association, combined with malicious gossip.

'As a general proposition, rumor and innuendo about crime and personalities are rife within the police force. I have found frequently that names are mentioned, quite inaccurately as it later turns out, but nevertheless this misinformation circulates on the grapevine,' Tanner said.

'Sometimes this is the result of malice, other times it is inadvertent, while at other times it can be the result of misguided enthusiasm. Facts and personalities change as the story does the rounds. It is an inherent part of the job that police will pry into the business of other people and this flows on to the individual lives of police.

'I believe now that at least one reason why my name has arisen in respect of this matter is because some persons know or learnt that I am an acquaintance of (former policeman) who was a friend of Moon and a good friend of (suspect detective) and wrongly speculated that I must have been connected with 'selling out' of the alleged Drug Squad job.

'The "selling out" of Operation Mint became a talking point, especially in CIB circles.'

Eleven serving and former police, from the rank of constable to chief inspector, told the board that Tanner was a 'trusted and valuable member of the CIB'. Support statements were gathered from five serving and former police.

Locals who were prepared to vouch for Tanner included a butcher, a local councillor, a supermarket manager, a school principal, a farmer, a publican and a car dealer.

His record sheet was filled with praise from senior officers. He was described over the years as well-conducted, efficient, reliable and enthusiastic.

On 4 May 1978 he was praised in the following terms: 'Commended with three others for dedication to duty, courage and persistence displayed, with scant regard for his personal safety, in the apprehension and subsequent conviction of a desperate criminal who exercised every violent means at his disposal endeavouring to effect his escape.'

Two months after transferring to Benalla in December 1988, Tanner hurt his knee on duty after a 'violent struggle' with a criminal in the cells. He was off work for 40 days from 17 April 1989 to 11 June 1989, suffering from stress and anxiety 'due to a variety of factors perceived by him, not the least being that he heard the allegations that he was suspected of serious corruption'. He had been disciplined twice in his career for inappropriate actions. In the early 1970s, he was counselled by senior officers for not following procedures and, at Benalla CIB, for using inappropriate language.

When he moved there he was in the process of buying a house for $147,000. In October 1989, he was 'very belatedly' interviewed by investigators over the Drug Squad leak. Tanner knew the ropes and the tone of the interview left him knowing that he was under suspicion.

He rang the head of the investigation, Superintendent Comrie, to find out where he stood. The future commissioner didn't mince words. Out in the cold, was the answer.

The board said Mr Comrie told the suspect policeman he 'was likely to be sent to Force Reserve'. Tanner allowed his offer on the house to lapse.

THE board warned of the dangers of listening to mess-room gossip. It found that a corrupt approach had been made to one of the targets but found there was nothing to link Tanner to the approach. 'The evidence which was available to the investigators did not afford any tenable basis for that conclusion. Nor was it such as to give rise to reasonable suspicion that Tanner was involved in the corrupt approach which was made. 'The evidence which was given and the statements which were received provided convincing evidence of the appellant's ability and efficiency, his value as a detective in the north-east of Victoria and his ability to integrate his CIB duties with his membership of the community in that area.'

The board overturned the decision of the chief commissioner to transfer Tanner to the force reserve.

Tanner gave impressive evidence at the hearing. He said he was financially secure, 'to refute the motive of greed attributed to him'.

Ron Iddles resigned from the force in disgust. He later rejoined and was given rapid promotion to become a senior member of the Homicide Squad.

CHAPTER 3

Red hot
The sudden death of two bandits

'The potential for disaster is always present in the planned confrontation'

IN underworld parlance, Paul Ronald Skews was running red hot. Skews, 35, was granted parole and released from Morwell River Prison Farm on 5 January, 1994, after serving two and a half years of a seven year term for armed robbery and attempted armed robbery. Police say that within weeks of his release he was talking big and trying to recruit others to commit armed robberies.

He had big criminal ambitions and a raging drug habit. It was a recipe for disaster.

Detectives had been told that Skews, who had also been acquitted of a 1991 murder, had bragged he would shoot it out rather than go back to jail. His criminal record went back to 1973 and included firearms offences, stealing cars, escape, burglaries and intentionally causing serious injury. He showed no signs of reform and went straight back to crime when freed.

Within weeks of release, Skews was picked up by police, who found amphetamines in the vehicle. Despite his record and his probable breach of parole, Skews was bailed to appear in the Oakleigh Magistrates' Court on 27 May. As an added precaution, he had to report to the Springvale police station daily. Being charged with a criminal offence did nothing to slow down the drug-addicted fringe dweller who wanted to be a gangster, but lacked the brains and contacts to be anything but a reckless fool. While on bail and facing more jail Skews, armed with a sawn- off shotgun, robbed a butcher at Hallam Square Deal Meats on 22 April, 1994.

The butcher, Brian Craik, was about to load up his van to deliver to a supermarket. He had just hopped into the van in a back lane when he was confronted by a man wearing a black balaclava, a blue, loose-fitting jumper and carrying a shotgun.

'He shoved the gun through the window and put it to my head. He said "Give us the money",' Craik said later. Told there was no money in the van, the gunman and his unarmed accomplice ran off. 'He was very cool and not really aggressive. He didn't appear to be excitable and wasn't worried. The gun didn't shake at all,' Craik said.

The butcher said he recognised the jumper worn by the man who threatened him as the same type worn by one of the balaclava-wearing men shot dead by police weeks later. 'I saw a picture of him on the ground in the newspaper and it looked very, very similar,' he said.

About seven hours after attempting to rob the butcher, police believe Skews robbed an Ampol service station in Springvale Road armed with a shotgun. The gunman grabbed the attendant and demanded money. 'He had a shotty and stuck it up his nose,' the proprietor said later. The attendant gave the bandit around $200 and a few phone cards. The gunman was chased by two customers who saw him get into a nearby car driven by another man.

The proprietor said he recognised Skews from pictures in newspapers as a regular customer. 'He lives around here and I know the face.'

If Skews thought he could keep his plans secret he was wrong, for he was a man with few friends but many enemies. He was desperate to recruit an offsider for further armed robberies, but the more people he spoke to, the more chatted to the police.

The Armed Robbery Squad targeted Skews, after being tipped off that he was planning to hit a $50,000 payroll from one of several factories in Blissington Street, Springvale, on 12 May. As part of operation 'Short Time' members of the Armed Robbery Squad got permission to enlist the surveillance police and the heavily armed

Special Operation Group, to try to trap Skews. Eight days before the robbery was expected police watched Skews hide a plastic bag containing 13 twelve-gauge shotgun cartridges in a stormwater drain. They knew he had a sawn-off single barrel shotgun and a .44 magnum revolver.

They found a stolen car nearby, at the corner of Nash and Sullivan streets, which they assumed was the getaway car. And they had information that he was ready. On 12 May Skews drove up Blissington Street with an unidentified man in another car. But it was a dry run. He didn't stop. Police were later told the job had been delayed a week.

Detectives believed they did not have enough evidence to arrest Skews and ordered 24-hour surveillance. But hours later they lost him. He was sleeping at different locations in the Springvale area and he eluded them.

Skews was about to pull a big job, but he also needed cash immediately. He owed $4500 to drug dealers and he was not sure if they would wait a week. People have been killed for smaller drug debts.

The following evening, about 6.30, he surfaced again. He was held by former policeman and part-time security guard, Jim Sheerin, 65, after he smashed the window of the Trewarne Antique Jewellery shop in Macedon Place, Lower Templestowe. He allegedly grabbed gold chains and diamonds valued at $25,000 which would net him about $8000 and clear his debts.

Travis Trewarne was in the shop with four other people when he heard the front window smash. 'He was still plucking things from the window when Jim got to him,' he said.

Sheerin, who had retired from the police force in 1986, chased Skews down a laneway into a carpark, then grabbed him. 'He was puffing when I was on top of him. He said he did the smash grab because he owed about $4000 for drugs. He said he had received threatening phone calls and needed the money. He said he had been told about the shop and how to do it.'

Skews was charged with burglary and theft and bailed from the Doncaster police station less than four hours later. 'The funny thing was that he was out before me,' Sheerin said. 'But the time I finished my statement it was about 10 o'clock. He was walking up and down outside the station waiting for a lift.'

For the second time since his release from prison, police had their man, but he was released on bail. The coroner, Graeme Johnstone, was concerned at the way Skews was given bail while he was running red hot. He said he understood why the Armed Robbery Squad wanted to keep the operation a secret but he felt that the police officer, Sergeant Michael Pearcy, who granted Skews bail, may have acted differently if he had been briefed by the squad. 'Had Pearcy been given (full) information, his investigatory and decision-making process would have been different.'

'Skews, having been granted bail, within a short period of time completed his plans and the end result is known. Whether a bail hearing by an agency independent of the police would have actually changed the events or merely put off the fatal day is a matter of conjecture. Had bail been refused and Skews sentenced he would not have been in a position to undertake the robbery on the 16th. It is a moot point as to whether he would have continued with his plans after his eventual release.

'It must be recognised this situation is a dilemma for police concerned with the overall safety of the public. However, that is a regular difficulty managed by police working within our legal system when dealing with potentially dangerous and violent criminals like Skews. The real problem in this case is that appropriate procedures in the circumstances were not taken. The consequences of that failure are unknown.'

Skews became suspicious when he went to report at Springvale police to report on bail and noticed his picture had been removed from his file. Police made up an excuse so that he didn't realise it had been sent to the Armed Robbery Squad.

The Templestowe arrest had not slowed him down. He cased a video shop and two service stations as possible robbery targets. At one point he returned his hire car and borrowed different vehicles, making it difficult for surveillance police. Detectives countered by getting a friend of the target to lend him a known car so he was driving so he could be identified and followed.

On Sunday, 15 May, the informant, code-named 'Mr Smith', rang police and said Skews was going to hit a real estate agency the following day, but he didn't know which one. At 9.30 am the next day 'Mr

Smith' rang and said it was Deacon Real Estate in Dingley. The office was also an agency for the Bank of Melbourne at the time, which made it a lucrative target. The SOG went to the scene and quietly checked the area, working out the best spot to grab the gunman. A few hours later they were confident that all was set. It had been done so quietly that the estate agent, Jim Farrell, said later he did not notice any police in the area that day.

At 11.45 'Mr Smith' rang and said Skews had just stolen a car from the Hallam railway station. Everything was going to plan. Five minutes later they got the call to say three members of the public had been shot by a robber who raided an Armaguard van at the Hoyts Cinema Complex in Chadstone Shopping Centre. It was not related to Skews, but it meant the Armed Robbery Squad's resources were going to be stretched that day.

At 12.40 pm 'Mr Smith' rang again and said the robbery had been switched to Finnings, a real estate office in Somerville Road, Hampton Park.

The plan had always been to intercept Skews before the job, but now time was running against the police. The SOG had to move to an area they had not checked. They had just over an hour to get everything set for an ambush. The job was a rush.

Surveillance police swept the area, looking for a getaway car. They found a stolen Falcon parked in Keppel Drive, Hallam, and sat off it. It had been stolen from Hallam railway station earlier that day.

Police knew there would be a second man with Skews. They did not know who he was, but had been told Skews would have a shotgun and the second man a heavy-calibre hand gun. Detectives don't know then that Skews had recruited Stephen Raymond Crome, 18, for the robbery. Crome had convictions for burglary, theft, possessing drugs of dependence and assaulting police. In June, 1993, he was driving a stolen car that crashed and killed his passenger, Ricky Carpando. Crome had suffered serious head injuries and walked with a limp afterwards.

At 1.56 pm Skews and Crome approached the stolen car and drove off. Surveillance police notified the SOG that the job was on. The surveillance police, known as 'the dogs', kept a loose tail on the two, who doubled back and drove up side streets to check if they were being followed.

Police were told the job was to be between 2 pm and 2.30 pm. About 1.45 pm, two members of the SOG arrived and cleared two staff out of the building and took them out a rear door. Minutes later, the arrest team of six arrived in a van and the driver also joined the group at the rear, along with another office worker from the agency.

Five SOG members, led by a sergeant and armed with five and seven-shot shotguns, stayed in the back of the van.

The two bandits pulled up in Lakeview Drive and changed into blue overalls and put balaclavas on their heads to look like beanies. At 2.19 pm, they arrived outside the agency and ran towards the building. According to police reports, the five SOG members attempted to intercept them, yelling 'Police, don't, move.'

They claim Skews turned and pointed his gun at the police. Crome, who was unarmed, allegedly had his hand in a blue linen sack. Four of the five police fired a total of 17 shots. They were using heavy SG cartridges, each of which contains nine heavy balls the size of a revolver slug. The member who did not fire his gun was the last out of the van and believed the threat was over. The shooting took less than five seconds.

Skews and Crome were both shot in the head, body and legs. At least 12 shots hit them, indicating that up to 108 lead balls were in the two shattered bodies.

One SOG member fired three times, the second fired seven, the third five times and the fourth, once. The two were dead when they hit the ground. Crome's hand was near the bag. Skews's single barrelled shotgun was loaded and he had spare ammunition. By luck, no members of the public were hurt. Bullet damage was discovered in a house 62 metres from the incident.

The Homicide Squad and the then coroner, Hal Hallenstein, were called to the scene. The SOG members were separated, their guns seized and the area cordoned off.

They were tested for gunshot residue on their hands and clothes. They all made statements after being advised by Police Association lawyer, Tony Hargreaves, who was called to the scene to act for the police involved. But they refused to participate in a video reconstruction of the event on legal advice. All received psychological counselling on the night.

The death of the two bandits, while publicly defended by senior police, obviously created dissent behind the scenes. On 31 October, 1994, the head of the State Crime Squads, Detective Superintendent Darryl Clarke, wrote a confidential letter to Detective Chief Inspector Ian Henderson, which stated in part: 'A question that may arise at the subsequent hearing is why Skews was on bail after being arrested on 11th May for drug offences and the 13th May for burglary and theft. On both occasions bail was on his own undertaking. An inference may be drawn that Skews was allowed bail in order to be permitted to commit an armed robbery and that the Armed Robbery Squad influenced the decision on bail,' he wrote.

Henderson's reply of 1 November, also marked confidential, clearly showed the tension in the police hierarchy.

'The Armed Robbery Squad did not request that Skews be granted bail for the Smash/Grab, nor did Detective Sergeant Watson nor any other member endeavour to influence that decision. The inference referred to in your report is totally incorrect and have serious reservations as to the propriety of raising it in the current environment.'

Under the new 'safety first' police policy ushered in with Operation Beacon, it is most unlikely that an operation such as Short Time would now be authorised.

WHAT the Coroner, Graeme Johnstone, found:

'Skews and Crome contributed to their own deaths and to each other's death by attempting to undertake an armed robbery. Crome's contribution must also be seen in the context of him being young, probably immature, intellectually slow and 'led' by the far more mature and experienced career criminal, Skews. Although he was clearly aware of Skews' plans and ready to assist.

'Skews was affected by drugs and Crome may also have been affected. However, as to the latter comment there is no certainty that Crome was affected by drugs.

'The shootings by members of the Victorian Special Operations Group was lawful and justified in that all members fired after being put in reasonable fear that their own lives were at risk by Skews and Crome. The fact that Crome was later discovered not to be armed, does not, of itself, alter the view of the police response at the moment of the shooting. 'Skews and Crome, by attempting the armed robbery put themselves, the public and the police at considerable risk and the eventual consequences of their actions would have been foreseeable ...

'In this case, whilst the management of the actual arrest situation was not unreasonable, it was the outcome that was not optimal. However, it must be remembered, the outcome was dictated primarily by the overt actions of Skews in presenting the shotgun in spite of police commands. In context of the management of an incident those commands inevitably occur rapidly with little opportunity for any rational thought by persons to whom they are directed. In that sense the potential for disaster is always present in the planned confrontation.

'No other person contributed to the death.'

CHAPTER 4

A fallen Starr
Inside a cocaine ring

*Starr was a cocaine dealer who
specialised in servicing Melbourne's
celebrities, nightclubbers and partygoers.*

DRUG abuse is not class conscious. Rich and battling parents alike
share a fear of the possibility their children will succumb to party drugs
with glamourous nicknames and a connection with the so-called
beautiful people. The children of Prime Ministers, high-profile business
people, judges and celebrities have been listed among the victims.

But while drug use knows no social boundaries, for police the sharp
end of drug investigation is aimed at the lower end of the socio-
economic spectrum. It is easier to grab heroin user-dealers, who work
of the streets in every Australian city, by getting young coppers to
wear scruffy clothes and buy a few grams (a technique known as 'buy-
bust'), than to infiltrate up the ladder to the major dealers.

For years international police intelligence has indicated Australia
was set for an explosion in cocaine. In the United States heroin was
considered a rather down-market street drug. Cocaine was the drug
of choice for the richer substance abusers. It was only when the
addictive and cheaper crack-cocaine flooded America that it became
available in the ghettos. Police intelligence predicated that as cocaine
production boomed in South America, and the market in the US

finally became saturated, the drug syndicates would have to find new markets. The countries identified as lucrative targets were those with high income levels in Europe and Asia.

Australia was considered an over-ripe plum, ready for the taking. Huge, unprotected coasts, cursory border checks and a culture which followed US trends without question or thought. It could be argued that throughout history Australians have been among the biggest drug abusers in the world, of both legal and illegal substances. For more than a decade there had an explosion in amphetamine abuse in Australia, a stimulant similar in some ways to cocaine. In America the cheaper amphetamine was often described as 'blue-collar' cocaine.

The conventional wisdom was that Australian authorities should brace themselves for a flood of cocaine. It would be big with wealthy followers of fashion, many of whom had travelled to the US and tried the drug, bringing their habits home with them. The fear was that as the role models for young people began to use cocaine, it would be seen as glamorous and so spread through society.

For police, the problem of infiltrating coke rings was a big hurdle. There is little street dealing of coke, unlike heroin. To infiltrate a drug syndicate you have to find an entry point. You must lever a protective shield away in order to get inside the main machine.

With heroin and amphetamines syndicates, police usually look for a criminal involved and then pressure him into a deal. He then introduces an undercover policeman to senior members of the syndicate. The undercover then gathers evidence over months, even years, before the trap is sprung.

In the case of cocaine, law enforcement officials were making the occasional big bust at airports and docks, which indicated there was a growing market in Australia, but they weren't seeing it at street level.

Police could hardly kick in the doors of the rich and famous in South Yarra, Double Bay and Brighton to see if the sugar bowls at dinner parties were filled with sugar.

A pornographic home video, involving a well-known female celebrity, in which the participants appear to be using cocaine, confirmed what police already know. In some circles, cocaine was readily available and used as a social lubricant. The syndicates tended to be a strange collaboration of violent, career criminals, business-

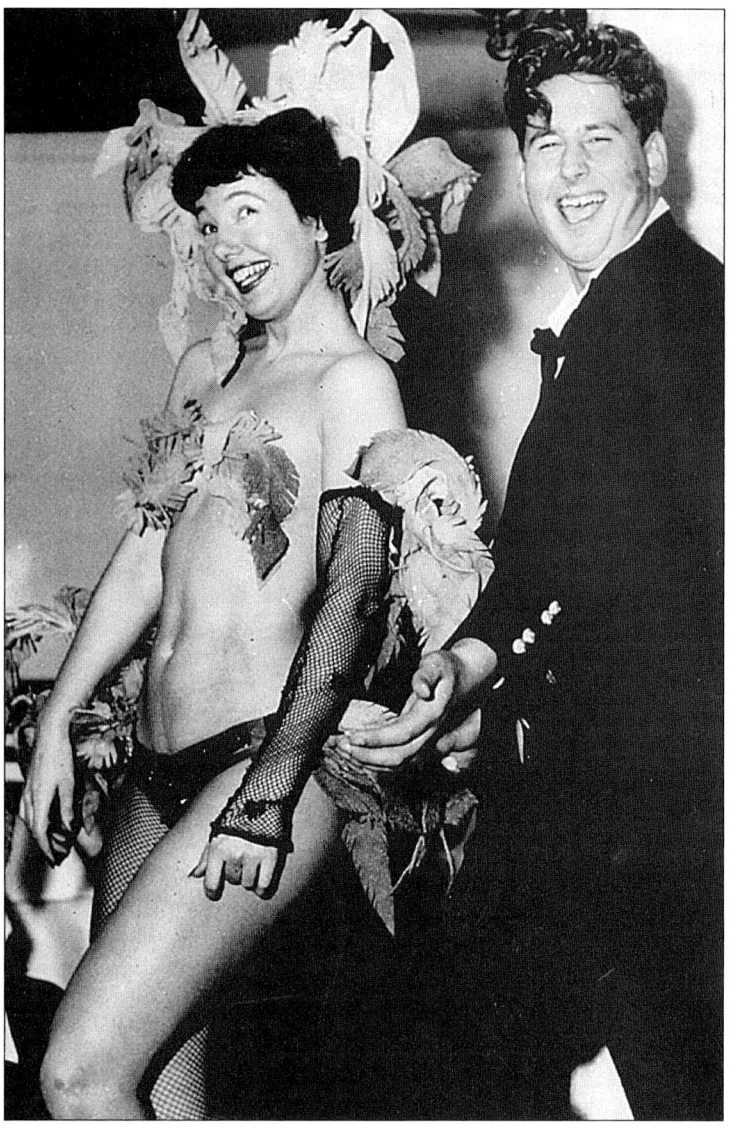

The late Lord Moynihan (right) ... peer of the realm, bongo player, informer, conman, drug dealer and journalist.

Stuart John Perry … believed thrown from an aeroplane following a financial misunderstanding.

LEFT: Howard Marks's marijuana brand, considered the best in the world.

Oxford graduate, international spy and drug dealer Howard Marks (above) … arrested with wife Judy. LEFT: Geoffrey 'The Engineer' Kenion (left), a key figure in the world-wide syndicate.

Stay there: Special Operations Group Police swarm around Stephen Asling, who was trying to escape at speeds of up to 80 kmh before his car was rammed by an SOG four-wheel-drive at Tullamarine airport.

Hold it: In these police surveillance photographs, Asling lies face down as two members of the Special Operations Group approach, guns aimed.

Walk this way: Asling is arrested by Special Operations Group officers. Two of his accomplices, Stephen Barci and Norman Lee, were shot by police after being thrown from the getaway car.

Getaway car rammed in collision with SOG blocking vehicle.

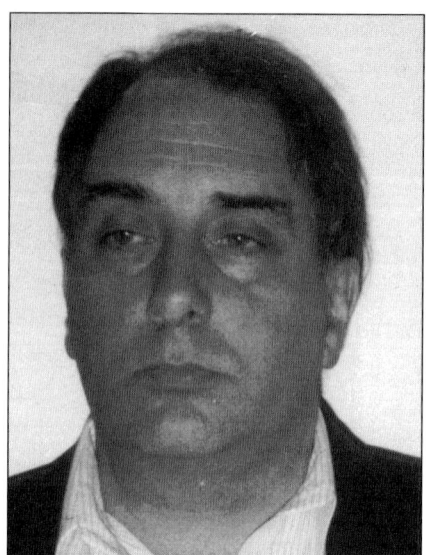

The *Full Frontal* television dummy (above and right) used in an elaborate sting operation to catch corrupt lawyer Philip 'Mr Laundry' Peters (left). He wanted an enemy drugged and murdered.

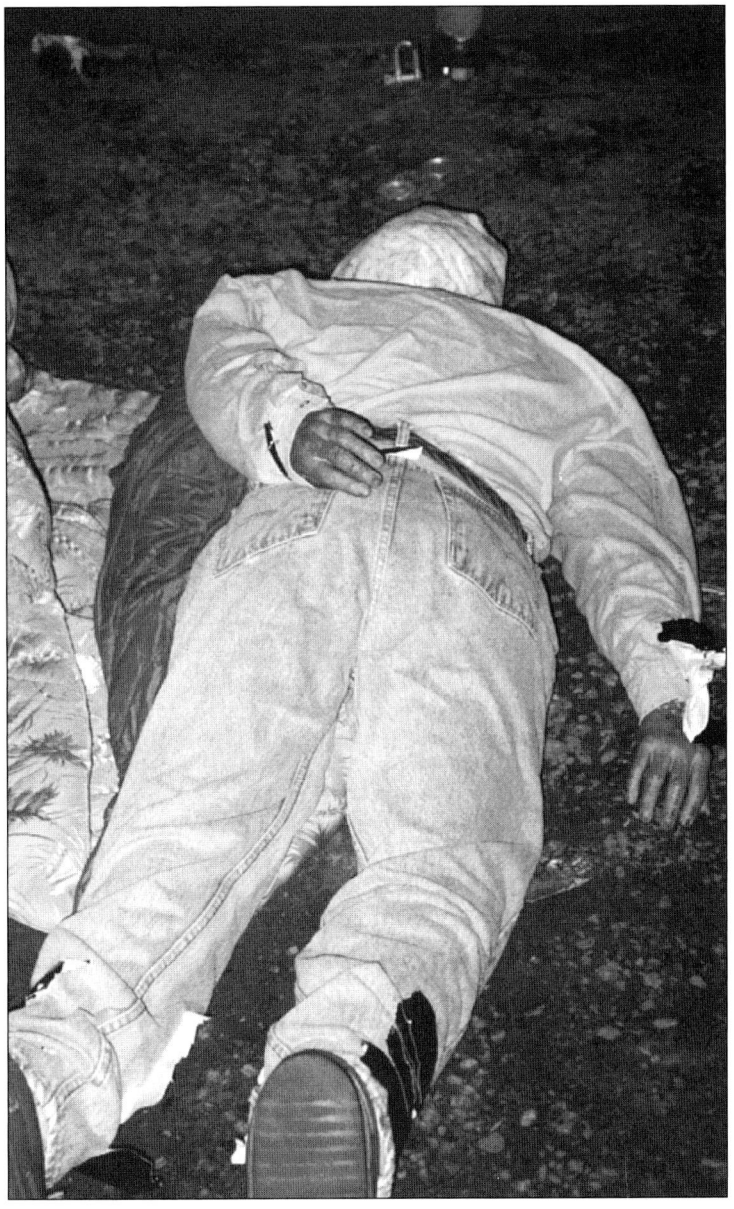

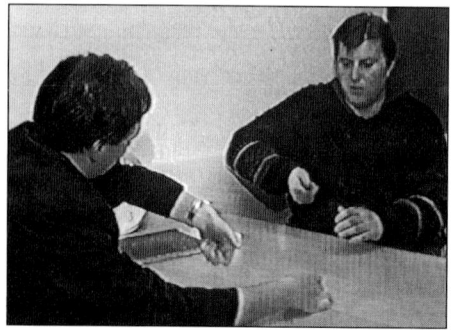

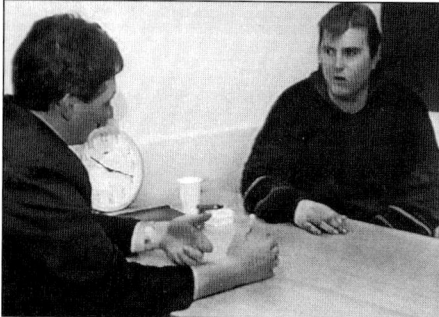

The moment of truth … video pictures capture the moment killer Paul Charles Denyer's story falls apart. He uses the wrong hand to describe how he cut his hand sharpening a knife, then realises his error. A fumbled explanation from Denyer prompts Detective Senior Sergeant Rod Wilson to remark in question 738: 'I don't think you're telling the truth.'

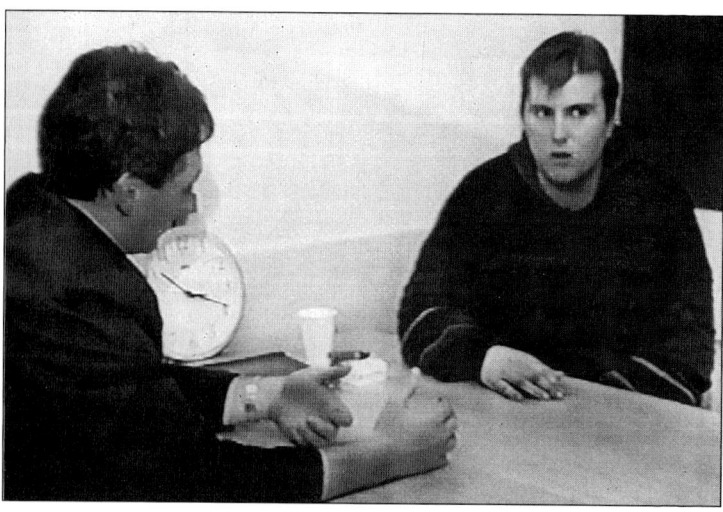

men, television celebrities and hangers on. In one case investigated by the National Crime Authority, a judge's son smuggled drugs from South America and his financier was one of Australia's highest profile businessmen. The man's contacts included a gangster with connections in Manila and Sydney hitman Christopher Dale Flannery, who was murdered in the NSW underworld wars in 1985. But he also dealt readily with a Melbourne real estate agent and an outer suburban veterinary surgeon who sold cocaine as a sideline.

By the 1980s and 1990s some strange types were being seen with celebrities. Dennis Bruce Allen, alias Mr Death, a drug dealer, police informer and murderer, was associating with a big Australian rock promoter and was a regular behind the scenes at huge concerts. It was long said that the tattooed career criminal provided the drugs required by visiting international superstars.

With the growing market for cocaine it was a chance for crims to jump into a new market with new friends and associates.

Paul Rick Marshall was one who saw the opportunity. By the time he settled in Melbourne, Marshall had convictions in three states for burglaries, false pretences and other minor offences. In Melbourne he soon gathered convictions for selling drugs.

It is a fair bet that many of his former associates now wish they had never heard of Paul Marshall – or his alter ego, Ricky Starr, night-owl, disc jockey and drug dealer to the stars.

He was popular in Melbourne's night-club scene, a personable figure often seen chatting with television identities, models and actors. But his greatest asset was not his line in conversation. It was a line of white powder.

Underneath the glitter, Starr was a big cocaine dealer who specialised in servicing Melbourne's celebrities, night-clubbers and party-goers. To do that he had to be connected to a reliable drug source, have hired muscle for protection and, above all else, he had to be discreet. Starr's clients were impressed with their dealer. He was friendly, not threatening, and seemed to able to supply any amount of high quality cocaine on demand.

But what they didn't know was that he kept a detailed contact list naming the television personalities and others he supplied with cocaine. Police have seized the list but will not produce it in court and will not divulge the names. As far as the detectives involved are concerned, the cocaine buyers are small fry, users who will not be singled out merely because they have high public profiles.

But others may not be so discreet. The head of the Drug Squad, Detective Chief Inspector John McKoy, said police were concerned that celebrities who dabbled in the cocaine scene were risking blackmail as criminals learned of their habits. 'They are leaving themselves wide open,' was his blunt assessment.

In investigating the Starr cocaine dealings police had to infiltrate a network that was suspicious of outsiders. He had an exclusive client base. But what police had on their side was the weakness most dealers share. Greed.

The Drug Squad used undercover operatives in an operation code named 'Turtle'. A policeman took on an elaborate false identity. He became 'Paul', a young wealthy man who wanted to set himself up as a cocaine dealer in the party scene. He was well dressed, good looking, suave, drove a Mercedes-Benz, wore expensive jewellery, carried plenty of cash, and acted as if he wanted to make more.

A second policeman became 'John', a surly, brooding type, a little rough around the edges, who acted as a full-time minder for 'Paul'. According to Detective Inspector Bob Armstrong, the head of the Covert Investigation Unit, few police have what it takes to infiltrate crime networks. They have to be able to think on their feet, weave a believable story and stick to it no matter what goes wrong. 'There is no safety net, and often there is no second chance.'

The two police selected for 'Turtle' were among the best. They needed to be. At least four times they were confronted with situations where their cover could have been blown. The operation ended with 16 members of the syndicate, including three major dealers, being arrested. Another 30 people connected with the ring were identified. One of the syndicate members suffered a broken jaw and another was shot when he attacked one of the undercover police.

After several meetings Paul and John won Starr's confidence. Paul said he wanted to buy cocaine and on 5 October, 1990, the men went to Starr's Brighton home, where the undercover police bought one gram of almost pure cocaine for $300. Starr was happy. He had a new client with money to spend. Police were delighted. The gram would only be the first in a series of buys designed to identify as many members of the syndicate as possible.

Operation Turtle illustrates the dynamics of the cocaine industry in Australia today. It is not made up of a regimented syndicate with a structured hierarchy, but a number of bit players, opportunists who drift in and out. They make a deal and move on, looking for new buyers and fresh suppliers. Starr had become involved in the drug scene in 1984, tapping into the growing demand for cocaine, and riding the wave of the drug's popularity.

The undercover police met Starr in a hotel in Caulfield three days after the first buy. They met two new members of the syndicate and bought cocaine valued at $6000 over lunch. Three days later, in a quiet Doncaster house, the police bought another 30 grams valued at $6000. Starr was so relaxed with his new clients that he started to big note. He dropped names of television and fashion identities who regularly bought his cocaine.

Starr was easily persuaded his new clients wanted to buy large quantities, and he went to a new supplier. The undercovers were introduced to Evan Tsiaris, a strongly built 25-year-old fashion designer turned tough guy. Covered in tattoos and with a long criminal history, he didn't look the type to make it to the cat-walks of Paris.

Tsiaris told the free-spending 'drug buyers' they would have to go to his boss's house to buy about 60 grams of top-quality cocaine. The pair were keen and ready to go – until they were told the address. It was the street where one of the undercover police lived.

It was one of the flukes that can cost an undercover office his life. If he had walked into the house he would have been instantly recognised – and possibly killed. Later, detectives found that Tsiaris carried a small pen pistol with him at all times.

The two detectives were in the Mercedes, heading for a certain ambush. They had to abort the meeting any way they could. They managed to get the attention of a passing marked police car and were pulled over and given a traffic ticket. This stopped the meeting – and the potential disaster.

The dealer they were supposed to meet was Ralph Peter Petruccelli, who worked as barman in a Collingwood hotel. The hospitality trade must have been good for Ralph, as he drove a Porsche with personalised number plates, even though he had lost his licence in 1990. In one incident during the operation Tsiaris wanted to meet 'John' to do a drug deal. For the heavy criminal the new kid on the block should have been easy pickings. In a late night meeting behind the Savoy Hotel near Spencer Street, Tsiaris demanded the cash from John. It was to be a typical rip-off. Promise the goods and steal the cash.

But what Tsiaris didn't know was that 'John' was a champion kickboxer. When he attacked John he was left unconscious in the gutter with a broken jaw. He had bitten off more than he could chew. In fact, he couldn't chew at all.

One evening, after another controlled drug buy worth $2000, 'Paul' was in a city night-club with members of the syndicate celebrating their latest cocaine deal. An off-duty policewoman walked over and recognised him. The wrong greeting could have blown the whole operation – or got the undercover pair hurt or killed. Before the policewoman could speak 'Paul' steered her smoothly onto the dance floor, confiding that he was working on the group.

In early 1991 'Paul' and his partner organised to buy 500 grams of cocaine for $80,000. By this time they were liked and trusted. To the dealers, the two men were just like them – young men keen on a dollar and who didn't care where it came from.

At a designated time back-up police moved in for a series of co-ordinated raids. One bit player, Michael Stephen Runje, attacked 'Paul' and was shot in the shoulder by the undercover officer.

In all, police bought cocaine from the gang five times. It showed that there were several inter-related syndicates operating in Melbourne. 'The operation was a major coup for us as it took at least three major dealers out of circulation,' the head of the Drug Squad said later. 'It revealed that cocaine was readily available in Melbourne on a large scale and huge profits were being made by dealers.'

The two policemen received Chief Commissioner's commendations, and later returned to orthodox police duties, which is standard procedure. Undercover officers must 'come in' to avoid burn-out from the stress of maintaining cover in dangerous situations.

The main players in the syndicates were convicted and jailed. But there is no doubt they have been replaced and that the cocaine market is still growing.

CHAPTER 5

The ghost who won't die
Gone, but not forgotten

'If this comes down to what you're implying,
I go to jail for the rest of my bloody life'

FOR years, Valerie Bordley dreamed of leaving her council house in Watford, England, and flying to Melbourne to join the sister she had last seen in 1972.

But, by the time she finally took the 40-hour plane trip, she knew the chance of a joyous family reunion had disappeared years before. She travelled 20,000 kilometres to sit in the No. 1 Coroner's Court in Melbourne during a hot summer in a bid to unravel the mystery that had tormented her for eleven years.

Since 1983 she has been trying to discover what happened to her sister, Edwina Boyle, who disappeared in suspicious circumstances from her Dandenong home and has not been seen since.

Valerie Bordley promised her ill mother that she would do everything she could to find out what had happened to her daughter. The family used private detectives, Interpol, the Salvation Army, international missing persons network and local police to try to find answers. Finally, Valerie borrowed about $4000 to fly to Melbourne for the inquest into her sister's disappearance. 'I have come here to find some answers,' she said. 'I have been determined to find out what happened since day one and I am not going to give in. Over the past eleven years, every time we have learnt something it has just led to more unanswered questions.'

The then Edwina Hobbs had been a shop assistant until the age of 17, when she became a bus conductress for the Cardiff City Transport System. She married Fred Boyle in February, 1972, and four months later, pregnant with their first child, and aged 19, she emigrated to Australia with him.

Valerie, who never saw her sister again, recalls: 'They were the normal type of newlyweds, very much in love and they really seemed to idolise each other,' she said.

Over the years, Edwina Boyle wrote regularly to her family in Britain. They read of the birth of her two daughters, Careesa and Sharon, and later of how Careesa became the junior ice-skating champion of Victoria at the age of ten. Edwina took the girls ice-skating four times a week and making their costumes for competitions.

But, in late 1983, the letters stopped. Late that year, as police were to tell the Coroner, Wendy Wilmoth, the family received a letter from Fred Boyle, telling them his wife had left him and not to be surprised if they did not hear from her at Christmas.

Boyle said in a police statement submitted to the Coroner's Court that he had twice tried to report the disappearance to police, but they did not list her as a missing person because they believed she had just run away. However, the first police record of reports that she was missing were made in mid-November, 1983, when a friend said she had not been seen for six weeks. Dandenong police went to Boyle, who said she had left him about 4.30 am on 6 October while he was asleep and had left a note saying she had run off with a man named 'Ray'. How he knew she had left at 4.30 am, given that he claimed to be asleep, is not known.

The court was told that it was only after Valerie Bordley reported the case to the Shady Lane police in Watford, who passed it on through Interpol to Victorian authorities in early 1984, did investigations start.

Concerned friends in Melbourne spoke to police and paid for advertisements trying to find the missing woman. Fred Boyle later said he paid for missing persons notices although police could find no record of them. The Coroner heard conflicting evidence about what had happened to Edwina Boyle. Police believe she is dead. Her husband maintains she ran off and is living under an assumed name. He told police: 'I got nothing to hide.'

Checks with the Immigration Department, Vic Roads, Social Security, Medicare, banking and financial institutions have produced nothing. Police investigations have shown she did not keep an appointment for a minor operation and did not turn up to collect her pay at the chicken farm where she worked.

She has not renewed her driving license or received social welfare. There is no record of her leaving the country or renewing her passport. There are no records of her having a bank account. She did not take her car or clothes. She has not contacted friends or relatives and, apparently, she has never inquired about her daughters, both now young adults. This does not fit well with the Coroner's finding that she 'was generally known as a devoted mother who was very proud of her children and apparently happily married.'

The inquest found that far from plotting to run off, she had indicated she was planning her future in the area. 'Mrs Boyle spoke of planning to open a second hand shop, and said she had already bought stock for it. She spoke of wishing to buy land and build a house with her husband.'

Police are convinced Edwina Boyle was murdered. They have used blood samples taken from her sister and dental records to mount an Australia-wide check on unidentified skeletal remains to see if they match those of the missing woman. All checks have proved negative. Fred Boyle, meanwhile, maintains his wife is alive, having run off with the unknown 'Ray'.

According to him, he fell asleep in his clothes on the couch of their flat on the night before she disappeared and when he awoke he found a note from his wife saying she was leaving him to move interstate with 'Ray' and that she would be in touch.

The Coroner said, 'The night before her disappearance, Mrs Boyle and the children were at the skating rink, preparing for a competition to be held that weekend. Mrs Boyle had apparently put a lot of time and preparation and was looking forward to it. The eldest daughter, Careesa, was Victorian Junior Champion. Her friend, Mrs Maureen

Gibb, saw her that night and as she left, Mrs Boyle said, "I'll see you tomorrow night."

'Mrs Boyle's friend found it extraordinary that she had left the children, and that as time went on she did not contact them. This was entirely inconsistent with what they knew of her.' The Coroner found a note had existed but that it had been destroyed. 'There may be some doubt as to whether Mrs Boyle actually wrote the note, with the possibility being that Mr Boyle forged her hand-writing.'

Boyle told police he suspected his wife of having an affair before she left. In the months before she disappeared, she had drastically lost weight, dropping from a size-18 fit in clothes to a size-10. He told police that he had confronted her with allegations that she was being unfaithful and 'she denied that she'd had affairs'.

About a year before his wife disappeared, Boyle began an affair of his own with a family friend, Virginia Gissara. The two families had met through their children's love of ice skating. The day after Edwina Boyle disappeared, Virginia Gissara moved into the Boyle home.

'I honestly believed that Edwina had left Fred,' Gissara told police. 'I was aware that Edwina was very close to her daughters, particularly the older one. I thought it strange, being a mother myself, that Edwina would leave her children. I am of the opinion that Edwina is dead. I didn't think that at the time when I went with Fred.'

Boyle and Gissara broke up in 1988. Boyle later blamed the pressure of the police investigation. He says he has been unfairly singled out as a murder suspect. In a videotaped interview with homicide detectives, he said: 'The whole investigation indicates and implies that I have something to hide. Now I don't bloody like that ... every day for the last ten years, we have had to live with (the possibility that) the next knock on the bloody door might be the police coming to pick me up for the murder of my wife.

'But I do not believe that woman is dead and nor will I ever. If she is dead, I have had nothing to do with it. But if she is not dead and I believe she's not dead, she is living quite comfortably, quite happy, somewhere else. And no matter what the outcome of this investigation is or the Coroner's inquest, even if you all, if you charge me and put me in Pentridge, I don't care. My children and I know or believe that Edwina Boyle is alive and I believe that, at some time in the future, you or someone else will discover where she is and the name she is living under.

'What she wishes to do with her life is for her to do but I am not going to be lumbered with being accused of being a bloody murder suspect in a murder investigation and let's cut the crap and the bullshit, that's what you believe, otherwise I wouldn't be in this chair now. Now, I've lived with this bloody cloud for all this time and I am not going to keep continue doing it.

'I'm not trying to make out I'm a saint, as I'm not, but for the last twelve years I've worked my arse off. I don't drink much at all. I have never gone out by myself and I've never hit her, so why it's happened, I'm stuffed if I know. But for whatever reason she has for going, why she has totally rejected the kids, I can't understand that part at all.

'If I knew where she was now and was in — I'd go down and punch her in the mouth, I bloody would. After living like I have for bloody as long as I have, and putting up with the bloody shit that I have, I think I have every right to get bloody angry. But as far as who she's with, whether she's rich or poor, bloody black, blue, green or orange and got 17 children, I don't give a damn. I am not interested. But I am interested in knowing where she is, only to satisfy you people, not for me.

'If this comes around to what you're implying, I go to jail for the rest of my bloody life. And within ten years, capital punishment will be back in. So I could well go to the bloody chair or be hung for something that I have not done.'

Senior Sergeant John Morrish of the Homicide Squad, known as 'The Pope' for his ability to help people confess, asked Fred Boyle a simple question. It was the 1030th of the interview. 'All right. Just one last matter I wanted to ask you, Fred, have you — are you in any way responsible for the disappearance or the death of your wife?'

Boyle: 'No. Absolutely not, other than the fact that I was her husband and at the time we were suffering difficulties in our marriage. So I will take a fair portion of the blame but I will not take any blame for her disappearance in a — in relation to what your people are implying.'

Morrish said bluntly: 'I'm not implying anything, I've asked you straight out.'

Boyle: 'You know, I — well, fine. And I answered straight out and I'll bloody answer that same question time and time again.'

Careesa Boyle told police that shortly before her mother disappeared, she had said she might have to go away for a while and that she hoped her daughter would understand. The court was told police suspect she was referring to the filming of a *This is Your Life* episode about her uncle, Lord Tonypandy, a former speaker of Britain's House of Commons, who died in 1997.

Valerie Bordley believes there were plans by the program's producers to fly her sister back to England secretly for the filming, but she disappeared before the episode was shot in late 1983.

Their brother, David, later made a police statement denying that he had provided his brother with information about the missing woman. Fred Boyle alleged that he had. He declined to answer questions at the inquest on the ground of self-incrimination.

Ms Wilmoth found it probable that Edwina Boyle was dead. She said it was unlikely the mother of two had vanished and created a new identity. She did not accept that she had committed suicide or died some time after she disappeared.

'The length of time which has elapsed since Mrs Boyle's disappearance, with no contact with her children or her family in Britain, makes it extremely unlikely that she is still alive, despite instances where missing persons have been found after many years. The evidence that Mrs Boyle was a devoted mother and not the sort of woman who would disappear for any reason was very compelling. Whilst it is possible for a person to vanish with the creation of a new identity, it is most unlikely in this case, to the extent that it can be reasonably discounted, and on the balance of probabilities, it is safe and reasonable to find that she is dead.'

She made pointed comments about Fred Boyle. 'The weight of evidence suggests the possibility of Mr Boyle being responsible for her disappearance by taking her life, although there is no · direct evidence of his involvement. It is a possibility which cannot be discounted. There is, however, insufficient evidence for me to make a finding on contribution on the part of Mr Boyle.'

For the Homicide Squad, the case remains open. Police have received a tantalising call with the promise of new information that may create a breakthrough. There is a $50,000 reward for information on the presumed murder.

Valerie Bordley headed back to England after the inquest, in debt and no closer to knowing what really happened to her sister. 'I am glad I came,' she said before leaving Australia. 'I have met some of Edwina's friends and I am convinced that she would not have disappeared and never contacted her children.

'I feel hurt and betrayed that her husband has taken a vow of silence when he may have some answers. I hope someone will have the courage to come forward so that we can find out what happened.

'I know this is not the end. I believe one day certain matters will see the light of day and someone will be charged. I will be back for the trial.' Fred Boyle declined to comment on the case

Three years later the Homicide Squad office on the ninth floor of the St Kilda Road police complex was looking a touch shabby. Senior police decided it could do with new carpet. They called for quotes from respected carpet layers.

Enter Fred Boyle, who carefully measured the offices for a quote.

He didn't get the job.

CHAPTER 6

Laughing Grass
The world's biggest dope pusher

'There's more money in dope than books'

IN an age in which anyone connected with the drug trade is painted as evil incarnate, Howard Marks should be one of the most reviled people in the world. Drug dealers do not come bigger — or more successful — than the Oxford graduate and former M16 spy.

Yet it is hard not to like the affable Marks, a man of legendary charm and generosity. Even the investigators who pursued him around the world stress he was never involved in hard drugs or violence. He may have been a drug boss, but he was never a gangster.

'Howard is an engaging, personable guy who makes people feel very comfortable with him,' says US Drug Enforcement Administration investigator Craig Lovato, who chased Marks around the world.

The agency once described Marks as the world's biggest cannabis dealer. At one stage he had links to 14 countries and 113 known associates involved in selling marijuana on an unprecedented scale. In a career spanning more than 20 years, he used sea-going tugs, freighters, giant rock concert speakers, ocean buoys and even US Navy containers to move huge shipments of cannabis around the world. When he used the Navy containers he cheekily made sure the

US military picked up the bill. He imported 1250 kilograms of hashish from Karachi to California in containers marked 'US Navy aircraft parts.'

It all came unstuck in 1988 when the 'gentlemen smuggler' faced the prospect of spending the rest of his life in an American jail.

But fortune does, it seems, sometimes favour the brave – or the reckless. The audacious dope dealer was released on parole in 1995, having served just seven years of his sentence. He moved to the Spanish island of Majorca, although his health seemed to be substantially better than that of another well-known fugitive, Christopher Skase, who lives only a few blocks away.

Unlike Skase, Marks doesn't dodge the spotlight. He wrote a best selling autobiography *(Mr Nice)* and was prepared to be photographed smoking dope. He even stood for parliament on a pro-marijuana ticket in the 1997 British General Elections.

With typical frankness, Marks says that if all else fails he may go back to what he knows best, smuggling dope.

It all began with a few university chums who shared joints in the mid 1960s. Within a few short years they had formed a cartel known as 'The Enterprise', shifting huge amounts of dope around the globe.

Key people, many of them relatives or 1960 hippy types, had code names. US court documents list co-offenders as The Chef, Mr Straight, The Vicar, The School Teacher, Mr Sewage, The Dishwasher, Mr Bliss, and The Rabbit. They were mostly sophisticated, well educated men, with no criminal records and mutual interests in dope, sex and rock and roll.

Marks was recruited by a former Oxford colleague, Hamilton McMillan, to be an agent for the MI6 intelligence agency and was used in a farcical attempt to infiltrate the Irish Republican Army. Marks was moving drugs with a maniac Irishman, Jim McCann, whom MI6 was convinced used the profits to help buy arms for the IRA.

In a classic double-cross, Marks managed to use his spy background as a cover for his lucrative drug dealings. After all he was risking his life by infiltrating one of the most dangerous terrorist organisations in the world. To make an omelette you have to break eggs.

The son of a Welsh sea captain, Marks used his contacts, wit and undeniable charm to build a formidable operation. Even when caught virtually red-handed in Britain with a shipment of 15 tonnes of Colombian cannabis valued at $40 million and brought across the world in an ocean-going tug, he managed a bizarre and audacious defence.

He told the jury that as an MI6 agent he had been working for the Mexican intelligence service to infiltrate a drug cartel and that, far from being a big-time marijuana smuggler, he was a fearless anti-drug crusader. He even produced a dark and mysterious Mexican law enforcement agent to back his claims.

It was a ridiculous defence that even his own legal counsel said was doomed to fail. It worked.

'I don't believe for one minute they (the jury) believed the defences presented to them. They just didn't want nice guys to spend years in jail for transporting beneficial herbs from one part of the world to another,' Marks said later.

After the trial, a retired senior British policeman, who had confessed to leaking information on Marks to the press, committed suicide by hari-kiri. 'No one was meant to die in all this nonsense,' Marks lamented.

During his drug dealing career he had 43 aliases, driving licences in the names of Waylon Jennings and Elvis Presley and a passport in the name Donald Nice. For years he was known as Albi (an anagram of bail). He planned to travel to Australia to discuss drug deals with a group of criminals but was refused entry under his real name because of a criminal conviction.

'A hundred years ago that would have guaranteed a trip to Australia; now it was enough to prevent it,' he wrote in his highly entertaining autobiography. Undeterred, he was later granted a visa under the name, Mr Tetley.

Marks was considering moving to Taiwan and smuggling drugs into Australia when he was finally arrested.

At his peak he had up to 89 phone lines and 25 companies around the world. He had a string of boutiques, bars, recording studios and travel agencies. To deal around the world in the 1980s you needed the phone and that was part of Marks' downfall. US police began to tap the phones and started the exhaustive process of building a case, but Marks was harder to catch than most. He kept finding new ways to smuggle and different markets to flood. One of his most successful scams was to import drugs inside giant rock concert speakers from Paris to California via New York. To complete the cover Marks recruited four out-of-work musicians to arrive with the gear and pretend they were on a US tour. He called them 'Laughing Grass'. What else?

There were several similar imports carried out by Marks' team, but on these occasions no fake bands were needed. The speakers were imported, unloaded and then sent back to Europe.

Marks had connections with the IRA, the Mafia, The Yakuza, the Australian underworld, Nepalese monks, the Thai army, the Palestine Liberation Organisation, English peers, US martial arts experts and the murky world of international espionage, including the CIA.

His links included a series of big Australian drug dealers whom he met in the Philippines in the mid-1980s, in the company of one of the world's greatest rogues, former Sydney bongo player and British peer, Lord Anthony Moynihan, who was protected by corrupt elements in the Marcos family. He wanted to persuade Marks to buy, or invest in an island in the Philippines to grow marijuana. Marks remained sceptical but he loved the bizarre lifestyles of the renegade Lord and the Australian criminals.

One of those he met was one of Australia's least-known, richest and most successful criminals, former Carlton identity, Laurence Edward 'The Boxer' McLean, a man with the rather boring alias of Joe Smith. But that was McLean: quiet, low key and out of the spotlight. That's how he avoided arrest for decades.

McLean and Marks liked each other. They talked in tonnes, not kilos. It was McLean who invited Marks to come to Sydney to talk business. Both owned international travel agents as fronts. McLean wanted more cannabis sources. 'I've been bringing dope into Australia all my life,' McLean is said to have told Marks. 'There's a huge demand for it back home. I don't need credit. I'll pay up front.'

Before he made it big in the world of drugs he was a known criminal in Melbourne with priors for false pretences, burglary, robbery, theft and assault.

Like many crims he progressed through the ranks by travelling to Europe and becoming one of the professional shoplifting group, the

'Kangaroo gang'. Australian police say that by the time he met Marks, McLean was worth about $20 million and moving regularly from Asia to Europe with his young girlfriend.

He had several British and Greek passports, including one under the name of Panos Logethetic.

He bought a Sydney travel agency for $500,000 as a money laundering front, and a subsidiary in Hong Kong. The Asian connection would simply send false accounts to the Sydney agency for group travel. The parent company then paid the fake bills with drug money and the transaction would appear legitimate.

Despite knowing a great deal about McLean police are not even close to catching him. National Crime Authority and state police force investigations were plagued with leaks and problems.

At one point, NCA surveillance experts from the top secret Operation Freeboot investigation travelled to Queensland to follow a key Marks-McLean identity. They were surprised when they saw the man they wanted to watch looking at them through the window of their motel room. It is believed he was tipped off by a senior Queensland police officer.

After the syndicate's Australian connection of the global syndicate was warned, it moved $8 million offshore in just six weeks using a corrupt Gold Coast lawyer. Investigators found that the money was brought into a bank in garbage bags, cardboard boxes and backpacks. Tellers were surprised when the lawyer brought in a cardboard box and told staff he hadn't had a chance to count the money. The box contained $600,000.

The information gathered by the NCA investigators sounded like the script from a B-Grade movie. Senior executives at the NCA were not impressed and eventually the investigation lost momentum and died.

Marks enjoyed the company of his Australian connections. 'I like Joe (McLean) very much,' he said from Majorca. 'I admired his wit and sense of adventure. He struck me as a man who had come from a heavier background who was happier in a gentler life. I wanted to be like him and stick in the same trade until I was in my 60s.'

The two men were similar in some ways. They were in the same trade, used the same fronts, shared similar senses of humour and loved the good life. But they were also opposites in a way. McLean made sure he kept a low profile. He had no family and moved from hotel to hotel. He hid his wealth and remained an obscure figure. Marks, on the other hand, loved a high profile. There have been three books, two television documentaries and a huge number of newspaper articles written about him. He was no shrinking violet.

Moynihan feted Marks. He named the best room in his hotel the Howard Marks suite. He threw a party where the guests were key military figures, Australian criminals, politicians and a bevy of young girls. There was even a full-grown tiger in a cage on the front lawn. It was no typical suburban barbecue. It certainly wasn't BYO.

For all the show, McLean took Marks aside and told him never to trust Moynihan. He should have listened to the quiet Australia, but the group was too much fun to ignore. Marks went out to dinner with an old Australian crim known as 'The Fibber.' They ended in an exclusive restaurant with a gang of beggars, some nuns, a group of dwarfs and a few other hangers-on. The Fibber picked up the tab.

While the Australians were fun, some of them could be ruthless when it came to business.

Stuart John Perry was an Englishman with a fearsome reputation. He told the Costigan Royal Commission into the Painters and Dockers Union and criminal-related matters he carried a gun for his own protection during an underworld war.

A fitness fanatic, Perry was devoted to his Melbourne family but spent long periods overseas on 'business'. As a 'hard man' he was given the job as the money collector by one syndicate in the Philippines. He went to Sydney to collect a huge payment. In a spur of the moment decision he raked off $1 million for himself. He was told by one Australian drug criminal not to worry as it was only petty cash. He hasn't been seen since.

It is alleged he was thrown out of a light plane in the Philippines,

Another associate of McLean was a fellow Australian made good in the world of drugs, Keith Albert Collingburn, now believed to be living in Holland.

Collingburn had 28 convictions, including assault, rape, arson and possession of a pistol, before he moved to Europe. His brother, Neil Stanley Collingburn, died two days after an altercation with police at the Russell Street police station. Two police were charged with manslaughter, but were acquitted. In 1969 Keith Collingburn took the alias of Terrence Plunkett, the name of a dead infant, and set out on an international life of crime. His criminal network spread to include France, Switzerland and England.

Police records show he was connected with the Kangaroo Gang and was arrested in Paris on suspicion of involvement in a big jewel robbery. He served three years in France after being found guilty of theft, forgery and handling stolen property. He then returned to England and moved into the drug industry. He began to enjoy the high life. International police documents show he was spotted at a Christies auction in Geneva and used a Rolls Royce in London.

British police believed he was the main player in a drug syndicate with connections in Switzerland, India, the Netherlands and Pakistan. On his return to Australia he rented a house on the Gold Coast for $2000 a week. It was pocket money in the international drug importing scene.

While the Australians were making big money Marks was ready to expand. According to the DEA, his cartel bought a 30-metre fishing vessel, the 'Axel D', for $665,000 to move cannabis around the world. This would enable the group to move massive amounts of cannabis to Australia, Canada, Britain, Europe and the insatiable US market.

Australia was seen as a particularly soft target.

'It is a bit of a joke, really,' Marks was to say. 'You can take as much as you like into Australia anytime you want and you have a high chance of being successful. The coast is so huge and there are no internal borders.'

The head of his Thailand operations, Phillip Sparrowhawk, a former English racing identity, made a detailed confession of 700 pages to US Drug Enforcement Administration and Royal Canadian Mounted Police officers which implicates several main targets of long-running Australian investigations.

It is believed the Australian Federal Police approached Sparrowhawk to come to Australia to give evidence against his former associates, but that he refused. Police have been able to establish that at least one million was transferred to one of Sparrowhawk's Thai companies from Australia after a successful importation. And it is understood Sparrowhawk was probably linked to one of the

Australian Federal Police's biggest seizures of cannabis from a trawler in Queensland. As the stakes got higher Marks began to realise he was hot, that police were moving in. But while he was not addicted to the drugs he sold, he was addicted to the rush of 'the deal.'

He had more money than he could ever use. He had boxes of it and a large number of legitimate investments. He always had several drug deals running at one time. He once nearly collapsed with the effort of carrying one million in a suitcase in Hong Kong humidity during a transport strike.

He was greedy, but it was the excitement and the thought of outwitting authorities that provided the charge. He also believed he was doing nothing wrong, despite various national laws he broke with impunity.

Marks said an electronic tracking device was put on the ship when it was searched in Australia. He could have walked away, but he kept dealing. That decision cost him seven years in jail.

The 'Axel D' was used to transport 30 tonnes of marijuana to a waiting market in Vancouver. A further ten tonnes made its way to California via Mexico.

The crew dropped the tracking device in the sea off Pakistan in a floating package to give the impression the ship was waiting to be loaded with hashish. The ship then headed to the Thai coast to load 30 tonnes of cannabis from small fishing boats.

While Marks preferred the company of his Australian rogue mates and counter-culture survivors of the 1960s university days (one of his drug syndicates was called The Brotherhood of Love) he was in the big time and had to deal with hardened gangsters, including killers from the Mafia and the Yakuza. But while he talked big, he never talked tough. He was prepared to be ripped off for millions rather than use violence. He would just move on to the next deal. Just as a department store factors in a percentage for shoplifting, Marks knew that not every deal would go smoothly. Drugs were sometimes seized by authorities, suppliers demanded extra cash, people had to be bribed and buyers were arrested before they could pay.

'It was just part of the business,' he said. 'You try not to take it all too seriously and keep a sense of humour. It was an amazing, exciting life. We made very good money. I didn't seem to be any good at any business other than dope dealing.'

With the sort of money he was making Marks could afford to keep a sense of humour. According to US law enforcement documents Marks and his associates smuggled 25,000 kilos of hashish and marijuana into New York in 24 separate deals between 1975 and 1978. They estimated the profit at $48 million.

How much Marks made out of drug dealing is disputed. The Drug Enforcement Agency maintains he has a fortune hidden away. Marks says it has all been spent. For years the agency followed a confusing money trail around the world, partially hidden by smart money launderers and partially by the anarchistic nature of Marks and his associates.

After years of investigation the DEA found a huge safety deposit box in Hong Kong. A DEA agent said: 'When we opened it there was just a jar full of dead flies. We thought that might be a message of some type.'

It wasn't. 'They were dead ants, actually,' Marks explained later. 'I bought an ant farm for the kids at Christmas but I couldn't find any big ants in Majorca. An Australian in the Philippines said he could get me some ants, but they were dead and completely useless. I left them in the safety deposit box in Hong Kong.'

He was delighted the DEA felt this was a secret message. 'I am quite happy to fly that one,' he said.

He eventually admitted in court to having made about three million, but he now candidly confesses he did not speak of other deals not proven in court.

'The DEA remains convinced I have $200 million buried somewhere in the Swiss Alps, which is, of course, complete nonsense. They may think I'm very clever, but the DEA have been known to hopelessly exaggerate things.' He said hundreds of millions of dollars had passed through his hands but had not ended up in his pockets. 'It's more like the money that a bank teller handles. It wasn't mine. It's always hard to work out profit. I was always involved in between three and ten deals at a time. Everyone is cheating each other and lying about how much money they have had to give up out front. It is a complicated business.'

Marks may not have been addicted to marijuana but he was addicted to the marijuana business. Even when some of his friends and associates started to be arrested he continued to deal. Even when he was warned by a corrupt American policeman that he was under investigation, he smuggled. Even when he was told, 'your dog is sick' (rhyming slang, dog and bone, phone. Your phone is tapped) he couldn't stop.

Like so many high-flying business types of the 1980s he didn't see the crash coming. But in his case it wasn't the stock market, it was his front door in Majorca. The DEA arrested him in 1988.

'I knew I was going to be busted. The trouble was I didn't know if it would be tomorrow or in 3000 years. I really knew nothing else but being a smuggler. I was like a boxer who need to be knocked out to stop.'

If Marks had stopped when he knew he was under investigation maybe he would never have been arrested. Greed keeps some criminals going until they are caught. The thrill is greater than the risk.

The DEA estimated Marks was responsible for 15 percent of all the cannabis imported into the US, a claim he says is nonsense.

He always thought he would be able to fight the charges in Spain, in a more sympathetic environment, where marijuana possession is hardly a hanging offence.

While Marks had not really changed in the 20 years he had been dealing, the world had. The Americans, probably the biggest dope users in the world, were frightened. In the late 1980s the crime rate was spiralling and courts were jailing offenders at an unprecedented rate. College athletic heroes were dying from crack-cocaine abuse. Most major cities had 'no-go' areas controlled by street dealers. Police forces were reduced to using armed trucks as battering rams to smash open crack houses. Colombian drug cartel bosses were seemingly beyond policing. South American judges, politicians and police who dared to investigate the groups were murdered.

One politician was even given a diplomatic posting in Europe after it was learned there was a price on his head, but he was hunted down and killed.

The Colombians brought a new level of violence to North America. The country had seen its share of gang wars, but the South American criminals had a ruthlessness not seen before. If they believed they had been betrayed, the mobsters would order the death, not just of the guilty party, but his whole family, particularly the children. The theory was the children could grow up to avenge the death and it was better to deal with the problem then and there.

What did all of this have to do with a rascal Welshman who liked to deal dope? The American politicians, frustrated by their inability to curb the cocaine syndicates, and disturbed by the crack problem infiltrating the school system, brought in tougher drug laws and harsher penalties.

The new laws took discretion away from judges. 'Narcotics' included all drugs, including marijuana, and Marks's crimes also fitted under the racketeering laws. There were no clauses for gentlemen smugglers.

He was in big trouble but, typically, Marks was looking to use imagination and lateral thinking to fashion a way out. If he fought the case and lost he would face up to 145 years jail with no minimum. If he did a deal, he could be sentenced under the old laws which would give him some hope of getting out.

He began to build his defence, not on a dry legal argument but on his view that if you give a jury a half-entertaining story and show them you're a half-decent fellow, you may get off, despite the weight of evidence.

And the evidence was compelling. The DEA had more than 500 phone taps. Lord Moynihan, as predicted by 'The Boxer' McLean, had rolled over and made a statement. Moynihan had some charges pending in England and was ready to do a deal if they would be dropped. He wanted to take his seat in the House Of Lords so that it would pass on to his son and not to the family of his half brother, Colin Moynihan, minister for sport in the Thatcher government.

Moynihan tried to re-invent himself as some sort of police spy who had infiltrated drug syndicates for the US and British authorities. The reality was that he was a charming, fat spiv who always looked after himself. Marks remained remarkably philosophical about his betrayal. 'I can't really blame Tony actually. I'm not bitter,' he said. 'I blamed myself for getting close to him. I am not surprised at what he did, like a cornered rat, he struck out. Who should I blame — him for doing what comes naturally, or me for misjudging the situation?

'I really liked his company very much. He was an obvious rogue. I would never have dreamed of getting into business with him. I wanted to use his contacts. He had no sort of morals. He would do anything for money. There are many things I wouldn't do but I don't think Tony would ever worry about the morality of the proposition.'

In the end Moynihan didn't survive to cut a deal to get him back to the House of Lords. He died in Manila of a heart attack. A legal bid for his son to take the Peerage failed.

Facing the weight of evidence, Marks went back to his intelligence background. He planned to cobble together a story involving the sinister Australian merchant bank, Nugan Hand, the CIA and his MI6 connections. 'I studied Australian politics, crime, drug consumption, drug trafficking and banking systems,' he said.

The defence was to be that Marks had imported huge amounts of drugs to Australia and used the CIA-influenced Nugan Hand bank to launder the funds. He had then reported the corrupt American intelligence agency to his MI6 connections. The corrupt US spies had to discredit him, so the story went, and had organised his arrest and fabricated evidence that he had imported the marijuana into America.

He even got old weather reports from Australia. For each of the 500 phone taps he fabricated an Australian angle. He would confess to the jury that he smuggled marijuana, but he would explain that none of the grass went to the US but was imported into Australia. This would mean, or course that he had not breached any US laws and would have to be freed.

'I was convinced this Australian defence could work,' he said. 'It wasn't even as bizarre as the successful Mexican secret agent defence. But did American juries have a sense of humour?'

All his research was, in the end, wasted. Using the traditional investigative method of divide and rule, DEA investigators and prosecution lawyers offered deals to key members of the Marks group. Married men were told their wives would be sentenced to 20 years jail if they didn't co-operate. Eventually Marks' most trusted friends rolled over on him and made damning statements. The Welshman knew that funny stories and bizarre excuses would not help this time. It was the cue to do what he did best. Strike a deal.

He agreed to plead guilty if there was light at the end of the tunnel. He was sentenced to 25 years in jail, later reduced to 20. But because he pleaded under the old laws he was eligible for substantial sentence discounts for good behaviour. He served seven years before being released on parole in April, 1995.

If the authorities thought that Marks had finished with cannabis, they were wrong. While he claims he doesn't deal, he now resides in a three-storey villa not far from celebrity asthmatic, Christopher Skase, and smokes marijuana every day.

'I don't know him personally but I know his family', he said of Skase. 'They are quite well liked on the island. They can understand why he doesn't want to go home. They don't take fraud too seriously over here.'

Marks is living off the earnings from his book and a film is mooted.

He said that he had no doubt marijuana should be legal. 'It would have meant that people like me wouldn't have made millions of pounds, but I have never seen any harm in it.'

Would he go back to smuggling? 'I could conceive of circumstances where I would. But so far those circumstances haven't come around. There's more money in dope than books.'

(Mr Nice —An Autobiography, Secker and Warburg, RRP $24.95.)

The life and fast times of Howard Marks

1964: Attends University of Oxford, begins smoking marijuana.

Late 1960s: Becomes professional dope dealer.

1972: Recruited by former Oxford colleague to MI6 to catch suspected IRA arms dealer, James McCann.

1973: Forms fake rock bands to import cannabis to US inside giant concert speakers.

1973: Charged in Britain for smuggling marijuana into the US, skipped bail.

1980: Arrested for importing 15 tonnes of Colombian marijuana to England on board ocean-going tug, Karob.

1981: Acquitted when he claims he is an international anti-drugs connected with MI6; sentenced to two years on false passport charges; with remissions, serves five days.

1984: Imports 1250 kilos of hashish to California in US Navy containers.

1985: Syndicate buys own ship, the Axle-D, with Bank of America cheque for $665,000.

1985 Decides to fly to Australia to meet contacts on drug dealing: refused visa but later gets one under false name.

1986 Hashish valued at $17 million dropped and then smuggled to California; police allege the brand on the packages was Marks's eagle brand.

1988: Considers relocating his business to Taiwan to concentrate on smuggling into Australia.

1988: Arrested in Spain.

1990: Pleads guilty in the US to drug smuggling. Sentenced to 25 years jail.

1995: Released.

CHAPTER 7

Life is cheap ...
(If you know where to go)
Murder Inc

'Can you bring me a part of her
... part of her hand, whatever?'

AROUND Australia police have become increasingly aware of a sinister new trend in murder cases.

Thirty years ago Homicide Squads were sneeringly known as the 'domestics', because most murders involved family members or close friends.

In simpler times the offender often rang the police minutes after the killing, filled with remorse, to report the crime and then confess.

Even in cases where the offender tried to cover his tracks, it was usually too late. Most murders were not premeditated, alibis could not be fabricated, forensic evidence was left untouched, offenders would panic and police would identify likely suspects within hours. In short, most killers were inexperienced in criminal matters, and had no idea how to avoid detection.

In the murder business it is planning, combined with ruthlessness, that can create the perfect crime. In the underworld, there is no shortage of gangsters who will kill . . . for a price.

Victorian police know of at least ten recent unsolved murders which they believe were contract killings, carried out by paid hitmen.

A recent study has confirmed detectives' worst fears. Not only career criminals, but lovers, former wives and husbands, fathers and greedy business partners are looking for hired killers to do their dirty work.

Police know cases of seemingly respectable men who have tried to organise the murder of their former wives. They will sit and calmly talk through the details of the crime with the hitman as if it were just another business deal.

Some even agree that the mother of their children should be raped and possibly tortured before being killed, to further push suspicion from them. Some practice their 'grief-stricken' response ready for when they are told of the untimely death.

In a Melbourne case where police thwarted an attempt by a businessmen to get a hitman to kill his former wife, they moved in at the last minute. Police arrived at the man's house a short time after the woman was supposed to have been murdered.

The husband's lips quivered and his eyes filled with tears. He had practised for this moment. Unfortunately for him, so had the poker-faced policeman at the door. 'I have terrible news for you, sir,' the policeman said. 'Your wife is alive — and I am arresting you for conspiracy to murder'.

The husband, all set to 'break-down' with the news his wife had been killed in a unexplained attack, suddenly found he didn't need to fake emotion. The shock real enough when he realised his scheme had failed and he was heading to jail for many years.

In some cases, men have been prepared to orchestrate circumstances so that their children find their mother's dead body as a way to keep police looking in other directions.

In one case in England a father persuaded his two sons to beat their mother to death while he set up his alibi by sipping beers and playing darts at the local pub. He promised his boys an overseas trip and a jet-ski as a reward.

The cold-bloodedness of some of the plots are disturbing. In one case a husband demanded a body part, such as a finger, be provided by the hitman after the killing as proof that the contract had been carried out.

The husband brought his wife and child to a meeting with a

supposed killer so that he would recognise the woman when he went to kill her. The husband, who had an injured wrist, had his wife drive him to the meeting even though she was unlicensed. He told his wife he was meeting the man because he wanted to buy a car from the stranger.

He manipulated his wife to pass within metres of the would-be killer by taking her and their child to a nearby shop to buy them chips.

To fight back against the spate of contract killings, police have begun to use undercover operatives to short circuit the plots before they are carried out.

In the first major research project carried out into contract killings in Australia, Detective Chief Inspector Ron Blackshaw has found that killers have been offered between $5000 and $50,000 to carry out murders.

'Victoria Police records indicate individuals are prepared to pay a contract killer up to $50,000 for their services,' Mr Blackshaw said.

He said police knew of several criminals prepared to kill for a price. Blackshaw, a former homicide investigator who has completed the research paper for his Masters Degree in Criminology, said some paid hits could go unreported.

'One cause for concern, is the possibility of a major "dark figure" of homicide.' Blackshaw, who also tutors in psychology and crime, said the person most likely to pay for a murder is a lover or spouse rather than a business partner or crime figure.

He said two undercover operatives had to be relocated after their identities were disclosed in court. One had received a number of death threats before being moved.

In one case, a paid hitman confessed to police that he killed a Melbourne man for $12,000 but as he had not been cautioned and the interview was not taped the statement could not be used in court and he was not charged.

In another case, a hitman was briefed on a victim and given details of the type of weapon to be used and the time and place for the murder. Police said he decided not to take the job, but a week later another man carried out the killing.

At least three women who had contracts taken out on their lives by their husbands have moved and been given new identities for added protection. In two cases the offenders have been released from jail after each served less than five years.

The law on incitement to murder was changed in 1993 so that an offender can be sentenced to life. Previously the maximum was five years jail.

In one case where police charged a man with plotting to have a hitman kill his wife, detectives believe another killer from Europe was flown in to complete the job. Police put the woman under protection and the suspected contract killer later left Australia.

Of the ten suspected unsolved contract killings all the victims were males, three were drug-related, one gambling, and one involved a struggle for power in organised crime.

The head of the homicide squad, Detective Chief Inspector Rod Collins, said once a hitman had struck successfully he was likely to continue to accept contracts.

'We know there are criminals who will kill for money. There a number of major rewards on offer for information on murders which look as if they may have been professional hits,' he said. 'These people know the law and become more difficult to prosecute as they become more proficient,' he said.

In the twelve cases detected over two years where undercover police posed as hitmen the proposed victims were wives, daughters, brothers, a former lover, a son-in-law, a business partner and a drug rip-off.

In one case a man charged with murder actually offered an undercover hitman money to kill him, in a bizarre 'suicide' plan.

His name was William James Robinson. He was charged, and later convicted, of paying $40,000 to a contract killer — actually an undercover policeman — to murder his lover's husband, Robert Purvis. After he was charged Robinson also wanted his lover killed, as she would be a key witness against him.

Realising that he would be convicted of the first murder, Robinson withdrew the contract against his lover and asked the 'hitman' to kill him (Robinson) as he did not want to spend years in jail. In the end, Robinson had to do the job himself. He was convicted and committed suicide in Pentridge in 1996.

Blackshaw found, not surprisingly, that criminals found it easier to find a hitman than non-criminals, who were more likely to be duped by an undercover police officer because they could not tap in to the network of 'Murder Inc.'

He concluded that using undercover officers posing as hitmen saved lives by stopping murder plots. 'Otherwise there is a presumption that the procurer will persevere until a willing killer is found.'

In England a man became so desperate to find a hitman to kill his wife he put an ad in the local paper. 'An opportunity to earn 250 pounds in a few minutes. A man of average intelligence with a tearaway disposition willing to take chances wanted for out-of-the-ordinary job which can be performed only once.'

When non-criminals tried to find killers they were usually thwarted but criminals, on the other hand, found it disturbingly easy to find killers without conscience who will murder strangers.

FOR the first time Homicide Squad detectives have ranked a series of ten recent murders as probable contract killings. A rating of ten indicates a certain hit, based on an off-the-record confession or ironclad evidence deemed inadmissible in a court. Less conclusive cases were given a lower rating.

CASE ONE

INVESTIGATORS rate this case ten out of ten as a professional hit.

Stuart Lance Pink was a 26-year-old drug dealer and thief. He was a street-level heroin dealer who could make plenty of money but, according to police, his ambitions exceeded his abilities.

Pink was, in criminal terms, 'overdue'. He had begun failing to pay his suppliers. In the drug world such failures can be fatal.

Despite warnings, he continued to run his own race and began to rip off fellow drug dealers, organising 'run throughs', forced entry raids on other sellers' homes, bashing them and stealing their drugs and money.

Crime syndicates don't like wild cards. If everyone stays in his place, there are profits for everyone. But Pink was greedy and treacherous, and this could not be tolerated.

About 1 am on 11 March, 1995, Pink was walking down Park Street, St Kilda, unaware that behind him were two paid killers, one in a car, the other on foot. The latter moved up to Pink and fired three shots from a .22 pistol, one to the back of the head and two to the left temple.

The gunman stepped into the waiting car and the two drove off. The whole incident took less than 30 seconds.

An investigator said there was no doubt it was a contract killing paid for by a drug syndicate. He said organised crime used the same principles as modern companies. 'Stick to the business you are in to make money, and if you have a crisis hire somebody with the expertise to fix it.'

Rating: ten out of ten.

CASE TWO

TOUGH Tony Franzone was a bad salesman, a would-be gangster and a big gambler with a history of minor crimes. He was well known around the illegal card games in Carlton and gave the impression of being 'connected' to organised crime. He like to pretend that he was a major player in the world of violence and gambling, but he was tolerated only while he paid his way.

He was given many chances to buy his way out of trouble but he kept gambling, hoping for the big win. By 1992 he owed $35,000 to legitimate gambling institutions and substantially more to criminal networks.

He decided to pull out of the peripheral crime world and married a woman he had known for eleven years. He hoped the criminal network would forget him and wipe the debt.

He was wrong. They wiped him instead.

Franzone started to get threats at work and an unidentified man started looking for him at his old Clayton address. Police believe the illegal gambling network decided to make an example of Franzone.

By killing him, they knew, they would not get the money back. But others would be encourage to pay their debts.

Franzone was shot dead outside his Mt Waverley home at 8.45 pm on 29 May, 1992. He got out of his car and was about to take his eleven-week-old baby from the rear seat when he spotted a lone gunman walking out of the shadows.

Police believe he knew the stranger was there to kill him. Franzone immediately began to run but was felled with two shots from a .32 handgun in front of his wife, who was in the driveway. The killer then walked up to the victim, who was on his knees, leant over him and fired two more shots into the back of the head, killing him instantly.

Police said the killer then calmly walked to a waiting car, believed to driven by a second man, and drove off.

There is a $50,000 reward for information on the murder.

Rating: ten out of ten.

CASE THREE

QUOCK Cuong Dwong, alias Alan Young, of Braybrook, 25, was a drug dealer on the make. According to police, he was two levels above the street in the heroin chain. Police believe he was killed by a rival heroin dealer who wanted to take over his distribution area.

'What was abundantly clear to investigators from their analysis of the crime scene was that Dwong died as a result of a cold-blooded execution. On 30th January, 1992, DC (Dwong) was taken to the Sandringham beach. Between 2 am and 4 am he was made to kneel on the sand and was then shot to death with three bullets from a .38 handgun at point blank range,' Detective Chief Inspector Ron Blackshaw wrote in his Masters research.

The letters I A N were scrawled in the sand near his feet. Police still don't understand the significance of the message.

There is a $50,000 reward for information on the murder.

Rating: seven out of ten.

CASE FOUR

CHARLES Francis Caron was looking forward to watching highlights of the 1990 soccer World Cup when there was a knock on the door of his house in Kendall Street, Hampton, a bayside Melbourne suburb.

Caron's wife, Sally, and ten-year-old son, Marcelle, had left the house and braved the Melbourne winter about an hour earlier to visit a friend recovering from heart surgery.

Police believe Caron must have been suspicious of whoever knocked on the door around 8.30 pm, because he walked up the hallway armed with a kitchen knife.

Detectives now know that the man at the door was a paid hitman armed with a shotgun and the knowledge that Caron was the only person in the house. He fired a single blast into Caron's chest at point blank range.

Caron was dead before he slumped forward and hit the ground.

About 9 pm his wife and son arrived home. The boy opened the front door, walked in and turned left into his bedroom. He saw the room had been disturbed and told his mother. She turned on the hall light and saw her husband lying face down.

Police examined the house and found two rooms had been ransacked with drawers pulled out and the contents dumped on the floor. There was no sign of forced entry.

Caron was a 53-year-old engineer who lived in a respectable suburb, but he had a reputation for violence.

The Coroner, Iain West, said, 'Inquiries by the police established that the deceased was a difficult, lonely and violent individual who was possibly mentally unstable. Family members stated he kept a knife beside his chair in the lounge room, it being readily available in that position for protection, with his wife stating that she believed he had been previously threatened.'

Mr West found; 'Several motives for the deceased's death have been canvassed at the inquest, these being:

i) a desire by an admirer of Mrs Caron to protect her from further abuse and assault;

ii) robbery, it being alleged that the deceased didn't trust banks and left large sums of money in the house, although several hundreds of dollars in his pocket was not taken.

iii) as a result of a reprisal by a disgruntled tradesman, it having been alleged by the deceased that the tradesman had performed faulty workmanship on the extension being built at the house.'

'There is insufficient evidence before the inquest upon which to conclude which of these motives, if any, is the reason for the deceased being killed.'

But, in a bizarre twist, police have actually found the killer, who has admitted to the crime but is unlikely to be charged. 'He admitted off the record to investigators that he was hired to kill (Caron) ... for a fee of $12,000. According to Victorian law, evidence of oral confession obtained in circumstances such as these is inadmissible at trial, and

DK (the killer) was well aware of that,' Blackshaw wrote. Police believe that a third person with an extensive criminal network paid DK the $12,000 for the hit to protect Mrs Caron from possible domestic violence. There is nothing to indicate she knew anything about the killing.

The State Government has offered a $50,000 reward for information leading to the arrest and conviction of the killer.

Rating: ten out of ten.

CASE FIVE

CHRISTOPHER Philips was a civil engineer with the Melbourne and Metropolitan Board of Works. He lived with his wife and children in Cheltenham, in the outer southern suburbs.

According to Coroner, Louis Hill, Philips 'was respected as a professional and family man.'

He had worked at the board's Spencer Street office but, on 1 May, 1989, the day of his death, he started work at the Mount Waverley office and was home by 5.30 pm, earlier than his previous routine.

After dinner his wife, Stella, and two children, aged eight and ten, left the house to go to music lessons. Philips, 42, was dressed in a blue tracksuit ready to go for a run.

When the family returned they found him dead on the kitchen floor. 'His head was found in a pool of blood and there was a pillow on his face and two kitchen knives lying next to his body,' the Coroner found.

An autopsy revealed he had been beaten around the head with a blunt instrument and his throat cut.

Police believe the killer tried to make the attack look like a burglary gone wrong, but they believe there was another motive for the murder.

'The family room of the house was in a disturbed condition, furnishings and books had apparently been strewn about. However, there was no evidence of theft and according to police the condition of the family room was inconsistent with an attempted burglary and theft,' the Coroner wrote. Police said Philips was a quiet man who was hardly known by his colleagues, even though he had worked for the Board of Works for 17 years.

Mr Blackshaw said police had interviewed two suspects who gave them false alibis and lied about certain known facts. They believe the suspects paid to have Philips killed, but detectives do not know the identity of the hitman. They are still investigating and have interviewed 250 people in connection with the murder.

'It was proved conclusively that (the suspects) conspired to mislead the investigation in several areas, and established false alibis ... investigators suspected their involvement as procurers of a third party killer.'

Rating: eight out of ten.

CASE SIX

GEOFFREY Engers was a teacher who met his wife-to-be on a trip to Thailand. They settled in Melbourne but later he dumped his wife and formed a relationship with her sister.

On 15 December, 1989, Engers, 42, was shot dead with a .22 rifle as he walked towards his car parked in the driveway of his house at 7.30 am. Four shots were fired, one hitting him in the head.

Seven days earlier, a man with an extensive criminal record had approached another man and asked him to kill Engers for $15,000. He said a .22 rifle would be supplied and the target should be shot as he walked to his car in the driveway of the house. The criminal said he knew that Engers always went to his car at 7.30 am.

The man who wanted Engers dead actually took the potential hitman to the Endeavour Hills house and briefed him on the target's movements. But the prospective killer shied off and police believe another hitman was recruited for the job. 'There is conclusive evidence that the recruit did not proceed to kill (Engers). Investigators believe that following the refusal, conspirators successfully procured an unknown assassin to kill (Engers) using the same plan. This case is still open and the investigation is active,' Blackshaw concluded.

Rating: ten out of ten.

CASE SEVEN

ALFONSO Muratore, 39, knew for at least a year that his death certificate had been signed. He just didn't know who would deliver it.

Muratore was heavily connected in the Honoured Society, an Italian-based organised crime cartel with influence in the Victorian fruit and vegetable industry for more than 30 years. Muratore's father, Vincenzo, was shot dead by the same group while on his way to the market in 1964. His son was killed in almost exactly similar circumstances in August 1992. Both were killed in Hampton, only a kilometre apart.

Alfonso carried an illegal .22 pistol for about a year after telling friends he knew a contract had been taken out on his life. He had left his wife, the daughter of alleged Melbourne godfather Liborio Benvenuto. Police believe this angered senior members of the Honoured Society. Muratore left his house with his friend and workmate, Ron Lever, the stepfather of his de facto wife. A lone gunman, armed with a shotgun, shot Lever in the legs to immobilise him. He could have easily killed the older man, but he was saving death for his real target. He stepped forward and fired four blasts into Muratore, who died instantly. The killer has never been found. There is a $50,000 reward for information on the case

Rating: ten out of ten.

CASE EIGHT

DIMITRIOUS Nanos was a well-known drug dealer who specialised in heroin and had progressed from street dealer to supplier in the narcotics chain. Police believe that on 6 April 1969 he was tortured, robbed and murdered after a tip-off from a rival drug dealer

His Hoppers Crossing house had been ransacked, consistent with a forced entry raid and drug rip-off. He had been bashed and tests showed he had been tortured before his death. He had severe head injuries, bruises covering his body, puncture marks to his left ankle, indicating a possible heroin injection, and his toe nails had been ripped off. He was beaten in several rooms of the house. A tooth was found in one room and blood in several others. Detectives believe three criminals went to the house for the rip-off. They think Nanos was tied too tightly around the mouth with tape and was beaten while taped to the cupboard doors in the hallway. It is possible he died too quickly as he had not told the gang he had $60,000 buried in the front yard of his house. Police believe one of the offenders actually rang the ambulance service asking for advice on how to resuscitate the victim.

Mr Blackshaw said there were six separate sources indicating that a notorious violent criminal and standover man accepted the job. Police said the killers stole jewellery valued at $45,000, including a $25,000

Rolex watch, and a ring with the number 69 set in diamonds, but they failed to find the stash of cash buried in the garden.

Rating: ten out of ten.

CASE NINE

SANTO Ippolito, a retired Italian fruiterer, was battered to death by a man who smashed his way into the victim's Springvale home in December, 1991. There were no demands for money and nothing was stolen. According to police the man broke down the front door, walked into Ippolito's bedroom and began beating him.

Ippolito's wife turned on the light and saw the killer, but did not recognise him. She was also bashed. Police looked at the possibility that the murder was prompted by a political dispute involving the Italian Pensioners' Club of Springvale where Ippolito, 71, was president.

Police believe the killer may have been a paid hitman because all known suspects who had a grudge or a motive to harm the victim had solid alibis. There is a $50,000 reward for information on the case.

Rating: seven out of ten.

CASE TEN

RAKESH Bhanot, 33, was helpless when he was stabbed at least ten times as he lay in a Parkville hospital bed on 8 November, 1993. Bhanot had been admitted to hospital after being found unconscious at the bottom of the Nunawading Swimming Pool two months earlier. He had been revived but suffered severe brain damage and doctors said he would never recover. On the night of the murder, a nurse on night shift at North West Hospital in Parkville saw a man wearing a balaclava.

Police and security were called but the man escaped. At 2.20 am, Bhanot was found dead in his bed. Police on routine patrol saw a red car, believed to be an early-1980s Toyota station-wagon, with P-plates parked in Poplar Road outside the hospital around the time of the murder. The two police underwent hypnosis to provide more information on what they had seen that night, but it wasn't enough to crack the case.

The head of the Homicide Squad, Detective Chief Inspector Rod Collins, said: 'This is a straight-out mystery. We don't know why he was chosen.' There is a $50,000 reward for information on the murder.

Rating: eight out of ten.

CLEVER undercover police work has foiled many murder plots. In 1993 a Melbourne man called Kemal Sahin started to plan the murder of his wife, Sevda. Through a go-between he was introduced to two undercover police who posed as hitmen.

Their first meeting was held at the Shell Service station at Kalkallo, on the Hume Freeway just north of Melbourne, on 13 June 1993 .The two police met Sahin and the go-between. Their secretly-taped conversations give an insight on how cheap life can be and the callous nature of some people who appear to be normal citizens in a civilised society.

UNDERCOVER (1): 'How are you, brother?'

SAHIN; 'Thank you, I'm good. I want my wife cleaned.' (Turkish expression for killed).

UNDERCOVER (2): 'What does he mean?'

SAHIN. 'Yes, I want her to be made non-existent, in other words, like, I don't want her to live. At this stage my money is at Turkey.'

He said he would report his wife as missing after she was murdered.

SAHIN: 'Nah, just that I want one, within 24 hours I'm going to report that my wife is missing to police, nothing else.'

He told the two hitmen he felt he had no choice but to kill his wife. 'Because if I don't do it to her she is going to do it to me.'

He said if the body was to be found there should be no evidence. 'It's not in an identifiable state.'

He said he was prepared to pay if she was left crippled but he preferred for her to be killed 'Without suffering, whatever is appropriate, the shortest possible way.'

SAHIN: 'The wife goes to school in the mornings. If you ran her over with a truck and killed her, I wouldn't care.'

SAHIN said he was prepared to take his wife to a place where she could be killed. 'I want to see her deceased ... Once she is made non-existent my assets in Turkey like, I'm gunna go with my child ... I don't want her to live.'

Saturday, 19 June. Meeting at Kalkallo service station.

Sahin drew a map of the house for the killer.

SAHIN: 'Do it but if you are going to do it like an accident, do it in my presence. I'll bring her wherever you want whatever position you want. Because I could help in that regard like, no-one can say anything at me.'

Sunday 27 June, 1993 Kalkallo service station.

Sahin has been injured in a fight with his nephew. At a previous meeting the undercover police ask for a photograph of the proposed victim. Sahin goes one better and gets his wife to drive him to meet the would-be killers.

SAHIN: 'My wife and child are at that car over there.'

UNDERCOVER: (1): 'Did she drive the car?'

SAHIN: 'Yeah, she drove the car, she hasn't got a licence as well.'

He then organises for his wife and child to walk past the 'hitmen'. 'At this stage I will go to buy some chips with them.'

UNDERCOVER: (1) 'What does she think you are doing?'

SAHIN: 'At this stage she thinks that I am negotiating a car deal.'

Monday, 28 June, 1993. Kalkallo service station.

UNDERCOVER: (1): 'Hello brother.'

SAHIN: 'Has the task been done?'

UNDERCOVER: (2): 'It's done, mate.'

SAHIN: 'So she's gone?'

UNDERCOVER: (1) 'It's done, Yes.'

SAHIN: 'Have you brought anything to prove that she is dead.'

UNDERCOVER: (2) produces eight gold bracelets and a gold chain with a pendant that reads 'I love you' and shows it to Sahin.

SAHIN: 'Okay, thanks. You killed her with a gun. It's finished in other words.'

UNDERCOVER: (2) Yeah, I shot her in the head. She's dead.'

SAHIN: 'Can you bring me a part of her ... part of her hand, whatever?'

UNDERCOVER:(1) 'Or part of a finger or something like that.'

UNDERCOVER: (2) 'That'll be hard for me to do, he wants me to chop off a finger.'

SAHIN: 'Like he's done it and it's finished like no-one is going to be able to find her, is that right?'

UNDERCOVER: (2): 'She definitely won't be found.'

SAHIN: 'I'm going to give $15,000 to you.'

CHAPTER 8

Breaking point
Death of a country cop

*'Us bloody one-manners are
a forgotten breed by most'*

TO Jim Wiggins, being a policeman meant more than locking up crooks. He believed he should be a leader in the community, a role model, someone to be relied upon.

Wiggins didn't want to be another anonymous cop who worried about the job in office hours. To him policing wasn't a job, it was his life. And, eventually, his death.

That was half a lifetime ahead on 2 April, 1972, when the young Jim Wiggins was one of 25 recruits who walked into the newly-acquired police academy, the former Corpus Christi College in Glen Waverley, to begin training. The recruits were grouped in alphabetical order. Wiggins roomed with a friendly young man named Ray Watson.

Watson, later a detective senior sergeant in the Armed Robbery Squad, was to remember his room-mate as a 'keen and decent man.'

'I joined the job with the hope of being a detective, but Jim was different. He wanted to serve the community in uniform in the traditional manner. He was pleasant, conscientious and friendly.'

He said he was not surprised when Wiggins took the job at the one-office station at Tarnagulla, an old goldfields town in central Victoria.

'It seemed to suit him, he was a down to earth person.' For Wiggins, it was a little like going home. He had been raised in St Arnaud, nearby, before moving to Melbourne when he was 16. He tried several jobs before deciding he wanted to be a policeman, but was on the borderline of the height requirements and had to undergo a series of stretching exercises before he made the limit.

Ray Watson last saw his old room-mate at the 20-year squad reunion. 'He hadn't changed. He was enjoying life and was the same talkative bloke I remembered. He seemed to be thriving.'

Jim Wiggins was no high flyer, but he seemed rock solid and unflappable. He had a steady, if unspectacular, career in eastern suburban police stations. His first marriage broke up, and he remarried in 1982. In 1989 he applied for the vacancy at Tarnagulla, 165 kilometres north west of Melbourne.

Those who knew Jim said he went bush because he thought he could make a difference there. In the city, policing was a round of grief and conflict. It meant shift after shift of trying to put a bandage on a weeping sore. In the country, he thought, it would be better. You could anticipate problems; try to deal them before it was too late.

'He felt that working at Ringwood was like being a repairman who was given a list of jobs as long as your arm at the start of a shift and just kept going until the end of the shift,' his wife, Helen, was to say.

'He wanted to be part of a community. We went to Tarnagulla because we saw it as a change of lifestyle, a chance to get out of the rat race.'

Tarnagulla, once a bustling gold mining centre, is a fly speck on the map, a town of 200 people in the dry farming districts near Maryborough. Jim and Helen and their two children, Kate and Tara, moved into the police residence there in February, 1990.

The station had not changed much since the grandfather of the Chief Commissioner, Neil Comrie, was the lone policeman there. The young Neil Comrie used to play in the station's lock-up, built 127 years ago to house drunken gold prospectors and would-be bush rangers.

There are 101 one-person stations in Victoria. About one per cent of the force is scattered around the state in these isolated domains.

It seems an attractive lifestyle. You are largely your own boss, with a car, a house and a position of respect in a close-knit community. But there is a downside. You live in a fishbowl where all your actions are open to scrutiny. Have a drink too many in the local pub and you're a drunk. Lock up a popular local and you're a demon.

As times have got tougher and the public purse smaller, the productivity demands on all police have become greater. In some areas one-man stations are expected to breathalyse 20 drivers a day in areas where they are flat out finding 20 cars.

Jim Wiggins' best friend and confidante was Senior Constable Con Geurts, who controlled the patch 15 kilometres away at Dunolly. They watched each other's back and kept in daily contact. Their families also became close. 'I've got two boys and he had two girls. His daughters were the ones that I never had and my sons were the ones he never had,' Geurts was to recall.

Geurts gradually became concerned about his mate. 'He went through a little hassle. He was overdoing it.' He said locals tried to get Wiggins to develop interests outside policing. They even got him to ride in the engine to Wycheproof on the wheat train as a distraction. His state of mind improved, but he was still obsessed with work.

'He always thought of the job first. He gave 110 percent. It got to him in the end. I think he thought he couldn't keep up his own standards. He had a big area to police with a small population. He was forever trying to justify the existence of the station because he was frightened it might be closed.'

He started a one-man road blitz and persuaded the local police command to give him a radar gun. 'He said he would get 30 bookings a month. He would sit there for hours on the side of the road. He loved that radar.'

Con, look after the radar, mate.

In Melbourne there are police psychologists who work around the clock on stress cases. There are social workers, welfare officers, doctors, chaplains, and mates to weave a safety net. But in the one-man stations, police claim they are often left to work it out for themselves. Each district has a welfare officer, but police are often reluctant to talk about their inner problems to a superior.

According to Geurts, in the last 12 months of his life, Jim Wiggins,

42, was confronted with more grief, trauma and tragedy than hard-nosed city detectives working in the high crime areas of Melbourne would be expected to bear – but he had to do it on his own. 'Death just seemed to follow him,' he said.

In one case, a local youth killed his step-father, then dumped the body in the bush, doused it with fuel and set fire to it. Wiggins had to guard the remains through a hot day, then escort them to Melbourne. He also had to spend a day guarding a cemetery after a grave robbery.

He found the body of a man who had suffered an epileptic fit and drowned. Later he found the remains of a man who had died several days earlier in a house, and organised a pauper's funeral for him. He also found a man who had committed suicide at the side of the road.

Wiggins talked a suicidal young man into giving up his loaded .22 rifle during a dangerous confrontation. After any incident with firearms, police are required to accept counselling. He drove to Melbourne for a session with a psychologist which, according to Helen, lasted three minutes.

While this was going on he still had the town's problems to fix. Police in one-man stations must try to walk the line between being everyone's mate and the law. Some residents grumbled when the district Traffic Operations Group nabbed a local drunk driver. 'Some people thought Jim should have warned him,' Geurts said.

Helen Wiggins said her husband loved his job and felt a deep-seated responsibility to the town. Even when on holidays he would keep running sheets and attend to jobs. 'It engrossed him. He became a policeman to the exclusion of everything else.'

The death message is every police officer's most dreaded assignment. In the one-man stations it's worse, because the policeman knows the victim and the family. It is nearly always much more personal. 'You can't walk away,' his wife said. 'Jim was a pall bearer at the funeral of people who had died in accidents he had attended.'

I served the people of Tarnagulla area to the best of my ability. I believe I've given all I can there's no more.

Barry Condick has been a motor mechanic, Justice of the Peace, and Tarnagulla resident for 44 years. He remembers Jim Wiggins as a 'special sort of man. He was the best country cop I have ever known and I've seen a few come and go. Everyone still wants to know why he did it. If he was unpopular it would be a different story, but he was well liked. If you had a problem he was always there.'

I'm not perfect, but I believe my life has been worthwhile – helping others.

'He would sit out on the road with his radar for hours. Time meant nothing to him,' Condick said. He seemed talkative and happy, and rarely spoke about police work. 'He didn't appear to worry about anything. Now I think he must have. He was never off duty. Maybe that was the problem.'

I'm so tired, I haven't slept much over the past four days since Sunday. I simply feel depleted – anxious and upset with myself for being so neglectful and careless.

It wasn't the big problems that sapped Jim Wiggins's will to live. It was little things that shouldn't have mattered. He charged two local brothers over not storing their firearms correctly, but felt a hypocrite because he had been doing the same thing for years. It evidently didn't occur to him to use his discretion and warn them.

I'm no better, being a policeman I should know better.

Wiggins went to the faintly ridiculous length of removing the police sign from the front of his car so it wouldn't forewarn speeding drivers. Then, racked with guilt, he drove to Bendigo headquarters to 'confess' to a senior officer over his actions. It was such a minor incident that it wasn't taken seriously. No-one seemed to pick up the signs that the country copper was beginning to unravel.

On Thursday, 4 January, 1996, Jim Wiggins woke up alone and depressed. The small police residence was quiet. His wife and daughters were in Eildon on a holiday. They were due back the next day.

He rang Con Geurts, who drove over for a chat. 'He was pretty low but after a couple of hours he ironed a shirt and said he was going to work.' He gave no indication he was considering suicide. Geurts has relived that last conversation with his mate a thousand times. 'I wasn't to know he was so stressed. He hid it. He was coming around for tea that night. Sometimes I think, I hate the bastard for what he's done, why did he hide it all from me? I could have helped.'

Sorry Con, I got worse as the day went on. Don't in any way blame yourself.

Jim Wiggins headed off to Bendigo to try and get the transfer letters to replace the police sign on the front of the car. When he decided to commit suicide no-one will know, but he clearly wanted his wife out of town in the hope it would minimise the trauma. She was due home the next day. It may have been a case of 'now or never'.

I couldn't bear to think you would find me.

He had last spoken to his wife two days earlier and had given no indication he was dangerously depressed. 'Jim was the last man on earth that I would have thought would take his own life. I am just lost for answers,' she was to say.

She said he'd been talking about getting a gun safe and was seen on the Tuesday in uniform, without his gun in his holster. 'Maybe it was a cry for help. Maybe he was trying to say, "Don't let me near a gun".'

She said she felt her husband may have become trapped in the role of the calm, rational policeman and could not talk of his depression. 'Jim and I had to appear to be always in control. We were the people that others came to for help and comfort.'

When he returned from Bendigo it was business as usual. Several locals spoke to him and he appeared normal. No-one sensed the inner turmoil.

Jim Wiggins was quietly disintegrating, but in his last few hours he completed mundane police charges. He filled out paperwork and dealt with routine queries. He drove to see a local man and delivered a summons, as if he wanted to leave a clean slate.

Sorry to the people of Tarnagulla. You are the best. To everyone I spoke with today I tried to keep up a happy appearance even though my gut was in a knot.

He returned to the station and at 2.40 pm began to tie up loose ends as he organised his own death. He tried to explain why a devoted family man, who was liked and respected and was doing a job he claimed to love, would end his life.

I have this feeling that I've let everybody down. The coward's way out. I couldn't go without leaving a note. I believe it is wrong not to leave an explanation. Now that I've written this down I feel much better and relieved. There's not much paper work to be completed.

He placed the keys to the police car on the table with a pencil and his sunglasses, next to his handwritten, four-page suicide note. Then, everything in order, Senior Constable Wiggins, still in full uniform, left the station and walked about 20 metres to the historic lock-up, unclipped his holster, withdrew his Smith & Wesson revolver, released the safety catch and, methodical to the end, shot himself dead.

The local community and the police hierarchy were shocked. The chief commissioner attended the funeral. But life goes on. Within weeks Helen Wiggins was told another policeman would be visiting the police residence the following day. He was considering applying for the Tarnagulla position.

It was no longer her family home. It was a house that went with a job – and the job was now vacant. She has since moved to Dunolly.

Helen Wiggins lost her husband and the father of her children. She also lost her identity. The police husband and wife are a team in small country town. The wife is as heavily involved in police work as the man in the uniform. She was the one who counselled victims, organised emergency accommodation, gave advice and helped where she could. But with her husband's death she was now the victim. Her role in the community was gone.

She was not pressured to move, but when the day came, leaving the police house hurt her. 'It was as though they were simply washing away Jim's blood and installing a shiny new happy family to carry on as usual. I felt I was leaving him behind. I half expected him to drive down the road and park in the carport.'

She thinks police in one-man stations are misunderstood, that their value to the community cannot be measured by cold crime statistics or kilometres patrolled and could not be quantified on a balance sheet. 'It is true community policing. They are everything from social workers to handymen. They are rung about anything and everything, from car accidents to fixing a globe on an outside light. It's not unusual to find a policeman chopping the wood or mowing the lawns for a widow.'

Jim Wiggins said in his suicide note he wanted to be buried next to his father at St Arnaud. At the church service 500 people turned up, more than twice the population of Tarnagulla. The locals even ran a bus so that the aged and infirm could pay their respects.

Everyone said Jim Wiggins was a good bloke. But for him, it wasn't enough.

WHEN police work alone they learn fast that the rule book doesn't have all the answers. So says a man whose beat for 17 years was 3200 square kilometres of isolated mountain country.

Bernie McWhinney was a legend as the old bush copper from Jamieson, a knockabout with a blue singlet under his blue uniform. He could be seen propping up the bar in the local pub or patrolling the area on horseback. He still believes common sense was more important than rules and regulations.

'I mightn't have always done it according to the book, but there were no complaints. It was effective policing,' he says of his remarkable career minding one of the biggest 'patches' in the state.

For 25 of his 28 years in the force McWhinney worked alone. In many ways he remained untouched by modern management theory. Commissioners came and went, district bosses were appointed and retired, but Bernie kept on being Bernie.

He would go to the pub and have a social drink in uniform, arguing he was always on duty, so what did it matter? When he was in the police residence next to the station he would always answer the door. Even when his marriage broke up in 1982, he still remained on duty and available.

A bad hair day … grandmother and drug dealer Kath Pettingill
on the day of her arrest..

Drug dealer Viet Le took no notice of a birthday party at the next restaurant table. He should have. It was the NCA.

Melbourne and Sydney heroin trafficker Mengkok Te (left) caught
by a police surveillance camera.

Dealer Steven MacKinnon with a woman now in police protection.

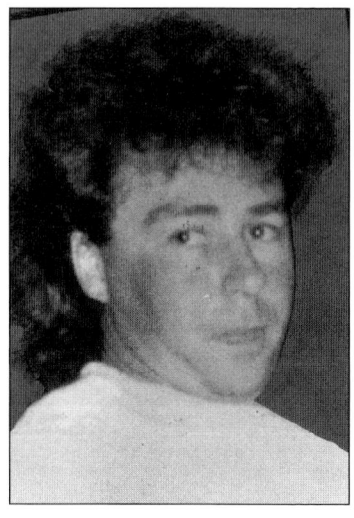

Wendy Peirce ... says she's
finished with crime.

Peter Allen ... ran a drug
syndicate from inside prison.

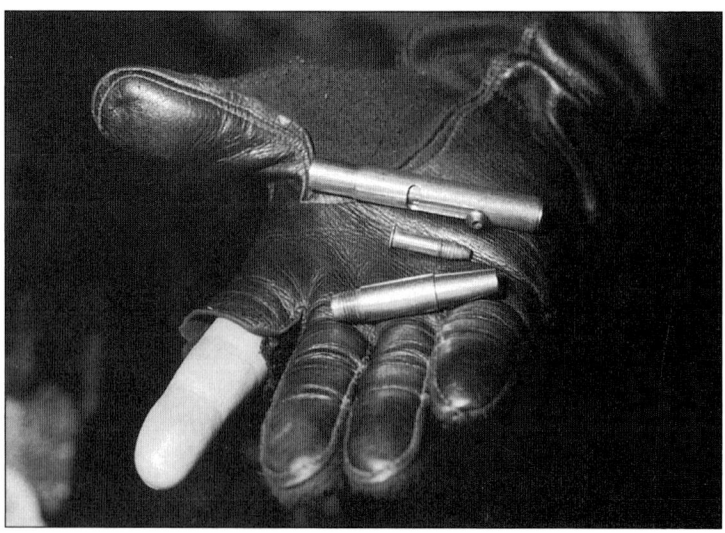

A pen pistol found in Kath Pettingill's knickers.

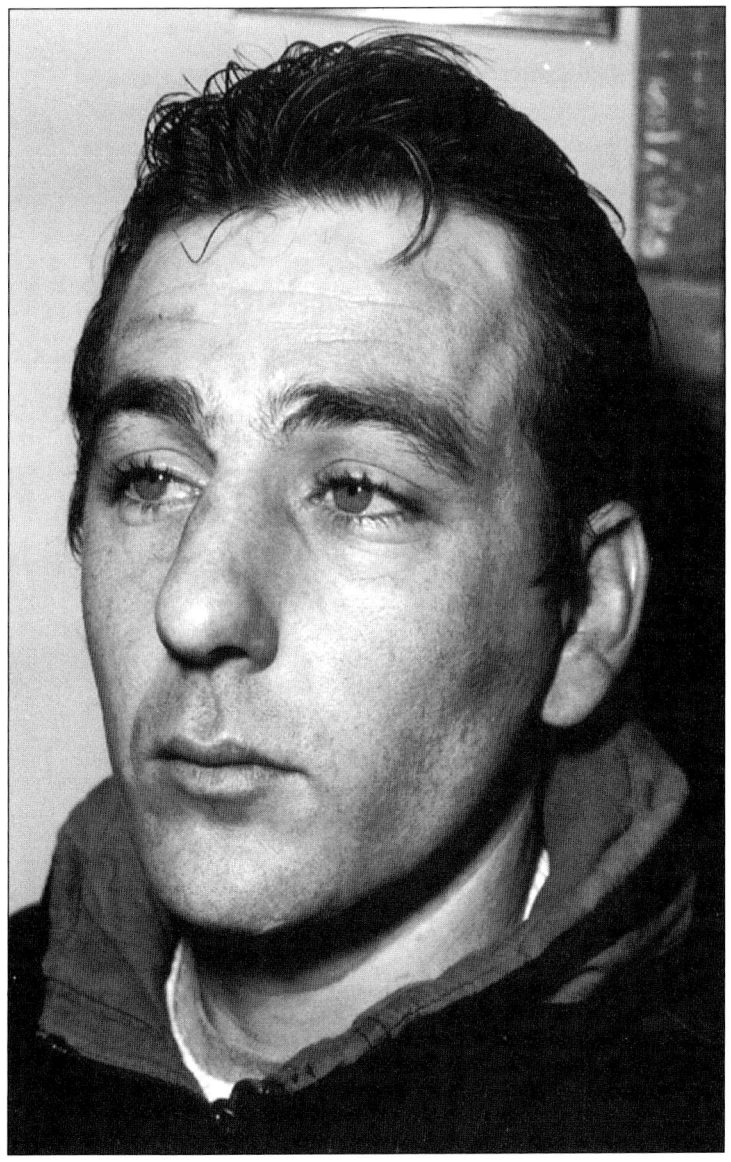

Trevor Pettingill … followed family tradition as a drug dealer.

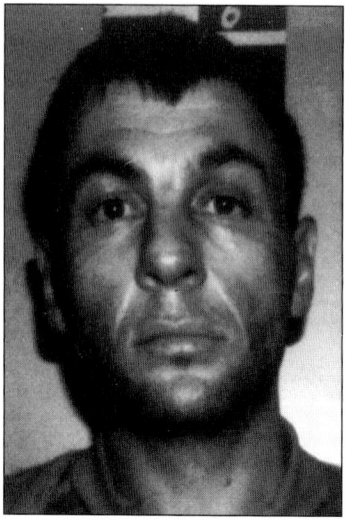

Victor Peirce … allowed out of jail to go bowling.

Dennis Allen … his mum would search him for a police tape.

Dane Sweetman … neo-Nazi and fashion plate.

Greg 'Bluey' Brazel … clever, charming, cold-blooded killer.

Missing … Edwina
Boyle with husband
Fred and daughters.
She has not been
seen since 1983.

BELOW: Kerry
Whelan …
disappeared from
a suburban carpark
in 1997.

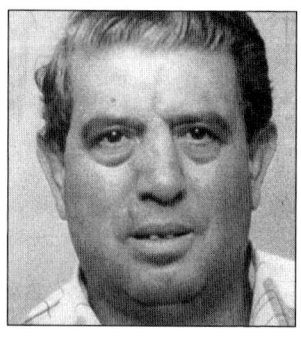

ABOVE: Multiple murderer
Sandy MacRae.
RIGHT: Two of his victims,
Rosa and Carmelo Marafiote.
BELOW: Their son Domenic
was buried by MacRae in this
pit at his Mildura farm.

'I was an old-fashioned kick 'em in the bum type of policeman. When the police force introduced computers I knew I was on the way out. I couldn't even start one, still can't. Today, if it isn't on computer it didn't happen,' says the man who retired to drive trucks.

A 'one manner' soon learns he is more than just the local copper. He is the marriage guidance counsellor, family psychologist, tourist guide and the person everyone leans on.

According to McWhinney's homespun wisdom, the first rule is always to have an answer. Even the wrong answer is better than none. 'I don't know,' is not good enough.

'There was an old bloke who was a little bit slow. He was in Melbourne when he was picked up by the locals for driving through a stop sign. He told them he couldn't read at all and they cancelled his licence. He came to me and said; "It will ruin my life, Bernie".

'They would have crucified him. I knew that he mightn't have been able to read but I knew he could drive. I got him the official written test, but he did my personal test over the kitchen table. I showed him pictures of the traffic signs and he could recognise them, even if he couldn't read them. I was satisfied so I filled out his test paper.

'Then I told him something which wasn't strictly true. I said, "Bill, this is a special restricted licence. You can drive in Jamieson and Woods Point and to the edge of Mansfield, but nowhere else." I even showed him where he could park at the edge of Mansfield.'

'He was happy, but then someone told him that was wrong and he could drive anywhere. He was nearly cleaned up by a truck on the way to Benalla. I got him and said, "Bill, I'm the policeman and listen to me. You can't go past Mansfield". He was as happy as buggery.'

But while the idea of being The Law was attractive, the reality of being always on duty eventually can grind down those who work alone. 'My door was always open. You would have someone come in and say he thought his kids were on drugs, and then someone who was worried his wife was playing up. You would counsel them, but who could you turn to? Welfare was three hours away in Melbourne.'

In 1987 McWhinney was severely bashed and spent a week in hospital. When the body healed he was left with emotional scars. 'I needed counselling. I was pig headed at first and denied it, but in the end I knew I did. But it was a three hour trip, and when I finally got there it was the last thing I felt like. Sometimes you would scream out for someone to talk to, to spill your guts, someone to have a bawl to. I admit there were a few times I took a box of stubbies into the hills and drank most of them. There's a couple of gay blokes up here who were probably the closest thing I had to counsellors. When I wanted a moan or talk about a problem I'd go to them.

'But sometimes police need to talk to police. To sit in the mess room with six or eight other police. You can't do that in a one-man station.'

He said even in the force, police didn't understand the pressures of being the only law in town. 'You might have to tell an old digger that his best mate has died in hospital. You spend an hour with him talking. You get in the car and over the radio someone will ask, 'where the hell have you been?' There was a lot of jealousy from the larger stations.'

But while McWhinney is full of tales of country people banding together, he still has the bitter after-taste.

'I remember having to deliver the death message after someone had died in an accident. There were 12 people, six men and six women. They were laughing near the water, having the time of their lives. At first I couldn't bring myself to tell them. Their day had been filled with laughter and I was going to turn it into a tragedy.'

That was more than 15 years ago. But Bernie McWhinney still remembers.

CHAPTER 9

They shoot horses, don't they?

Drug dealing from the inside

'Did you, did you knock him?'
'Good Friday. Yeah.'

'FRANK' was a devoted family man and volunteer firefighter who worked in the Melbourne wholesale fruit and vegetable market when he was asked to deliver a package, no questions asked.

The father of three did as he was told, although he knew the package contained cannabis. He was given $1000 cash for his trouble.

For Frank, it was the start of a decade in which he went from a low level courier, carrying drugs and cash, to become the confidante of the bosses of five drug syndicates.

Frank was also to became one of Victoria's most important police witnesses. Known by the code name Informer 108, he gave detectives entree to drug syndicates that had proved virtually impenetrable.

Confidential police documents say that 108 provided enough evidence and information to short-circuit the drug rings that provided the majority of the drugs in the western suburbs.

One expert wrote, 'It is accepted by many that it would have taken up to eight years by conventional policing methods to achieve what this operation has in eleven months.'

According to Detective Sergeant Stephen Cody, Frank became

known in drug circles as a man of his word. The major dealers loved him. He wasn't an unreliable junkie, he didn't try to rip them off and he kept his mouth shut.

He acted as a human buffer for the syndicate heads. He handled the money and the drugs so that if there were any arrests, they remained a step removed. Informer 108 took the risks, but he was always assured that if things went wrong his family would be looked after.

Eventually he was arrested and sent to jail. As a man of his word he did not implicate any of his superiors. He was prepared to take the rap. But, his family was left to fend for itself, even after his daughter was hit by a car and suffered brain damage.

Late in 1990 police raided Frank's house and he was arrested again. His wife was furious. She saw the family being dragged into the underworld. A few months later, aged in her late 30s, she suffered a stroke and became paralysed on one side of her body.

Normally police have to pressure low-level criminals into giving evidence against members of a drug syndicate, but this case was unique. Frank approached police and offered to become an informer. 'He wanted to make sure he didn't go back to it. He wanted to burn all his bridges so that he would be forced to make a new start,' Detective Sergeant Cody said.

As a unique go-between, 108 introduced police to five separate drug syndicates. It began as Operation Pipeline in 1991 but expanded into Operations Advance, Exceed, Extra, Overflow and Bluestreak. Even though the operation itself ran for eleven months and resulted in 68 arrests it was not completed until late 1995 when the final court cases ended.

It involved more than 30 police from the Drug Squad and the Altona District Support Group and more than 80 police were called in when the final arrests were made.

Police seized or purchased cocaine, heroin, amphetamines, cannabis and hashish to the value of $6 million and observed drug deals totalling $7.5 million. It resulted in the arrest and conviction of two drug millionaires, solved a previously unknown murder and led to the discovery of an Uzi machine gun.

Police seized assets, including a farm at Laverton valued at $350,000, nine cars, including a Porsche and a new $47,000 four-wheel-drive, two motorbikes, including a Harley-Davidson 'Fatboy', and $500,000 cash.

Pipeline provided a snapshot of the real drug world in any big Australian city: a fluid, turbulent mix of individuals and syndicates always on the make. It wasn't a neat pyramid structure with one Mr Big or a series of criminals who run separate organised crime groups.

Rather, it showed how different gangs dealt with each other when it suited. It also showed how a generation of minor criminals, who in another time would have just been bottom dwellers in the underworld food-chain, were able to make millions from drugs.

The five syndicates were basically broken into ethnic groups — Chinese, Italian, Lebanese, Greek and Anglo-Saxon — but while they were independent, they were all prepared to co-operate on major deals.

'They were into everything and anything. Greed was the only common interest they had,' was the pithy judgment of the head of the operation, Detective Inspector David Reid.

An example of the wealth that can be made from drugs was the rapid rise of John Falzon.

In the mid-1980s Falzon lived in a housing commission flat in Sunshine. In 1984-85 he put in his only known tax return and declared an income of $10,000. He has not claimed any social welfare and did not work since yet, according to police, he acquired assets of more than $1 million, including two farms, houses and cars.

Police watched him dig up $230,000 in cash, hidden in a plastic drum under a sleeper in the back yard of a friend's parent's house in Sunshine. Days earlier he had loudly criticised his wife for spending $20 too much at the supermarket. 'She used to have to provide receipts to him after she'd done the shopping,' a policeman said.

'He was a miserable, self-centred, selfish, secretive individual,' he said. 'Falzon spoke in code when discussing drug transactions within his network and refused to deal with anyone he didn't know,' a confidential police report said. He would only deal with informer 108. It was to be his downfall.

Informer 108 introduced undercover policeman David Barlow to the syndicates. The second time he met millionaire amphetamines distributor Atilla Erdei, the drug dealer stuck a gun in his ribs. 'He nearly broke them,' Barlow was to recall. 'He was a violent man with no regard for anyone else,' he said.

Before Operation Pipeline police were unaware that Erdei, a clothing manufacturer and millionaire property owner, was a major drug distributor. During the investigation they found he had already killed one man and was planning to murder a second.

Erdei was eventually arrested and convicted of murdering Anh Mal Nguyen on Good Friday, 1992, by strangling him with his bare hands and then dumping the body in a concrete-filled 200 litre drum in Pyke's Creek Reservoir, near Ballarat.

After the arrests police were told that a $100,000 contract had been taken out on David Barlow's life. He was married during the undercover operation and spent his first anniversary in the witness protection scheme. He eventually was forced to sell his heavily fortified eastern suburbs home at a loss of $24,000.

Some members of the syndicates were not content with making threats. They also offered inducements. Drug Squad detectives were offered $100,000 in cash for the undercover operative's original secret tapes. They were promised the money in two $50,000 lots, one before and the other after the committal.

It was no idle promise. When Senior Detective David Harley from the drug squad parked his car near the corner of Park and Nicholson Streets, North Fitzroy, to meet syndicate member Frank Dimos, he was ready to gather evidence for the bribery sting.

He didn't have too wait long. Dimos walked along the road clutching his stomach. When he hopped into the car his shirt was unbuttoned and $40,000 cash was spilling from around his belly. He said that he was ten pair of 'socks' short and would pay the rest the next day. He threw the bundles of cash into the driver's side foot well.

The group also wanted police to raid selected drug dealers, keep a small percentage for evidence and then return the rest to be resold. Police were to be paid a retainer and a share of the profits.

Two of the men were arrested in a Melbourne motel room viewing 40 kilos of cannabis valued at $72,000 they thought they were buying from corrupt drug squad detectives.

Three men involved in the syndicate were later charged with attempted bribery and conspiracy to pervert the course of justice. Two received no effective jail terms as the sentences were made concurrent with drug terms and the third, Dimos, received an effective sentence of only four months.

Police privately say the courts should be tougher on criminals who offer bribes. 'The crims have nothing to lose. If someone cops a bribe they can get away with it, but if they are arrested for it they don't do any real jail time anyway,' comments one investigator.

After appearing in court, a process that took five years, informer 108 moved interstate with his family under a new name. According to Detective Sergeant Cody: 'He is doing well. He is one of the success stories of the system. He has a full-time job, is looking to buy a house and is supporting his family.'

But while confidential police documents described Operation Pipeline as 'one of the most significant drug operations undertaken in modern Victoria Police history' detectives remain convinced they were not backed up by the courts. They believed that light jail sentences and flawed asset seizure laws made it impossible to make serious inroads into the drug racket.

Detectives, who arrested the 68 people in Operation Pipeline, claimed some of the major dealers were back selling drugs even before the five-year operation was completed.

Police in Pipeline said that though they arrested the main dealers in heroin, amphetamines, cocaine, hashish and cannabis, the operation had no long-term effect on the drug industry.

'As soon as we arrest a major player there is someone else who is prepared to walk in and fill their shoes,' complained the then acting head of the Drug Squad, Detective Inspector Reid.

Police in the western suburbs reported that there was a slight increase in price and minor supply problems for about four months after the arrests, but then the industry returned to normal.

'The profits are so great. People can amass more money in a few short years than they could ever acquire in a lifetime of legitimate work,' Detective Inspector Reid said.

Some of the major drug dealers arrested through Operation Pipeline were fined or given jail terms of two years or less. The longest sentence was for one of the main targets, John Falzon, sentenced to seven years with a minimum of five.

'I think everyone agrees there is a need for the major dealers in the drug industry to be subjected to severe jail terms but it doesn't seem to regularly happen,' Detective Inspector Reid says. 'I know we are fair-dinkum about doing something. I just wonder if others are.'

The maximum sentence for drug trafficking is 25 years jail and a fine of $250,000.

'In Operation Pipeline more than 80 police were involved. It involved time, resources and effort and personal risk for a number of people. An undercover officer, an informer and their families were placed at great risk and the maximum sentence for any of the offenders was seven years with a minimum of five,' Detective Inspector Reid said.

'I think the only way to make inroads is when people selling drugs at the highest level go to jail for long periods and come out broke.'

Police in Operation Pipeline and associated investigations tapped into a group of drug cartels with links in China, Thailand, Western Australian and South Australia. One gang ran a separate drug syndicate inside Loddon prison.

The operation, which began in 1991 and finished in late 1995, identified hundreds of drug deals worth more than $13 million and resulted in the seizing of assets of more the $1.1 million, although further assets of more than $1 million allegedly acquired with drug money could not be seized.

Police believe at least three Melbourne legal identities help organise removal of assets so they cannot be traced to drug purchases.

In Pipeline, a new four-wheel-drive vehicle bought with $47,000 cash of drug money and with 40 kilometres on the clock was kept in a police compound for nearly three years before it was sold at a heavily discounted price.

FOR most police, it is possible to move on after a major arrest. The brief of evidence has to be completed and there may be several court appearance to come, but largely the hard work is over.

In some ways the detectives are like film directors. They plan and control the whole production, but they are not the stars. It is the witnesses and the hard evidence that ultimately matters. Confessions are recorded, tapes produced and witnesses swear statements.

But when an undercover policeman is used, the stakes become higher. Undercover work is specialised. Recruits have to be gregarious, likeable and able to think on their feet. They can't make a mistake or freeze under pressure. A slip can be fatal.

Undercovers have to be carefully controlled. In New Zealand and the US some have gone 'wild' and crossed the line. They often see a different world, well away from the humdrum life of a wage earner. No mortgage problems, no saving for a holiday or a second hand car. It is cash city. If you want something, then buy it. The restaurants, the bars, the girls, and the partying seems to be all on tap.

Often, when the sting operation is completed the criminals caught in the net are doubly outraged. It is a personal insult that someone they trusted and liked turns out to be a policeman who betrays them. The added concern is that the undercover is the key player in any successful prosecutions. It takes the police-criminal relationship to a different – and dangerous – plane.

In one big Victorian police operation into a Griffith-connected Honoured Society group, the cartel took out a million-dollar contract on the undercover operative.

In Operation Pipeline the undercover, David Barlow, actually had to slip out of his role to get married. At the time he looked more like Frank Zappa then a clean-cut police sergeant.

Barlow was introduced to the syndicate as a major drug dealer and was soon accepted by the main players. In a restaurant in Carlton in May, 1992, he was on the mobile phone to a drug dealer in Hong Kong when Attila Erdei walked in. 'I said I was talking to my Chinese connection and he said he had a Chinese problem, but it was gone,' Barlow said.

What Erdei had referred to was the cold-blooded murder of an Asian victim. 'I always knew he had the capacity to do it. At one meeting at a service station near Westgate bridge he pulled out an Uzi machine gun and started waving it about.'

He said that when he realised Erdei was talking of a recent murder he tried to get him to provide details without appearing to be too pushy, 'I went into evidence gathering mode.'

'I put my finger up to indicate pistol. He put his hand up to indicate he had strangled him. He said his thumbs were sore for three days.'

'He said it took about ten minutes and the victim kept screaming and fighting. He called him a dirty little monkey.'

Barlow said Erdei told him he put the body in a drum and filled it with concrete. The next morning the concrete had shrunk and the head was visible. 'He said he gave it a pat on the head and filled up the rest of the drum with concrete.'

Erdei told the policeman that when he rolled the drum into the dam it had bounced on rocks before disappearing. Police divers were able to estimate the point of entry and recover the drum with the body.

After the arrest, Barlow's wife started to get strange telephone calls. The family started to receive letters about pre-paid funerals.

Police installed two security systems, bullet proof glass and a video surveillance system. Armed police moved into their house. His wife was followed by police. Barlow was armed 24 hours a day. Every time he arrived home he would check outside and inside looking for gunmen. 'It was like living in a fishbowl. Every time I went home I was waiting for someone to jump out of the bushes.'

The couple's first anniversary was spent in witness protection with armed police. Eventually things began to settle down. They were at a formal ball enjoying themselves when a work call came through for Barlow.

The Coburg police had received a tip. 'You've got an undercover named Dave who lives in Ringwood. There's a $100,000 contract out on him.'

For the Barlows it was the end. They decided to sell their suburban home with the security systems more in keeping with a city bank than a family house. They sold the house for a loss of $24,000. They were glad to get rid of it.

Meanwhile, the wheel of crime and detection turns on. By the time the Barlows had regained a semblance of normal life, some of the men convicted of dealing drugs had been released from prison and were back in business.

TIME: 12.22 pm, 1 May, 1992.

PLACE: Genevieve Cafe, Faraday Street, Carlton.

PRESENT: Informer 108, Police undercover operator, David Barlow and target Attila Erdei.

Edited transcript of Erdei bragging of killing Anh Mal Nguyen on Good Friday, 1992, by strangling him with his bare hands, then dumping the body in a concrete-filled drum.

The three men are sitting at a table and have ordered lunch of soup and chicken parmigiana.

ERDEI: 'My problem, my problem, gone my little problem.'

BARLOW: 'Is he? What is he?'

ERDEI: 'Holiday.'

BARLOW: 'Where.'

ERDEI: 'Long tour.'

BARLOW: 'Did you, did you knock him?'

ERDEI: 'Good Friday. Yeah.'

He then indicated he strangled the victim.

BARLOW: 'Yeah.'

ERDEI (a body builder): 'My hands .... hurt for three .... days.'

BARLOW: 'Do you know what? You're .... mad.'

ERDEI: 'He .... owe me 60 grand.'

ERDEI: 'I start squeezing his throat like hell you know. And he going 'Err' like that and 15 minutes I got him down on the ground.'

He said that he put the body in a drum and filled it with concrete but the following morning the victim's head was still visible. 'His head a little bit out.' He then poured more concrete on top before taking the barrel to Pyke's Creek and dumping it in about 14 metres of water.

Informer 108: 'That's life, murder.'

ERDEI: 'Yeah, so what.'

108: 'I'd hate to see if you got upset with me, mate.'

BARLOW: 'You'd have to get a bigger drum.'

108: 'Bigger drum all right.'

ERDEI: 'No, you just chop into four pieces . . . with a chainsaw.'

ERDEI: 'Five years ago we go to hunting. And I shoot one horse, not me, one friend of mine. White horse, I like horses and the ....

shoot him. And I go to him (the horse) and you know, he not die, so I put five or six bullets in the head. And believe it or not, I never go hunting after because I so sorry for the horse. And after three weeks, four weeks, believe it or not, I start sleeping, always come that horse in my mind. I can't sleep.'

Then Erdei talks about the difference in killing the horse to murdering Nguyen. 'I feel nothing, man ... Believe me, I feel nothing.'

ERDEI: 'Now it's two weeks ago tomorrow morning, exactly, tomorrow morning. And once not he comes into my dreams or something. I got good sleep and everything because he is a piece of shit, not a human being.'

Police recovered the body on the basis of details from the taped conversation, sixteen days after the murder.

Erdei was convicted of murder and sentenced to twenty-two years with a minimum of seventeen.

CHAPTER 10

Born to be old
Motorbike gangs in Australia

'It must have been good stuff.
The weeds were gigantic and the
mosquitos were as big as helicopters'

TED is a man in his 40s who lives with his family in an eastern suburb of Melbourne. He likes to collect antiques and tend his garden, but for years he was forced to live the life of an outlaw bikie.

He was a member of an outlaw motorcycle gang that refused to let him drift back to conservative, mainstream society. He would rather have been home planting geraniums, but he had to go to the parties, ride on bike runs and fight people he didn't know who had offended the honour of a club 'brother', a person he probably didn't even like.

According to police, Ted is one of a growing group of aging bikies trapped in a lifestyle they have long since outgrown. But you can't retire from an outlaw motorcycle gang, not without paying a huge price.

'To be honest, I was sick of it,' he told police. 'But if I quit they would have come around here with a truck and cleaned me out.' So, as infrequently as possible, he kisses his wife goodbye, dons the colours of the club and rides his bike to another booze and drug filled night out.

The traditional retirement gift for a bikie who wants to leave his club is a beating from fellow members and the loss of his bike and other assets. Ted finally found a way out. He was released without punishment after he found he had a life-threatening disease.

'They join because of the parties and the image but they end up getting ripped off by their so-called brothers,' a policeman says.

Only colour-wearing members are allowed to know the secrets of the clubs. There are hangers-on who are used for a purpose, the girls, the users and the potential recruits known as prospects, who are treated as virtual slaves.

One prospect was ordered to take a package of drugs across town with the lights of his motor-bike off. It was done to see what he would do if he was picked up by police.

No wonder police have had massive problems trying to investigate the groups. Traditional methods such as using undercover operatives can't be used. Those close to the bike gangs are often required to commit crimes to prove their loyalty, which effectively protects the groups from being infiltrated by undercovers.

One of the few non-members in Australia to be accepted as an equal by bikies was Frank, who helped produce amphetamines for one outlaw motor cycle gang. For years he helped produce the best speed that money could buy and he watched as some of the toughest bike groups moved from being good-time boys who loved parties and fights, to sophisticated gangsters in leather jackets.

'In the gangs there are two types of blokes. Half of them are dead set tough and the others need to be in a big group to survive. They wouldn't know what to do if they were on their own.'

Frank has known bikies for decades. He believes some of them just love the image. They have the bike, the belt, the colours and all the T-shirts. They go to the parties, ride on the interstate runs and will brawl for their bothers.

'If you are a H A (Hells Angel) and you walk into a pub you have immediate respect. Everyone knows that if you fight him, the rest of them will come after you,' he says.

But there are others who are in the clubs for themselves. They ride their bikes only when they have to and exploit other members of the gang as cheap labour and low level runners for their drug activities.

'Some of them are very smart and very greedy,' says Frank.

At one time a Melbourne bikie group was producing the purest amphetamines in Australia, with four 'cooks' producing five-kilogram batches in shifts.

The chemical overflow from the operation was poured into the garden. 'It must have been good stuff. The weeds were gigantic and the mosquitos were as big as helicopters,' Frank says.

He said the Australian bike groups began to use and sell amphetamines in the 1970s after seeing the profits made by US gangs. 'At first the speed was sent from America through the post wrapped up in T-shirts. Then they got a recipe from the Hells Angels in the States.'

The links between Australian clubs and their US counterparts have long been established, and it is believed that Australian bikies were taught how to cook speed in America. The money to be made was so great one group wouldn't even stop while on trial over amphetamine charges. They would cook overnight and then go to court. To stay awake through the hearing, they used their own 'gear'.

Bill is a policeman who investigated bikies for years in Melbourne. In the 1980s he had a price on his head and kept a loaded shotgun in his car.

'They are total misfits who band together because they don't fit in anywhere else. Many of them are just hypocrites. They say they never use the needle, but some of them sell heroin,' he said.

'Years ago some of them were real hard men you respected, but most of them are long gone, either dead or in jail. Now crims just use some of the clubs as fronts. Most of the members aren't too bright and are led around by the nose by the few who are in it for the money,' he said.

The Hells Angels were the biggest suppliers of amphetamines in Australia in the 1980s. They recruited a brilliant eccentric, dubbed 'The Mad Professor', Colin Fleet, who produced 27 different types of illicit drugs.

Fleet was convinced police were firing micro-waves at him, so he wrapped his head in tinfoil. He also sanded the bottom of his bath, believing that this would sabotage police bugging methods.

Ultimately, he committed suicide.

The Angels were convinced that one policeman was responsible for investigations of their drug-producing empire. Police received information that an international gang hitman was to be flown to Australia to kill the officer in question.

They intercepted one of America's top US Angel members, James Patton 'Jim Jim' Brandes. He had been charged and acquitted of attempting to murder a US undercover policeman, Bill Zerby. Zerby lost his hearing in his left ear and 75 percent in his right after a remote control bomb was detonated next to his car.

When Brandes arrived in Australia his luggage included thumb cuffs, a de-bugging device, instructions on how to tap telephones and a confidential copy of a US Treasury book, *Forensic Handbook*. Hand marked in the book were passages on 'Explosive Substances and Devices' and areas devoted to fingerprints on chemicals.

Brandes was kept in a holding cell at Melbourne Airport, then sent back to the US.

At one stage Australian Hells Angels sent their US brothers the Chemical P2P, a vital ingredient of amphetamines. It was smuggled into America in pineapple juice cans.

An internal struggle sparked a gang war in Melbourne. At one stage gunmen burst into a member's house and, using a shotgun, blasted the television, fishtank, furniture and walls. They then set fire to a bike and car. Police gave chase to a group on its way to a fire fight. Gang members threw their weapons out the windows. Police later recovered an Owen sub-machine gun, a .357 magnum, a Colt .45 automatic, a .38 revolver and a pair of thumbcuffs.

One enemy had every major bone in his body broken. Two members of another gang had their kneecaps shot and their clubhouse burnt to the ground. But the Angels have long since lost their stranglehold in the amphetamines market. According to police, the delicate power structure of the outlaw motorcycle gangs is changing in Australia and has resulted in an upsurge of violence.

Police know of at least 14 violent incidents in 18 months connected to inter-gang rivalry, and they believe many more attacks have gone unreported. Detectives believe one unsolved murder and an attempted murder in country Victoria are related to bikie gangs.

Drive-by shootings, violent raids on opposition clubhouses, bashings, sophisticated targeting of rivals, bombings, and predatorial takeovers of smaller gangs, have become part of the scene.

In 1995, police were told that five men in a car had been spotted wearing balaclavas in a quiet Melbourne street. Police moved in to stop what they believed may have been a planned armed robbery. What they found were members of a bikie gang, all carrying firearms, about to conduct a military-style raid on a rival group.

Police have now found that gangs are producing detailed dossiers on enemy members, which include pictures, work details and likely movements, in order to plan future attacks.

Detectives fear that the undercurrent of violence is part of an undeclared battle for control in Victoria. For two decades the Hells Angels have been considered the strongest gang, but in the last few years the Bandidos have developed a strong power base.

'The Hells Angels are an endangered species in Australia. This will all end in a big blue,' a bikie associate predicts.

Police intelligence reports indicate that several smaller country gangs have been absorbed by outlaw motorcycle groups with strong interstate connections.

Police believe the smaller gangs are forced to close and hand over their assets, which include club houses and property, to the major national gangs. A bikie was shot dead, another abducted and tortured and a third attacked with a tomahawk before one club was absorbed in one regional Victorian city.

Detectives say dominant elements in some of the big clubs have been involved in the production and distribution of amphetamines, debt collection, counterfeiting and being paid to commit assaults. At least one lawful and respected club is being pushed into organised crime by a few members, according to police.

Money from illegal activities has been laundered through motor cycle shops, concerts, strippers, property and bike shows, according to police intelligence.

As the likelihood of violence has increased, the gangs have begun to fortify their club houses against attacks from rivals. The club houses are normally located in industrialised areas. The gangs buy or rent small factories or warehouses and turn them into garrisons.

Police say some of the buildings have been fortified with internal walls made of layers of railway sleepers. 'They have surveillance cameras, strong lights and monitoring devices to protect buildings which are really just big tin sheds,' a detective says. 'When they have meetings they usually have two members on foot-patrol outside the building who wear headsets equipped with state of the art communications gear,'

'They don't have that sort of gear to protect them from police raids, because when we go in there's nothing much of interest there. It is designed to protect them from raids from other gangs.'

The head of the organised crime and task force division in Victoria, Detective Superintendent Ian Thomas, says some gangs encourage young factory workers to become involved. 'They have Friday night parties for the local workers where there are strippers and drinks. The workers end up being the unpaid eyes and ears for the clubs.

'This may seem innocent enough but with the tension between rival gangs there is a real chance of these people being caught up in violence. The main reason for some of these clubs existing is for criminal activities.

'There is a group of criminals in the bikie community and they should be treated as any other criminal group. It is pointless to glamorise them. Many of them exploit the image of a bikie and use and exploit their fellow bikies.'

The National Crime Authority had to fight the bikies in and out of courts to proceed with the investigation. Operation Panzer began in May 1995 on the instructions of the state and federal governments as reference 23 for the NCA. Under a special reference the NCA is able to use its coercive powers, which include demanding answers under oath to questions in secret hearings.

The NCA was instructed to investigate gang members suspected of murder, drug trafficking, armament dealing, extortion, fraud and tax evasion. But in June, 1996, the Federal Court ruled in favour of two gang members and found the reference was too general to allow use of the coercive powers. It is not known who paid the massive legal fees.

The NCA appealed the decision, but continued the investigation without using the special reference authority. A year later the Full Federal Court found in favour of the NCA.

The authority established a national task force involving state and federal law enforcement agencies to investigate bikie groups. For the first time, ten years after the Australian Bureau of Criminal

Intelligence found some bikie groups were linked to international crime gangs, there was a national approach to the problem.

By the end of 1996, NCA-related investigations had resulted in the arrest of 169 people charged with 454 offences including the manufacture of amphetamines, possession of steroids, supplying cocaine, possession of ecstasy, counterfeiting currency, possession of firearms, explosives and a stun gun.

Police were amazed at the new methods bike gangs used to try to protect their criminal activities.

In one case a gang built a large brick barbecue to conceal an underground concrete bunker designed as an amphetamines laboratory at a luxury property near Frankston.

The gang used a local concreter to build the bunker. The night after he completed the job his clients stole his truck and removed the hydraulic lift on the tray. The hydraulic system was fitted below ground level to lift the barbecue to expose the secret trapdoor.

BIKIE VIOLENCE IN VICTORIA

January, 1993, Geelong. Shootout between members of the Warlocks and Black Uhlans results in one death and several injuries. Police said the dispute related to a dispute over drug distribution. The Warlocks were taken over as a Rebels chapter opened.

August, 1993, Horsham. Rebels gang tries to take over the Cougars. Rebuffed at first but takeover later completed.

April, 1995, Ballarat. Bandidos Gang absorbs the Loners Gang. No major violent incidents reported.

April, 1995, Ballarat. Several shots fired into the Vikings clubhouse in Ballarat. Police believe it was a show of strength by the Bandidos.

April, 1995, Kyabram. Bandidos take Broke Brothers Motorcycle Club.

May, 1995, Ballarat. Hells Angels attack and bash members of the Bandidos gang at a bikie function. The Bandidos have a set of their colours stolen. Police say this confirms world-wide tensions between the two groups. They have reports of an international war between the gangs, culminating in an anti-tank missile attack in Amsterdam.

May, 1995, Ballarat. Bandidos fail in a takeover attempt on the Vikings. Tensions rise.

May, 1995, Ballarat. A Bandidos member's business is bombed with a home made explosive device. Believed to be in retaliation for a takeover bid.

June, 1995, Thomastown. Four members of the Bandidos arrested near Hells Angels (Nomads) Chapter clubhouse armed with various firearms. Police said the Bandidos had planned an armed raid on the Hells Angels to try and get their colours back.

August, 1995, Melbourne. Two Hells Angels (Nomads) arrested in possession of pistols. In a search of their house, police found a book which contained personal profiles and photos of 14 Bandidos' members. A confidential police report on the incident said 'It is likely the Hells Angels had these details for use when targeting the Bandidos members for violence.'

November, 1995, Ballarat. Bandidos member knocked from his motorcycle by a car as he leaves the clubhouse in a hit-run 'accident'. Police later told it was part of an ongoing bikie war. The hire car which struck the man was found to have been rented by the girlfriend of a Hells Angels Nomad member.

February, 1996, Ballarat. A hotel brawl between Vikings members and a Bandido leads to heavily armed Bandidos firing between 12 and 20 shots with a .223 rifle from a passing car. One Vikings member hospitalised. One bikie involved made a statement to police, breaking the code of silence.

May, 1996, Ballarat. The man who had made the statement over the February incident goes to police to withdraw his allegations, saying he was under the influence of drugs at the time. Police later find he has received a number of threats, and rival gang members continually drive past his house as a form of intimidation. Police received intelligence that the Vikings plan revenge.

May, 1996, Ballarat. Witnesses see a Vikings member being bashed on a street corner at 4 pm. Offender's vehicle registered to Bandidos' associate. Four hours later two cars spotted with front seat passengers pointing shotguns out of the window in nearby Sebastopol. Believed to be Vikings gang members.

July 1996. Members of Bandidos (Sydney) chapter spotted in Portland. It is believed they are attempting to take over the Bros club as part of an expansion into south-western Victoria.

CHAPTER 11

How far is too far?
To catch a thief

*Blessed are the peacemakers, for they shall be
called the sons of God. — Matthew 5 (ix).
Motto of the Special Operations Group.*

IT was the heist professional armed robbers dream about. The bandits
had inside information about a million-dollar soft target. The guards
would be unarmed and there was an easy escape route, or so the
theory went.

But there were two groups of trained, armed and ruthless men who
descended on Melbourne Airport the cold, windy July day chosen for
the robbery of the decade.

Both had done their homework. Both had conducted repeated
surveillance operations and dry runs. Both knew that precision and
timing would be the keys.

But there was one big difference: one group was made up of three
career armed robbers, while the second was the police's major strike
force, the Special Operations Group. And only the police group knew
that the others would be there.

On the face of it, Operation Thorn was right out of a Hollywood
script. Armed baddies move in on helpless target, terrorising innocent
victims, only to be trapped by the good guys in a shootout that leaves
one bandit dead, a second permanently disabled and the third lying on

his stomach at gunpoint after a high-speed car crash. But Operation Thorn was not a B-grade movie script, it was an officially-sanctioned Victoria Police operation, one that raised serious questions about the philosophy of law enforcement in Australia.

Operation Thorn exposed a police win-at-all-costs mentality that placed innocent lives at risk because police deliberately allowed criminals to stage an armed robbery rather than move in to stop the raid. Some of the bandits' victims remain traumatised years later, unable to understand why they were drawn into becoming cannon fodder in a life and death drama.

The Coroner, Jacinta Heffey, was left to pull together the pieces of an operation which took months to plan — and only seconds to end in death. The inquest had to look at the death of bandit Norman Lee. Along the way it shed light into the world of hard men playing out a drama in which the safety of innocent people was treated as irrelevant.

Evidence at the inquest showed police being quite prepared to set up an ambush in a public place, where they couldn't be sure that arrests could be made without risks to outsiders.

Police had intelligence, phone taps and physical evidence that a robbery was to be carried out at Melbourne Airport by a group of bandits suspected of being prepared to shoot anyone who got in their way. They suspected the target was the Ansett freight office.

The question is: Why did they wait for the crime to be committed before stepping in?

ON 28 July, 1992, the police lay in wait. It was the culmination of a four-month operation involving the Armed Robbery Squad, the Special Operations Group and the National Crime Authority. On the day of the armed robbery, 52 police were mobilised to catch the robbers at the airport at Tullamarine.

The targets were no cleanskins. The driver, Stephen John Asling, then 32, had previous convictions for assault and dishonesty offences.

Stephen Michael Barci, then 35, had convictions for armed robbery, selling drugs, assault, aggravated burglary, and intentionally causing serious injury.

Asling and Barci were close mates. So close that, in 1990, Barci was charged with using Asling's passport. The charge was later withdrawn. Police believed they were the core of one of Victoria's more proficient armed robbery teams, a group that relied on inside information and was prepared to use firearms to succeed.

The two planned and executed the armed robbery of a Brambles armoured van in Port Melbourne in May, 1990, in which a shot was fired. They also robbed a Greensborough McDonald's store in 1992.

In the Port Melbourne job, Asling and Barci ambushed two security guards, who were having breakfast, and forced them at gunpoint to lie in the back of their armoured truck. They were taken to a darkened warehouse in nearby Swallow Road where they were bound, hand and feet, before the gang took the payroll of $426,169.81 and the crew's revolvers.

One of the abducted guards was David Lapworth, who later admitted to being the inside man for the robbers. After Lapworth's arrest in April 1992, the Armed Robbery Squad went after Asling and Barci. They obtained warrants to bug four telephones as part of the operation.

Police said that, while conversations between the men indicated they were planning another robbery, they would never discuss the location over the phone.

It was clear that three men were needed for the job. Police were convinced they knew the name of the third man and even had his phone tapped. He had been in on the Port Melbourne job and was set for the next big robbery. But, with just weeks to go, the third man pulled out. Asling and Barci needed a replacement and quick. A man who knew the stick-up business and could be trusted.

They turned up a wild card, a small businessmen with a minor criminal history, Norman Leung Lee.

Norman 'Chops' Lee was one of the greatest enigmas of the Victorian underworld. He was the only man ever charged over the infamous Great Bookie Robbery, and one of few to survive the carnage that followed it.

Lee was charged by police with the robbery at the Victoria Club on 21 April, 1976. The actual amount of money stolen will never be known, with estimates ranging from $1.4 million to $12 million in untraceable cash.

Lee's best friend was Raymond Patrick 'Chuck' Bennett, the

acknowledged mastermind behind the robbery. Bennett was eventually shot dead inside the Melbourne Magistrates' Court, on 12 November, 1979.

Lee was alleged to have laundered $110,000 through a solicitor's trust fund, bringing $60,000 into the office in plastic bags.

The allegations were never put before a jury. Lee was released at a Magistrate's Committal over the bookie robbery because of insufficient evidence.

The then head of the armed robbery squad — now retired deputy commissioner, Paul Delianis — said Lee had always appeared quiet and cool.

'The question is whether he was quiet between the bookie robbery and the incident at Tullamarine or whether he was always too clever to come under notice. I think it was probably the latter,' he said. 'He moved in a circle of top crims. It would be a reasonable hypothesis that he was simply not caught.'

Lee was of the old school. Police seized an expensive safe from his business when they were looking for the money from the bookie robbery and took it by truck to the Russell Street police station. Detectives asked Lee what was in the safe. He remained silent. They asked him for the keys. He remained mute. Police phoned a safe expert who drilled out the lock, rendering it useless.

It was empty. But, on principle, Lee refused to assist.

Police used the National Crime Authority surveillance team to follow the key men, Asling and Barci, for three months in 1992. According to evidence from Detective Sergeant Stephen Brown, of the Armed Robbery Squad, the two men were seen watching cash deliveries from armoured vans at the ANZ bank in Mount Alexander Road, Essendon; at Westfield Shopping Centre, Airport West; the Gladstone Park Shopping Centre; Tip Top Bakeries in Brunswick; and the Ansett freight terminal, Melbourne Airport.

The best bandits use a combination of planning and gut feeling when plotting big jobs. They may check one target for months and then, for apparently no real reason, walk away. It is if living on the edge of a kill or be killed world heightens animal instincts for survival. Police have watched bandits, armed and ready to go, virtually sniff the air and leave a payroll after months of planning. It is always a battle between the two competing elements in a robber's mind, greed and survival. The ability to walk away from a job separates the elite bandits from the dangerous and desperate who invariably get caught.

Police eventually narrowed the likely armed robbery targets down to two, Tip Top and Ansett. But what police did not know was that the bandits had the most precious of all contacts, an inside man. They knew an Armaguard security officer.

The guard, Dean Rook, had known Stephen Asling for more than ten years. They had run into each other at the Golden Fleece hotel in South Melbourne in the months leading up to the attempt at Melbourne Airport as the gang was looking for its next target, weeks earlier. Rook mentioned the type of work he did and what was carried in his Armaguard van.

'I had a couple of beers in me and I was mouthing off,' Rook later told police, admitting he had told Asling details of airport and Tip Top runs. He claimed he was offered a cut of $100,000 from the takings but declined. Crucially, he did not pass any information of this alleged approach to the authorities.

The information provided by Rook must have been enough for Asling. On four occasions in three weeks, the robbers were seen at the bakery, but they were also seen four times at the airport. Normie Lee used to walk around the airport in a suit and carrying a clipboard like a professional efficiency expert. In a way he was, secretly observing the movements of the armoured van at Ansett's freight depot.

A few weeks earlier Barci and Asling slipped in and robbed the McDonald's store in Greensborough of $3500 and a security guard's gun. The bandits held guns to two people's heads during the robbery and so terrorised the manager that he could not remember the safe combination.

But it was just pocket money, although they would later use the security guard's gun in the big one they were planning.

Each week on a Tuesday, an Armaguard truck with three guards would arrive at the Ansett freight terminal with huge bags filled with cash. Airport protocol meant the guards would lock their guns in the truck before delivering the bags. As regular as clockwork, the van would arrive between 1.20 pm and 1. 45 pm for the cash to be loaded on to a Kendall's Airline flight to Mildura.

On 21 July the gang was observed parking two getaway cars near the airport, then parking a stolen Ford panel van in the airport. As the armoured truck arrived, around 1.20 pm, the driver of the van got out and lifted the bonnet, appearing to check the engine while watching the cash truck. Police suspect a loose engine wire forced the three bandits to abort the mission. The gang could hardly call the RACV to fix the van. It was torched that night. After the false start the gang decided the next cash drop, one week later on 28 July, would be the chosen day.

Police found out that the gang had even driven to Bendigo to test fire their weapons in readiness for the job. If the guns were to be used only as a bluff, why did the bandits need a day to make sure each was capable of killing efficiently?

Later, at the inquest, Barci and Asling said the plan to carry extra weapons and ammunition was Lee's. 'If this is true then it supports an image of Norman Lee as a person more likely to try and shoot his way out of a confrontation than to surrender when commanded to,' the Coroner found.

On the day Asling parked a gold BMW in the car park at the Gladstone Park Shopping Centre and Barci parked a Toyota Corolla in Derby Street, Tullamarine. Both were clearly planted as getaway cars for a job.

The three bandits arrived at the airport in a panel van armed with three pistols and two rifles. The bandits had a .38 revolver, a .357 magnum, a .380 pistol, a .223 self-loading rifle with 26 cartridges, and a .308 rifle. They also had three rubber masks — two Michael Jacksons and a Madonna — for disguises. It was a toss-up which was the more frightening. Barci and Lee also carried spare ammunition. Lee had 12 rounds of .357 cartridges in his pocket. It would do him no good.

The SOG arrest team also brought along a small arsenal, including a 12-gauge pump-action Remington shotgun with pistol grip, semi-automatic pistols, knives and gas masks. No-one could accuse the 'Sons Of God' of being under-prepared.

On the day of the robbery, the bandits drove their stolen van to a parking spot about 80 metres from the Ansett depot. The SOG arrest van was parked about 100 metres away in Depot Drive.

Police believed that because of a twist in the law, it would have been fruitless to arrest the men as they were just seated in the stolen van, even though the bandits were armed and clearly about to commit a robbery.

Police were not prepared to charge the men with lesser offences; they wanted them on charges that would result in long jail terms.

They believed a High Court ruling in 1983 precluded police from charging people with conspiracy to commit an armed robbery, without establishing the actual target. But while evidence at the inquest disputed the police impression of the law, it was clear the detectives wanted no chance of any loopholes in their case.

'Thorn' investigators decided they needed an 'overt act' before they moved. They wanted the bandits to put on their masks, or grab their guns, to make a move that couldn't be disputed in court.

Much play was made at the inquest that police should have moved days or weeks earlier. They could have chosen the least risky time and place to arrest the three.

But the Armed Robbery Squad, perhaps tired of seeing some of the dangerous men in the country walk free or be sentenced to only a few years, were going for broke. They wanted their case air tight; to do that they wanted to catch the offenders in the act. This would guarantee that the robbers would be put away for ten to fifteen years.

Police often criticise lenient sentencing because they have a vested interest in keeping criminals behind bars. And, for the Armed Robbery Squad, who hunt the hardest crooks, the stakes are always high. At Tullamarine they couldn't have been higher.

The police plan was to grab the three gunmen before the robbery, but the position of the SOG van left them too little time to intercept the bandits. They would not move in during the robbery because of the fear the gunmen might take hostages.

This meant they were forced to let the raid take its course, despite a risk the bandits could shoot Ansett staff while it was happening.

The bandits arrived around 1.16 pm and parked near the Ansett depot. The armoured van was late. It arrived about 1.45 pm.

Asling reversed the stolen van within 30 metres of the Armaguard vehicle. Barci and Lee jumped from the back of the van and ran into the office and grabbed three large red bags containing $1,020,000.

The five-man SOG team was parked in a disguised police van at least 100 metres from the Ansett depot. The police had no chance of stopping the job: the bandits had committed the robbery and were back at the van by the time they arrived. Lee threw two bags in the back of the van and Barci dragged his along the ground. 'As I dragged the bag down the steps I noticed a man in a van to my right. I fanned the gun past him and I was surprised that he grinned at me,' Barci later told police.

'When I got to the van Norm was inside the van on the rear passenger side, squatting. I then picked up the bag I was dragging with both hands and put it in the back of the van. I was pushing the bag in and Norm was pulling it. I then spun around and sat on the rear of the van on the driver's side with my legs hanging down. At the same time Norm grabbed me by the collar of my jacket to help push me in.'

The SOG arrived as the two men were settling in the back of the getaway van. A witness heard the bandits scream, 'go, go, go', but the catch on the back door was not in place. 'It was then that Steve hit the accelerator and Norm and I were thrown out the back of the van,' Barci said.

'We were screaming, 'stop, stop, stop!',' Barci said, as Asling tried to outrun the police. Not only had the two bandits been thrown out, but one of the three cash bags had fallen, too. Suddenly, it was every man for himself.

Barci and Lee chased the van as the SOG arrest team jumped from its vehicle. According to police, Lee, armed with a .357 magnum, lowered his gun and appeared to be about to give up. He then raised the gun. 'His actions left me no choice but to fire my weapon to protect myself,' one SOG member said later.

Two SOG police fired, hitting him in the back of the head and to the left side of the chest and left wrist. He was dead by the time he hit the ground.

Another SOG member fired five shots at Barci, hitting him at least three times — twice across the back and once in the left shoulder. He has been left permanently disabled.

It was later found that Barci's gun had fired one shot, probably discharging when he fell to the ground. Asling sped off, reaching a speed of up to 80 kmh. An SOG marksman fired one shot at the tyres, blowing out the rear passenger wheel. The bandit's car was then rammed by an SOG four-wheel drive. Police had left nothing to chance. If the bandits had escaped the inner net, there were road graders on standby to block the only road out.

Barci later pleaded guilty to three counts of armed robbery and was sentenced to 15 years jail, with a minimum of ten. Asling was also sentenced to a minimum of ten years for the three armed robberies.

ONE of the main concerns arising from Operation Thorn is that police, armed with the element of surprise and outnumbering their quarry 17 to one, chose to let the robbery go ahead before moving to arrest the criminals.

Up to 80 staff were counselled after the incident. Ansett and airport staff had been left dangerously exposed during the shoot-out.

Some say Operation Thorn was fatally flawed because it involved an armed confrontation in a crowded area. The operation was not as controlled as police would suggest: a shot from the SOG went through the window above a meal area of a nearby office, the bullet lodging in a noticeboard.

Barci made it clear to the coroner what he thought of the operation.

'I believe that the police knew about this robbery well before these events and it could be said that in allowing the robbery to actually take place they participated in a situation that was not only dangerous to the public but which was also a well-planned execution.'

His apparent concern for the public rang a little hollow considering the gang used five high-powered weapons it had test fired a week earlier. The bandits, were prepared, at best, to terrorise anyone who got in their way. At worst, they were equipped to murder.

Some Ansett staff were disappointed with police handling of the robbery, but one placed the blame squarely on the bandits. 'They were the ones who put the lives of innocent people in jeopardy. It's a shame they (the police) didn't shoot them all.'

One of the Ansett staff members at the front counter during the robbery, Darren Attard, complained that no-one had been warned of the raid.

The chief commissioner, Neil Comrie, disturbed at the number of police shootings, ordered the total retraining of the force under Operation Beacon, where safety became the first priority of any police raid.

Under Beacon 'the safety of police, the public and offenders or suspects is paramount'. The guidelines also specify, 'The success of an operation will be primarily judged by the extent to which the use of force is avoided or minimised.'

Strict new procedures were put into place stipulating when the SOG could be used. Under the new rules, an operation such as Thorn is unlikely to be authorised again.

What the Coroner said:

'The fact that Norman Lee contributed so substantially to his own death by undertaking a violent enterprise would not interfere with the making of an objective judgment as to whether the conduct of the Armed Robbery Squad did not also contribute to his death. The same consideration and criteria should apply as if the person killed was an innocent member of the public whether by accidental police fire (and we know that three rounds of police fire were unaccounted for on the day and windows in a nearby recreational building were shattered by gunshot fire) or by indiscriminate shooting by robbers. What occurred at Melbourne Airport on the 28th July was both foreseeable and avoidable.

'Whether Lee was in fact raising his gun in order to shoot will never be known.

'The three robbers were in possession of far more weaponry than they could need to perform an armed robbery alone. In addition to loaded handguns, they carried extra handgun ammunition; in the rear of the panel van were two Armalite military style rifles, both loaded. Mr Asling carried a loaded handgun and extra ammunition even though he did not enter the terminal building. Both Barci and Asling agreed in evidence that they had been to Bendigo with Lee to practice using some of the weapons. In evidence they said that being equipped with extra weaponry and ammunition was Lee's idea. If this is true then it supports an image of Norman Lee as a person more likely to try to shoot his way out of a confrontation than surrender when commanded to. 'That a death could result in the course of an apprehension of violent armed offenders in the course of committing an armed robbery on an unknown target in a busy public place in circumstances in which it was known that the robbers had rehearsed by test-firing weapons was not in my view a remote possibility. It was highly foreseeable.'

'The possibility of the unexpected occurring, the previously observed unpredictable behaviour of the offenders, the large area to be secured and contained, the possibility of some member of the public behaving heroically and complicating the apprehension — should have all served to demand greater reflection and more objective decision making.

'In their single-minded focusing on catching these "career criminals" the members of the Armed Robbery Squad overlooked their overriding responsibility to ensure the safety of the public. They are given substantial powers including in this case the power to direct the highly trained members of the Special Operations Group to apprehend their suspects at gunpoint at a time of their choosing. They had been available to them from the 22nd June onwards an option to arrest their suspects quite legitimately and in circumstances that posed no risk to the public and little or no risk to the offenders. Their failure to do this prior to the 28th July coupled with the forseeability of death or serious injury in the course of the arrest on that day in my view amounts to contribution to the death of Norman Lee.'

Postscript: Norman Lee was a fit-looking 44-year-old man of 73 kilograms and 171 centimetres. During the autopsy it was discovered he had a serious heart problem, including a 70 per cent blockage in his left coronary artery. If he hadn't been shot, chasing the getaway van and the shock of confronting armed police arrive at the scene could have killed him.

3/5/1990. Brambles armed hold-up in Port Melbourne; 426,000 stolen. Armed Robbery Squad commences 'Operation Thorn'

25/3/92. As a result of Crime-Stoppers publicity information is received by police that a Brambles employee by the name of Lapworth was involved in the Port Melbourne job.

10/4/92. Lapworth arrested and confesses his involvement. Names Barci, Asling and a man named Kendrick as robbers.

21/4/92. National Crime Authority commences periodic surveillance on behalf of Armed Robbery Squad of addresses, vehicles and movements of Barci and Asling. The investigators decided that Asling was the principle target.

28/5/92. Lawful telephone intercepts placed on Barci's home.

2/6/92. Lawful telephone intercepts placed on Asling's home.

20/6/92. Armed hold-up at Macdonald's Greensborough (for which Barci and Asling are later sentenced after pleading guilty)

9/7/92. Special Operations group becomes involved to conduct reconnaissance with the view to arrest at the appropriate time.

17/7/92. Lawful telephone tapes placed on the robber's safe house at 10 Dumas Street, Avondale Heights.

21/7/92. The 'dry run' at Melbourne Airport.

28/7/92. Norman Lee shot and killed at Melbourne Airport.

CHAPTER 12

A routine call
Life after death

*'All we wanted to do was to get her to be a
little bit quiet and then we would have gone.'*

FOR eleven months Senior Constable Trish Carl had to live with the allegation that she was a murdering racist. When a coroner finally cleared her of any wrongdoing, nearly a year after she had shot a woman three times, the country police officer thought what had blown into an international political controversy was finally finished, and she could get on with life. She was wrong.

The day after Trish Carl was officially exonerated, her daughter, Jessie, then six, walked out the front door of family's comfortable home into the neat front garden and found, freshly daubed in paint on the lawn and the front fence the words; 'COON KILLER'.

'It was supposed to be the first day of the rest of our lives, but it started in tears,' Trish was to recall. The brutal graffiti was probably the work of local youths, several of whom were seen around the area. But for the Carls it was a double blow. Their privacy had been violated, and it was the first indication Trish had that some people would always doubt her version of what happened.

All police shootings create controversy, but the events in Wodonga, in north-eastern Victoria, on that early November morning in 1995 conspired to turn a tragic death into an international incident. Senior Constable Carl shot dead a black woman, a Papua New Guinean national with strong political connections, at a time when Victorian police had a reputation for being gun happy.

It was the 25th police killing in Victoria since 1988 and the second since police had undergone a massive retraining program, called Operation Beacon, designed to minimise armed confrontations.

The Coroner, Jacinta Heffey, found the victim, Helen Merkle, was armed with two knives and that she had chased and attempted to attack Senior Constable Carl, who fired three shots in self-defence.

'I am satisfied that in all circumstances that the shooting of Helen Merkle by Constable Patricia Carl was justified,' the Coroner found.

Trish Carl was working night shift at Wodonga early that Sunday morning. A few hours earlier she had been called to the Wodonga Hospital, where a man had committed suicide by jumping from the roof. At 1 am she went to the dead man's home to speak to his wife. She wanted to know answers to the unanswerable. These are the tragedies of night shift that appear as only a few lines on a police running sheet. A man dies, a family is left devastated, but there are no suspicious circumstances to report, only heart ache. By 1.10 am Carl and her night shift partner, Barry Randall, were back on the road. By 2.30 am they were back in the station, hopeful that things would begin to slow down. After all, this was Wodonga, a relatively quiet country town, not Kings Cross or King Street. It is a good place to police and bring up a family.

About 2.55 am the station telephone rang. It was a call to attend a noisy party at 17 London Road by irate neighbours. They had reasons to be upset, having called the police in similar circumstances on the two previous Saturdays. For police it was a routine call. There are hundreds like it throughout the country every night.

But this one would be different.

As the police pulled up they could see light behind the front blinds, They could also hear a baby crying and loud, aggressive adult voices.

For the police, this was a simple matter. Knock on the door, have a quick chat, ask people to quieten down, write down the owner's name and then go away. They went to the porch and knocked. Two men came to the door, but behind them was Helen Merkle, 27. She began to scream abuse at the police. It was only because the two hefty males were unintentionally blocking the doorway that she couldn't get out. As the abuse continued the men held her back.

'All we wanted to do was to get her to be a little bit quiet and then we would have gone,' Trish Carl said later.

The screaming woman's husband, Mark, an army corporal, stepped out onto the porch to talk to police. He was carrying their two-year-old son, Joshua. Like so many routine police calls the lines become quickly blurred. Police went to the house to quieten down party goers. Now they were on the front porch acting as social welfare experts and marriage guidance counsellors. Mark Merkle was telling them he couldn't control his wife, and pointed to a scratch on his face claiming she had attacked him earlier.

Trish Carl had her back to the front door. She then felt her partner grab her jacket and pull her backwards and say, 'Let's get out of here, she's got a knife.' Helen Merkle had gone into the kitchen and armed herself with two knives. She then ran screaming at the policewoman.

Senior Constable Carl began to run backwards down the driveway. With her torch in her left hand she could see one of the knives in Helen Merkle's right hand. She screamed at least three times at the woman to drop the knife. But Merkle, irrational with alcohol, kept coming, and gaining. It seemed that a crazy woman running forwards travels quicker than a frightened one going backwards.

Trish Carl unholstered her firearm, automatically slipped off the safety catch and fired when Merkle was within one metre. One shot from the hip, a second as she brought the gun up and a third from in front of her body. Each shot hit Helen Merkle, the third hitting her heart, killing her almost instantly.

Senior Constable Carl said: 'She could have stopped. I fired once and she kept coming. I fired again and she didn't stop. I fired the third time and then she fell.' Her husband came to the fallen woman. Her breathing was erratic. She was dying. He found a knife in her hand and threw it way. Trish Carl moved the second knife away from her. Mark Merkle was with his wife. He was crying. The last thing he said before she died was, 'I love you.' A large group of Papua New Guinean friends of the dead woman gathered and their grief soon turned to anger. The situation threatened to turn ugly. Senior police who attended ordered Trish Carl to get inside the divisional van and lock the doors. The dead woman was the niece of Papua New Guinea's Foreign Affairs Secretary, Gabriel Dusava. Senior PNG officials, including the then Prime Minister, Sir Julius Chan, and the PNG high commissioner to Australia, Sir Frederick Reiher, disputed whether Merkle had been armed, even though her husband was adamant that she had carried the knives. Even the then Foreign Minister, Senator Evans, saw fit to express an opinion. 'It just staggers the imagination that something has not gone fundamentally wrong in the way in which the police are administering themselves.'

The Chief Commissioner, Neil Comrie, said he hoped that the people who condemned the police actions would be as quick to apologise when all the facts were known.

When Trish Carl was cleared the Police Association wrote to Senator Evans asking for an apology. He responded: 'While I am pleased from the point of view of your membership and Senior Constable Carl in particular, that the Coroner found that there was no wrong doing in the Merkle incident, I remain of the view that my comments of 15 November were fair in the circumstances as they were known at the time.'

In the days and weeks that followed the shooting Helen Merkle's friends and relatives eulogised the dead woman. She was, according to them, the victim of a police force that no longer valued human life and was too quick to go for the gun. Trish Carl had to suffer in silence. With an inquest scheduled, she could not speak out in her defence.

The headlines in the local paper read: 'Police Shoots Mother Dead'.

'They didn't say: 'Mother Shoots Mother Dead,' Senior Constable Carl, a mother of two, said.

A headline in a PNG paper was even more judgmental. 'It was Murder,' it stated.

What emerged from the coroner's hearing was that Helen Merkle was a bright, well-educated former teacher with a drinking problem.

Sober, she was a lovely woman. Drunk, the Coroner was told, she was a 'walking time bomb ready to explode and kill someone.'

An hour before she was shot, she was disarmed when she tried to stab her husband with a carving knife. She had previously attacked people with fists, broken stubbies, knives and a truncheon.

The international after-shocks from the incident continued. Expatriate Australians in PNG were warned by the Foreign Affairs Department to be careful, as they feared a revenge killing as a payback over Helen Merkle's death.

Australian Military Intelligence feared that PNG soldiers, training with the army at a base near Wodonga, could also plot a revenge. They feared a raid on the military armoury followed by an attack on the police station. The armoury was quietly emptied of all weapons and guards placed on the area. The Wodonga police station was locked every night from 11 pm to 7 am even though the station was a 24 hour centre. The tension was great.

But in some ways Senior Constable Carl was lucky. Her husband, Andrew was a local policeman, so she has been able to discuss the shooting with a partner who understood the mental torment. She developed a shorter temper and her memory deteriorated but she and her family worked through the problems.

Some police involved in shootings don't recover well. Several in Melbourne have resigned after being involved in killings.

'I haven't suffered from the what-ifs, what if this happened or that had happened? I know I had no choice,' she said.

In America one policeman lost the use of his right arm, although there was nothing wrong with him physically, after an armed robber shot his partner dead. He returned fire and killed a child playing in a park behind the bandit.

Police and so-called experts have been trying to find non-deadly weapons to use against mentally-disturbed offenders. The New York police have tested a spiderman-type sticky net which can be fired from a gun or thrown by hand. The net is designed to immobilise offenders. Capsicum spray, which temporarily blinds offenders, has been introduced as standard issue for Victorian police. Stun guns have been given trials, but the facts remain straightforward.

Police are paid to do a job and have the same rights as anyone else. If their lives are in danger they can kill on the grounds of self defence. They do not have to be heroes.

Trish Carl's duty that morning was to stay alive and to come home to her family. While she knows she did nothing wrong, the events of 12 November, 1996, have left their mark on her family. Having always told their children that police don't hurt people and are there to help those in trouble, the Carls had to tell the youngsters their mother had killed a woman.

Jessie seemed to understand. She drew pictures of her mother and wrote of a lady with a knife who died. At the time, they thought her younger brother, Jake, then three, was too young to understand.

Almost 20 months after the shooting the family was playing. Trish asked her son, 'What does dad do?' Jake replied proudly, 'He's a policeman.' Then she asked 'What does mum do?' He answered, 'She kills people.'

'It sort of knocked me for six,' said the boy's mother.

But Jessie obviously dwelled on the matter, too. She was at a family friend's house when she helped clear up after a meal. An adult commented on how helpful she was and she said, 'Oh yes, I'll do anything except kill someone.'

Even though Trish Carl wanted to tell her story publicly, she was advised by her lawyers not to give evidence at the inquest, a decision she understood, but it still left her frustrated.

'I feel I was deprived of my chance to say what happened, to have my say. All I wanted to do was to say what happened'.

For a year after the shooting she dreaded policing. 'I loved it before the shooting, but I lost interest in work.' She admitted that if she could have found another secure job, she would have quit.

She decided to throw herself into her work, to get the buzz back. 'I've started to enjoy it again, but it's not the same.' With both partners working in the same station there are ups and downs. They understand the pressures, but are acutely aware of the dangers.

When his wife works nightshift, Andrew drifts over to check the roster. If her partner is a good copper he rests a little bit easier, but if he has doubts about the ability of the partner he worries and is restless until the week of shift work is over.

Trish says she cannot sleep when Andrew is on nightshift. 'It's worse than doing the shift yourself.'

Nearly two years after the shooting, Trish Carl was called to a mundane disturbance. She found a mentally unstable woman with a knife. She talked her around and took her to hospital, where she was certified. It was all in a night's work.

CHAPTER 13

A criminal clan
The granny

*She used Salvation Army emergency petrol to
fill the car she drove to do her drug deals.*

AT times she was a doting grandmother, clucking and fussing over her children's children, but under pressure she showed the ruthlessness that made her a feared underworld figure for more than 30 years.

It took a heavy police taskforce, a tough female criminal and an undercover police officer posing as a yuppie snow skier to bring Kath Pettingill to justice, exposing her as an active drug dealer.

None of it might have happened without Rosina Power. She was a big, powerful woman with a tough streak and a keen sense of justice. When she heard that a man who lived near her was a suspected paedophile, she took matters into her own hands. Her husband was serving eight years for armed robbery, leaving her to bring up their three children alone. But he had hidden a double-barrelled shotgun inside a door in their house.

Rosina grabbed the gun, and she made a Molotov cocktail. She went to the man's house, threw the fire bomb at it and blasted the front door with two shots. The next day the house was still standing so she bombed it again and fired more shots. She was arrested when she attacked the house on the third night.

She was sentenced to four years jail. While in Fairlea Women's Prison she met Kath Pettingill, a grandmother, whose sons were considered among the worst criminals in Australia.

In 1993 Rosina Power was trying to make a new start. She moved into Wedge Crescent, Rowville, in Melbourne's outer east. By a twist of fate one of her neighbours turned out to be Kath Pettingill. Like all good neighbours, Pettingill was soon on the doorstep to say hello. But instead of the traditional chat over coffee and cake, she came straight to the point. Would Ros like to move some drugs for her old prison buddy? Like a good host, Rosina walked into the kitchen to make her guest a cup of tea. But while she was there, she picked up the phone to ring a drug squad detective to tell him of the new neighbour from hell.

At 6.30 pm Pettingill returned to the house with her little grand daughter, but it was no Neighbourhood Watch meeting. She asked Power how much cannabis she could sell at $400 an ounce.

Kath said another of their close neighbours was also a dealer. On 15 May Rosina met Kath and the neighbour in a car outside the local milkbar and bought six small plastic bags of amphetamines for $300.

It was no big deal, but it sowed the seeds of Kath Pettingill's destruction.

Rosina Power began to talk regularly to the Drug Squad detective. She agreed to introduce him to Pettingill as 'Lenny Rogers', supposedly a snow skier who wanted drugs to sell to yuppies on the slopes.

In May Pettingill went to Rosina Power's home and gave her a plastic bag with an ounce of cannabis and several bags of speed. Power paid the grandmother $350 for the drugs the following day.

Kath Pettingill was a cunning old lag and she knew the way police worked better than some police did. She knew the best way to deal drugs was through a tight network, and never to strangers. But when Rosina introduced the man who called himself Lenny Rogers, she decided to take a risk. After all, Rosina was an old jail friend and Lenny seemed harmless. He didn't look or act like a policeman or a crim. He didn't talk tough and he appeared to be from another, more civilised world. In other words, to the street-smart Kath, he was a soft touch. A harmless mug.

But Kath knew the underworld was full of traitors and one night she turned on Lenny and demanded to search him, looking for a tape or gun. She always searched people, she explained. Even her own son, Dennis Bruce Allen. The feared underworld figure, known as 'Mr Death', was one of Australia's biggest drug dealers and was involved in several murders before he died of heart disease.

Pettingill's instincts were right. The conversation was recorded. It was a tense moment.

KATH: 'Nobody's guaranteed.'

LENNY: 'I know.'

KATH: 'Dennis never trusted me one hundred percent and I never trusted him one hundred percent, and he's my son.'

LENNY: 'Yeah, I know.'

According to police, Kath made further enquiries about Lenny, going as far as contacting corrupt former NSW detective, Roger Rogerson, to run a check on him. It came back clean.

Once Lenny had Kath on side, it opened all sorts of criminal doors to the undercover operative. If he was dealing with Kath, many criminals reasoned, then he was obviously worth knowing.

With Lenny working on the inside, police set up a task force that branched into two major investigations. Operations Earthquake and Tremor resulted in police moving in on amphetamine, heroin and marijuana rings, arresting sixteen people who were convicted and sentenced to a total 42 years jail.

In a series of buys Lenny purchased amphetamines, marijuana and heroin from Kath, her son Trevor Pettingill and their associates.

Most purchases were for at least $4000, but this wasn't enough for Kath. She used Salvation Army emergency petrol coupons to fill the car she drove to do her drug deals.

Although she was making plenty of easy money, old habits died hard. She remained an active shoplifter.

She told friends the story of stealing a toy dinosaur for one of her grandchildren. She had slipped it under her clothes, next to her armpit and as she paid for other items at the checkout, the stolen toy began to slip and she had to squeeze it to make sure it didn't fall. The pressure made the soft toy let out a growl. She pretended she had a bad case of wind and was making the growling noise herself. It worked. No store detective was prepared to confront an elderly woman making noises like an extra in Jurassic Park. Another shoplifting trip resulted in a haul of cosmetics and lingerie later sold at a discount through a suburban massage parlour. The grandmother took to wearing a see-through crochet white top in what was a rather bold fashion statement. Police were determined to make an airtight case. The fact that two of Kath's sons, Victor Peirce and Trevor Pettingill, had been acquitted of the notorious 'Walsh Street' murders of young policemen Damian Eyre and Stephen Tynan in 1988, added to the detectives' determination. They knew that any defence would be that police had planted evidence as a payback for Walsh Street. The taskforce wanted tapes and photographs that could not be disputed.

Kath Pettingill was like no other criminal. She called everyone 'Love', as if she were a friendly tea-lady. But she was often armed and had intimate knowledge of at least a dozen underworld murders.

On 26 July Kath went to Power's house, produced a pen pistol from her knickers and said 'have a look at my toy.'

At another meeting with Power, she chatted about business.

KATH: 'Come in, love.'

ROSINA: 'Hi Kath, how are ya?'

Rosina followed Kath into Victor's room. The grandmother sat on her son's bed, produced a small Wizz Fizz spoon from a confectionary packet, and carefully used it to measure white powder into about six aluminium foils.

KATH: 'I'll just shut this door 'cause all the kids'll hear . . . Is your bloke happy with it (drugs) love?'

ROSINA: 'Not too bad. He reckons if it was a bit better he'd be able to jump on it (dilute) a bit more. But he wasn't, you know; he'll make a bit, but not much.'

KATH: 'What, complainin' about it?'

ROSINA: 'Yeah.'

KATH: 'Fuckin' kiddin'.'

ROSINA: 'No. no.'

KATH: 'We'll look after ya, love, don't worry . . . I made $2800 last night, love.'

The drug dealing in the street was an open secret. One night Rosina had every window in her house smashed and the words 'DRUG DEALING SLUT' daubed on her door. She could hardly defend herself by saying she was working undercover for the police.

During the operation Rosina walked up to Kath's house with $1000 she had been given by police to buy amphetamines

KATH: 'Yeah; oh, how are ya love.'

ROSINA: 'How are ya.'

KATH: 'All right.'

Rosina handed over $1000 to Kath.

KATH: 'Oh, it's the best love.'

ROSINA: 'Yeah.'

KATH: It's the best. I only get the best, you know that.'

Rosina was later to be put into witness protection, where she became one of the program's success stories.

SLOWLY the police operation moved up the drug chain. It was nearly blown in August when Lenny was supposed to buy heroin worth $12000 from a drug dealer, Steven MacKinnon, known as 'Stacker'.

Lenny arrived for a meeting at the corner of Johnstone and Hoddle Streets, Collingwood in a white Holden Commodore.

Stacker arrived on foot. He was furious, saying he had seen a man in a lane photographing the scene. He said the photograper had to be a policeman and he smelled a rat. Lenny remained calm and kept talking even when Stacker said he wanted to use a bottle to open the undercover's head.

The group moved on to Footscray to meet the Chinese connection to get the gear. This time the Asian dealer spotted a police photographer. Stacker was livid. He began to shake with rage and accused Lenny of being an undercover policeman.

The butt of Stacker's gun stuck out from his jacket. He wanted the money and he wanted it now. This was a deadly dilemma, a time when the only thing that stands between an undercover and a bullet in the brain is the ability to talk under pressure. No back-up police can move in quickly enough to help when flashpoint arrives.

If Lenny backed down his credibility in the criminal world would be ruined. Lenny took the risk and stood his ground, refusing to hand the money over without the gear. Stacker threatened to put Lenny in the boot of his own car. The deal was blown and MacKinnon stormed off. As Lenny became more accepted he was able to deal directly with the

Chinese connection, Viet Le. He bought a quarter ounce of rock heroin at a Housing Commission flat in Collingwood for $3500. Later that day he bought a pound of amphetamines for $8500 from Trevor Pettingill.

That afternoon Le made contact to say he had given half an ounce rather than a quarter and wanted the balance back. In the drug world the idea of asking for drugs back was laughable, but Lenny did go back and hand over the difference.

Le was so impressed he dropped his guard and embraced his new found honest friend. He said that Lenny no longer needed an introduction, he could deal directly with the Asians. They would go to restaurants in Victoria Street, Richmond to deal.

Senior police were getting nervous. Stacker was still a loose cannon, and the longer the job went the greater the chance of it running out of control.

Le said he could sell Lenny eight ounces of heroin for $65,000. It was time to move after more than 15 controlled drug deals.

On 15 September Lenny bought two ounces for $21,000 from Le, with a promise of the balance to be provided the next day.

That was the day picked as the day to make the arrests. The key was to grab the offenders without letting anyone from the gang being warned. A series of co-ordinated raids were planned. Each offender would have to be arrested and isolated.

MacKinnon was arrested by Special Operations Group police at a Food Plus store in Preston and taken to the drug squad for interview.

Lenny and Power met Le at the Van Mai restaurant at 1 pm. The undercover had $56,000 to buy the drugs. Le said he could not get six ounces of heroin until the evening but he could get one ounce immediately. Le made a call on his mobile and then left the restaurant. He was handed the drugs by his dealer, Mengkok Te. He returned and handed Lenny an ounce of rock heroin. Lenny handed over $10,500 for it.

So happy was Le with the deal that he gave Lenny a small amount of amphetamines as a bonus. He said he would provide the rest of the heroin later that day and a pound of amphetamines in a few days. No-one was taking much notice of a group of twelve raucous office workers celebrating a birthday at the next table. The multi-cultural nature of Australia meant that a group of Anglo-Saxons shovelling down cheap Vietnamese food did not raise an eyebrow, although the diners made enough noise to raise the roof. The drug dealer and Lenny had to strain to hear each other as the nearby group sang 'Happy Birthday' and the guest of honour blew out the candles on the cake to loud cheers.

Le told Lenny they would be able to do business together and they were special friends. As the smiling Lenny was about to leave he made a pre-arranged gesture and the birthday party broke up.

The office workers were actually undercover National Crime Authority officers planted for the bust. Two pretended to head to the toilet, and as they passed the complacent Le, they swooped. The supplier, Te, was walking towards the restaurant to get his cut. He actually passed Lenny on the street. Surveillance police moved in and grabbed Te, who was also wanted in Sydney as a major importer of heroin.

Meanwhile, Kath Pettingill's house in Venus Bay was searched. She might have seemed a charming old scallywag but she didn't get a reputation as a gangster for nothing. When police searched her they found her pen pistol in her knickers.

Lenny had played his role so well that even as the boom was being lowered one dealer was trying to undercut Trevor Pettingill's marijuana price by $400 a pound. His name was Edward Fiorillo, and he agreed to sell Lenny five pounds of marijuana for $22,000.

They arranged to meet near a cafe in Lygon Street, Carlton.

Lenny and Fiorillo met in a laneway. Fiorillo had a purple sports bag with the marijuana sealed in one pound lots. Lenny had $22,000. Police moved in to arrest Fiorillo, but he saw them and ran down Rathdowne Street. He was eventually arrested in a dead-end lane.

Police checked the dealer's St Albans house. They found marijuana matching the drugs offered to Lenny. They also found marijuana hidden in the school cases of Fiorillo's de facto's child.

The Special Operations Group arrested Trevor Pettingill that evening in his flat in Collingwood. He was fairly relaxed as he had only a small amount of cannabis in the flat. His mood changed when he finally learned that one of his best clients, Lenny, was an undercover policeman.

Trevor Pettingill was sentenced to five years for drug trafficking, and his mother Kath to nine months. Le got three years jail, Te seven years and MacKinnon two years.

The mum

'I've got a heart'

WHEN Wendy Peirce's brother-in-law offered to shoot her in the foot for 'the good of the family' she thought about it for a while before declining the offer on the grounds that she was pregnant.

The brother-in-law was a notorious drug dealer, police informer and killer, Dennis Bruce Allen. The motive was to get Wendy's husband, Victor Peirce, bail on compassionate grounds while he was awaiting trial for drug trafficking.

'If I wasn't pregnant it would have been all right. Dennis would have known how to do it without doing too much damage. Dennis shot himself in the leg once, when he didn't want to go to jail. He wouldn't trust anyone else to do it,' Wendy Peirce said later.

Welcome to the world of Melbourne's most infamous crime family, the Allen-Pettingill clan. Theirs is a world of violence, greed and betrayal, in which family members would take up arms against outsiders but then turn on each other, virtually on a whim.

Many criminals isolate their families from their 'work'. The family home is sacred and safe houses are rented for underworld activities. But the Allen-Pettingill gang was different.

For them it was all mixed together. Children were brought up in households where people were killed, armed robberies plotted, drug deals struck, and guns as commonplace as stuffed toys. The kids grew up knowing Santa came down the chimney once a year, but armed detectives crashed through the front door a little more often.

Wendy had a massive falling out with Kath Pettingill when the older woman published her memoirs, *The Matriarch*, in 1996. It is purported to be the true story of Melbourne's underworld during the past 20 years.

Few knew the workings of the underworld like Kath. She has worked as a brothel madam and a drug dealer. Six of her sons have been involved in virtually every serious crime on the statutes and some which should be. Two of the sons are now dead. Three of the remaining four were serving long jail terms by the mid 1990s.

But Wendy Peirce says her mother-in-law is an exploitative old woman, recycling family stories she has picked up over the years.

'She's a great grandmother now. She should be sitting down and doing the knitting not dragging up what has happened to us,' she says. 'She has brought my children into her book. She gave me a copy and wrote, "Wendy, if I have embarrassed you in this book I apologise, love Kathy." When she rings I just hang up on her now. She's written about things that have happened to me when she wasn't even there. I'm disgusted.'

The Allen-Pettingill brood will always be associated with one of the worst crimes in Australia's history. On 12 October, 1988, two young police, Damian Eyre and Stephen Tynan, were ambushed and murdered in Walsh Street, South Yarra. It was alleged to be a payback for police killing an armed robber, Graeme Jensen, during an attempted arrest in Narre Warren the previous day.

Two of Kath's sons, Victor Peirce and Trevor Pettingill, and two family friends, Peter McEvoy and Anthony Farrell, were charged and acquitted over the Walsh Street killings.

Both Peirces had reasons to grieve over Jensen's death. He was Victor's best friend – and his wife Wendy's secret lover.

One of the police task force's main strategies in trying to gather evidence against the Walsh Street suspects was to get inside the close-knit Richmond tribe. First Jason Ryan, a nephew, turned to the prosecution, then Jason's mother and Kath's daughter, Vicki Brooks, agreed to give evidence for the police.

Police thought another key witnesses would be Wendy Peirce, who had made statements to detectives that her husband had admitted to her that he was one of the Walsh Street killers.

But for reasons Wendy finds difficult to explain, she changed her mind. When it came to the Supreme Court trial her story had changed. The police case was largely blown to pieces.

Police confidently predicted that Wendy had made the biggest mistake of her life and would ultimately pay for it with her life. But eight years after the murders and five years after the trial, she was still healthy and still married to Victor, the man she originally declared was a cop killer.

'I was never going to give evidence against Victor. I don't want to go into that all now. I think I had a mental breakdown, I was on heavy medications and I can't recall all of what happened. I really don't know why I did what I did,' she said.

'I love Victor and I know he loves me,' she said. 'He is a gentleman and a devoted family man. We had another child after that (Walsh Street) so it shows we are still together.' The couple have four children ranging from voting age to kindergarten.

In 1992 Wendy was sentenced to 18 months with a minimum of nine for perjury over her evidence regarding Walsh Street. Her youngest child, Vincent, was five months old and went to jail with her.

Vincent was named after the Walsh Street trial judge, Justice Frank Vincent. Victor Peirce was sentenced to eight years with a minimum of six for drug trafficking. He had been in jail since his son was born. He was moved from the maximum security Barwon Jail to medium security at Bendigo and his earliest parole date was May, 1998. He was allowed to go ten pin bowling, cycling and long distance running outside of the jail while in custody.

Wendy maintains that Victor really had no choice but to go into crime in a big way. The Peirces lived in Chestnut Street, Richmond, next door to Victor's brother Dennis Allen, who was making up to $70,000 a week through drug dealing. Allen once shot a bikie, Anton Kenny, and then severed his legs with a chainsaw in his Chestnut Street garage. It was not the ideal family environment.

Wendy met Victor when she was a business college student in 1977 and moved in with him shortly after. 'I didn't understand what sort of life we would lead,' she said later. 'I have come across murders. I've seen people shot, with their throats cut and bashed. It was a nightmare. I had to bring kids up during this. I was 17 when I got into this. I should be in a mental home.'

Peirce said she lived in a climate where any day a family tiff could be fatal. She recalled the day that Dennis Allen fought with his wife, Sissy Hill.

'Dennis opened the boot. Sissy was in there with her throat cut. It wasn't ear to ear, but she lay there just gurgling. It was awful. I was helpless. He just slammed the boot shut and I spun out. He told someone to drive her somewhere and just leave her in a dumpmaster. I got her dropped off at a railway station so someone would find her

Neil Gordon Wilson … no one knows why he wanted to be a fish.

Neil Wilson (above) self-portrait and (below) self-destruction.

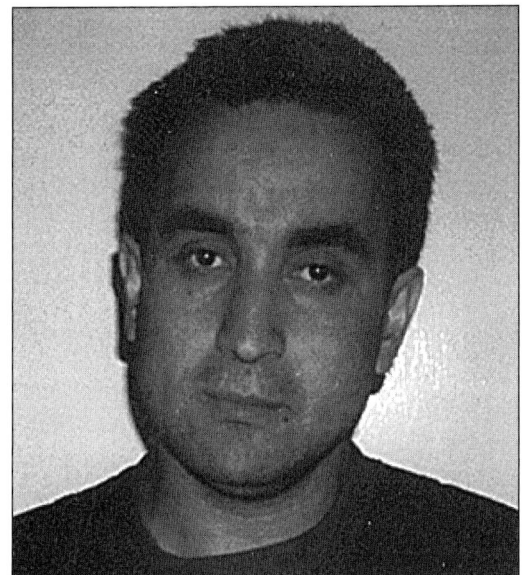

Kemal Sahin … wanted his wife's finger delivered to him as proof of her murder.

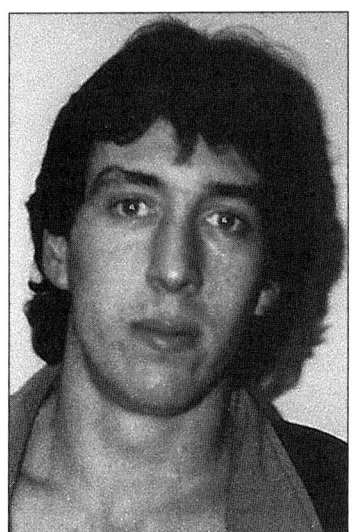 

Victims of hitmen … Stuart Lance Pink (left) and Tony Franzone.

Eight more hit victims: Charles Francis Caron (left), Christopher Philips.

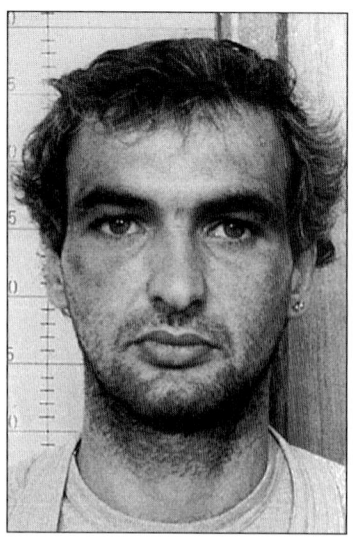 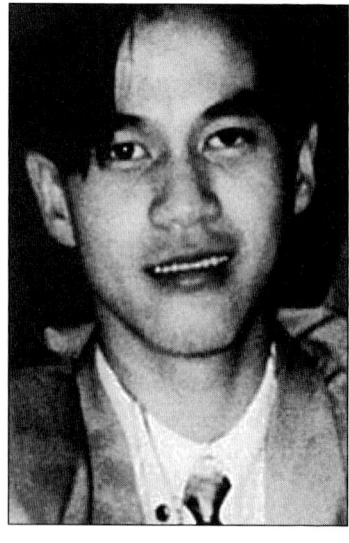

Dimitrious Nanos.

Quock Cuong Dwong.

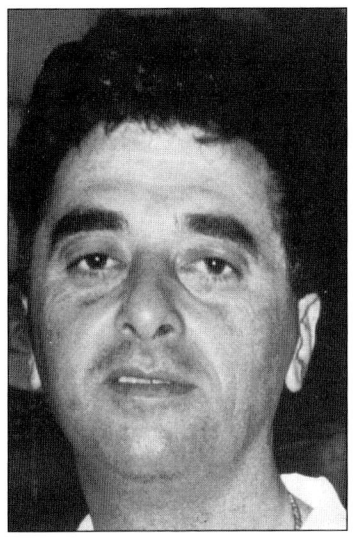

Alfonso Muratore.

Geoffrey Engers.

Santo Ippolito.

Rakesh Bhanot.

Double
murderer and
multiple
rapist
Raymond
'Mr Stinky'
Edmunds.

Edmunds'
victims
… Abina
Madill
and Garry
Heywood.

Bikie barbecue … hiding a massive concrete bunker used as an amphetamines laboratory in a suburban backyard.

Jim Wiggins and wife Helen … the pressure of one-man
policing led him to suicide.

and take her to hospital. That saved her life.' Or what was left of it. Sissy later committed suicide.

On another night Allen brought home a woman he suspected of informing to police on a series of burglaries and car thefts. 'He put her on a bed and beat her with a baseball bat. She was crying out for water and Dennis gave me some petrol and told me to make her drink it. When he went down the Cherry Tree (hotel) I sat her up and gave her some water and let her go. I just told Dennis she had escaped. I've got a heart. 'Later, we were in the same cottage in jail and she said "Wendy, I can never repay you for saving my life".'

While Peirce sees herself as the victim of her in-laws' propensity for violence she was not kept there against her will. She was an active member of the family and accepted its peculiar ethos of rearing children in an environment of danger, police raids, drugs and death.

When Victor was arrested for drug trafficking in 1985, he wanted bail. Wendy, heavily pregnant at the time, purposely urinated while in court and announced to the stunned judge that her waters had broken and she was having a baby. Bail was granted.

'I wouldn't leave Victor and he was there. I was so young when I moved in with him and I adapted to what was happening. It was our biggest mistake moving into Chestnut Street. None of this would have happened if we had gone off on our own.'

A policeman who got to know her when she was in witness protection said: 'She could be a real bitch. She had a savage temper and could flip out. She was sort of sucked into the gangster mentality of the family.

'But she has a soft side as well, and really loves her kids. She came from a decent family but was drawn into their (Pettingill) way of life and had no way out.'

When she was in witness protection, one of the worst chores for police was to take her shopping. 'She would shoplift things. She couldn't help herself. She was always testing us, trying to push the boundaries.

'She was in witness protection for nearly two years. I thought she had a real chance but it (the case) took too long to come up. She got in touch with Victor and that was the end.'

Another policeman is less sympathetic. 'She is a manipulative woman who actively embraced the life of a gangster's wife. She would do anything for the family and had the privileges that came from the profits derived from her husband's drug dealings and armed robberies.

'She agreed to go into witness protection when the family seemed to be disintegrating. It was a huge decision and she gave damning evidence at the committal. She was in protection for two years and she got sick of it. The family turned her again before the trial. If the trial had been quicker it may have been different,' he said.

But Peirce denies having the trappings of the gangster days. She lives the life of a struggling single mother in an outer Melbourne suburb, struggling to pay the bills. She cannot use her telephone because of failure to pay previous accounts.

She says her children were victims of the family's gangster background. 'None of my kids have been in trouble with the law. Parents don't want my kids mixing with theirs. What do they think? I've got a machine gun under the apron? I'm just a housewife.'

'Katie's a good kid, but she hardly ever gets invited to a birthday party. Another kid said at school the other day, "at least my dad isn't in jail".'

Peirce said a book about the Tynan-Eyre killings had been passed about at school. 'I know the Walsh Street thing will never die down. I don't care. I can live with that, but it is unfair on the kids.'

She said she knew that she had a temper and had convictions for crimes of violence. 'I know I can get aggressive and fly off the handle but animals protect their young like mothers protect theirs.'

She said that all she wanted was for her husband to finish his jail sentence and come home.

'He is the father of my kids but I've told him if this happens again that is the end. But it won't happen again, I know it. When he gets out this time then that will be it. He adores his wife and children and he just wants to come home. We are just a normal family.

'My daughter wanted to join the police force, but I told her to be realistic. There is no way known they would let one of Victor's kids do that.'

The brothers

'We are the heart of the family,
we keep things pumping'

PETER John Allen was a hard-working small businessman determined to get ahead. He had a product that was eagerly sought after, a strong distribution network and a captive market. His product was heroin, his customers were fellow inmates at Pentridge prison, and his supply line was managed by his half-brother, Victor George Peirce — one of the most dangerous criminals in Australia.

Allen controlled a large slice of the drug market to Pentridge, Bendigo and Geelong jails and he ran it using a telephone network inside the jail system.

Allen, then 41, was convicted of drug trafficking after a five-month trial costing about $960,000 in 1994. The jury of eight men and four women heard how a career criminal had been able to manipulate the prison system.

They were told Allen had made a total of $22,610 from 17 June, 1991, until 3 April, 1992, while inside prison.

According to police, he controlled a large section of Victoria's main prison, using a combination of violence, drugs, a sinister reputation and cunning.

Allen had been convicted of being a heroin dealer in 1988 and sentenced to 13 years, with a minimum of 11. But for a career criminal, being in jail was only an inconvenience when it came to running a drug syndicate.

He developed a network using a corrupt prison officer, codenamed 'The Postie', three female couriers, five TAB accounts and his brother as his banker and drug buyer, all to supply inmates with drugs to order. The brothers trafficked heroin, amphetamines, Rohypnol and cannabis to prisoners.

In business, communication is the key, and Allen had no trouble talking to his outside network. He was allowed to work in the F division laundry, which he turned into a personal kingdom. He manipulated the system to the point where he had control of a telephone, which phone taps revealed he used to order drugs through an unsophisticated code and to 'talk dirty' to his girlfriends.

A group of prisoners worked in the laundry four hours a day. Allen used the telephone there for two hours a day. For a prisoner who should have been earning $20 a week, it was big business.

Police set up phone taps on the laundry phone and the telephone at Victor Peirce's house to record conversations in which drugs and finances were discussed. The tapes were later used to break the network. As part of Operation 'Double N', police recorded 17,850 phone calls, including 1760 from the jail, and documented hundreds of hours of conversations.

During one phone call, Allen made it clear that it was he and Peirce who controlled the most feared crime family in Victoria.

'Exactly. Yeah, 'cause we've got it all together. Yeah, we're the nucleus of the family. Yeah, we are the heart of the family, we keep things pumping,' Allen said.

At one stage Allen lost contact visits for three weeks and rang Peirce in a rage. He asked his brother to organise the fire-bombing of several prison officers' private cars as a payback.

He bragged on the phone that he certainly wouldn't be broke when he got out, and spoke of paying 'The Postie' $300. 'Not a bad effort for a poor boy in jail with 20 bucks a week ... I've got people that want to help me out, that's my business.'

As part of his business he organised inmates to get relatives or friends to deposit money (usually in multiples of $50) into one of the TAB phone accounts before the drugs were handed over.

The records, admitted in court, showed that cash deposits were made across Melbourne within minutes.

On 22 August deposits were simultaneously made to an account in the name of Peirce's wife, Wendy, in Boronia ($50) and in Lonsdale Street ($52) at 1.49pm. One week after that, deposits were made in Blackburn at 11.36am and Balaclava two minutes later.

Police say Allen was able to control the network because prison officials put him in D division, an area for remand prisoners easily dominated by a man with Allen's reputation. He had been placed there for his own protection from other career criminals.

In one telephone conversation he speculated whether the laundry telephone was tapped before dismissing the idea, believing that police might be monitoring his friend's telephone: 'His phone must be off.'

Detectives spent 13 months investigating Allen, from August, 1991, until September, 1992. Three months after the investigation began, Allen was transferred from Pentridge to Bendigo prison but he continued drug operations there. Police believe he also trafficked drugs while an inmate at Geelong.

'We had no doubt that Peter Allen was a major drug trafficker within the system. He knew the system inside out and was able to build a network using jail telephones,' the head of the Tactical Investigation Group operation, Detective Senior Sergeant Peter De Santo, said after the trial.

'He was ambitious, and used hired muscle inside the jail to protect his business.'

The court was told that Allen had used five TAB accounts to hold the money. They included accounts in the name of Victor Peirce and Wendy Peirce, under her maiden name of Ford.

Allen bought a four-bedroom house for cash in 1985, after trafficking heroin for only four months after his release from jail.

According to fellow prisoners, Allen is intelligent, with a good grasp of the law, and has often acted as his own defence counsel. In the latest case he used a barrister paid by legal aid, but it did him no good. The jury took less then a day to find him guilty.

While Allen could be ruthless, prisoners said he lacked the violent streak of some other members of his family.

Victor Peirce did not confine himself to dealing in drugs for his brother. He also ran his own syndicate on the outside. In a separate case he was charged and convicted of heroin trafficking and sentenced to eight years with a minimum of six.

The Office of Corrections has changed the telephone access rules for prisoners, allowing inmates to ring only four different approved numbers. But drugs are still getting into every jail in Victoria.

The family

Kathleen Pettingill: Former barmaid and massage parlour madam. Heavily connected in the underworld for 20 years, she had one eye shot out by another woman in 1978. Police codenamed an investigation into the family 'Operation Cyclops', a sly reference to the one-eyed giants of Greek mythology. Has written her memoirs, *The Matriarch.* Had six sons and a daughter, all with criminal records. Two have died.

Dennis Bruce Allen: Kath's son. Drug dealer, murderer, pimp, police informer, and gunman. Allen was investigated over 11 mysterious deaths in the 1980s. Was believed to have been protected by corrupt police. Was making between $70,000 and $100,000 per week from drugs. He was on bail for 60 different offences in the early 1980s. He would inform on criminals to keep out of jail. Died in 1987 from heart disease. One death notice read: 'Dennis the Menace with a heart so big. Sorry you're gone, you were such a good gig.'

Peter John Allen: Kath's son. Probably the most intelligent of the family. Considered one of the best 'jail house lawyers' in the state. Has often defended himself in complex criminal trials. Ran a heroin empire while in jail using a corrupt prison officer code named 'The Postie', three female couriers, five TAB accounts and his half-brother Victor as his buyer on the outside. In custody on drug trafficking. Release date, July 1999.

Victor George Peirce: Kath's son. String of convictions. Charged and acquitted of the Walsh Street killings. Involved in armed robberies and drug trafficking. His best friend was Graeme Jensen, who was shot dead by police on 11 October, 1988. Has four children. In custody on drug trafficking, release date, May 1998.

Wendy Margaret Peirce: From a respectable South Melbourne family. Was to give evidence against Victor over Walsh Street but later changed story. Convicted for perjury. Says her life of crime is over.

The spotted dick

How a top cop turned

*'He was on top of everything
when he was in the job'*

GARY Robert Whelan was never going to be a high flyer in the police force, but he was a goer. Whelan was the sort of officer experienced police love to have in every station and squad. He didn't complain about the hours or the danger. He loved the work and did what was required, no questions asked. The sort so keen that if he had been a dog he would have chased cars, snapping at the tyres. Most of all, he wanted to fit in.

'He was a keen kid who wanted to be the world's greatest crook catcher,' recalled a former colleague. He was desperate to get into the CIB.'

Whelan wasn't one of those who look for a comfortable clerical job where they can wear cardigans and potter about in an air-conditioned office. For them, the biggest excitement is winning the office football tipping competition and the biggest danger they face is getting home late for dinner.

Whelan didn't want to work in the comfort zone. He wanted to be at the cutting edge. He joined the Victoria Police Force in 1977 and within four years he had moved to the busiest crime area in the state,

St Kilda in the inner suburbs. It was the early 1980s when drugs were taking hold.

St Kilda, like its Sydney equivalent, Kings Cross, was full of opportunities – and temptations – for police. It was a place where police earned reputations – one way or the other.

When Whelan walked into the chaotic St Kilda station he looked to those with experience who could guide him. One of his sergeants was Dick McLean, an accomplished officer on the way up. Although McLean was only four years his senior, he became a father figure to the ambitious, easily-led young policeman.

In May 1982, Whelan was called to a guest house in St Kilda over a complaint about the behaviour of one of the guests. It was a routine call, but for the eager young police officer, it was like winning Tattslotto. In the room he found 154 grams of heroin in condoms and caps. It was 75 percent pure, indicating this was no street dealer's stash. This was close to the source.

For the early 1980s it was considered a huge bust, headline material. In the so-called war against drugs this was considered a victory. Whelan was congratulated by senior officers. It could have been his ticket to the fast track.

It wasn't.

The following year, Whelan got his wish and was promoted to senior detective and was transferred to the Stolen-Motor Vehicle Squad.

Meanwhile, the heroin found by Whelan was supposed to be kept under lock and key in the drug security cabinet at the St Kilda station until the court case. In police and criminal circles it was widely known that security at the St Kilda station was a joke.

Property and drugs tended to disappear from the cabinet. It was suggested, though not proven, that some junkies who provided information might be rewarded with a 'taste' of seized drugs.

As Whelan was celebrating his promotion to the CIB, rumours reached senior police that all was not right at St Kilda. They decided to re-weigh the heroin from Whelan's day in the sun.

It was 42.5 grams shy.

Whelan was charged with trafficking, selling and stealing heroin. The trial judge directed to acquit him of trafficking and the jury found him not guilty in 1985 of all other offences. He remained suspended until 1986 and was then found guilty before the Police Discipline Board with failing to account for property, fined $700 and demoted to constable.

In the police force, most coppers never live down that sort of black mark on their record. When Whelan returned to duty he was transferred to the Russell Street reserve, a pool used to fill holes in the force. It was generally considered the road to nowhere.

In 1989, Whelan was moved to the audio-visual section. His job entailed videoing crime scenes and crime re-enactments for later court cases. It was important, but hardly taxing work.

But, in 1993, there was a reorganisation in the crime department and Whelan's section came under the Bureau of Criminal Intelligence, which dealt with organised crime. Whelan's job was to set secret cameras to help build cases against some of Australia's top gangsters.

The days where police could jump into the witness box and be instantly believed were gone, partly as a result of 'verballing' and other abuses by investigators who wanted to take short cuts to get a result. Now they needed irrefutable proof, such as video and audio tapes, to make their cases. Suddenly, the policeman with the questionable past was back in from the cold and privy to some of the force's most confidential operations.

A touch of electronic expertise and a stroke of the bureaucratic pen helped Gary Whelan re-invent himself from suspected drug seller to top crime buster. He was back at the big end of town – and he was ready to run red hot.

DICK McLEAN was a policeman in a hurry. He was on the fast track for promotion and was openly spoken of as a future commissioner. But for him, that wasn't enough: he wanted it all, and he wanted it soon.

McLean was a good policeman, so good that he was appointed in 1987 to the staff of the elite Airlie Officers' College in South Yarra, where he instructed the future top-ranking members of the force on matters such as leadership and management.

His lectures were polished and informative and he excelled in the field during training operations, where his practical experience could be used to the fullest. He was a born leader.

McLean was seen as a shining example of the modern and progressive police officer. He had made his mark in the tough areas of the force, including St Kilda and the Homicide Squad, yet he was no rough diamond. He had the personal skills and diplomacy needed to deal with every stratum of society. He was as comfortable talking to career criminals as captains of industry. Sometimes they were one and the same.

But the policeman on the make was restless. 'He saw himself as a bloke who could cut it in the business world,' a former colleague was to say. 'All during his career he dabbled in business.'

He had a furniture factory, a financial interest in a waterbed shop and even had an international diamond importer's licence while a serving policeman.

A detective who worked with him said: 'He was generous and always would give police furniture and beds at cost. He was always being touched for a cheap deal. He was never around the office to do any mundane stuff but when there was a major job on he would be as hard working as the next bloke.'

McLean once interviewed a murder suspect for 16 hours until he cracked her story. 'Dick was a good investigator, there was no doubt about that,' a senior policeman said of him.

From the time he joined the force, in 1969, there was never any suggestion he was anything but squeaky clean. But being a good policeman and a future leader was not enough to hold McLean. Business called and, in December 1989, McLean, then a Chief Inspector and a 20-year veteran, left policing to make his fortune in the outside world.

The first sign for McLean that private enterprise was not a guaranteed road to wealth came when his waterbed business sprang a leak.

He may have been lacking a little on the cash front but he certainly wasn't short of ideas. He moved straight into the restaurant trade.

A former colleague recalls 'There was a lovely fellow we all knew from the St Kilda days. He had a little pizza parlour in Fitzroy Street. Dick was always at him with big plans, to extend it into the next shop and turn it into a flash restaurant. Eventually he went along with Dick and they became partners. They both ended up broke.' It was a humiliating experience for the polished policeman. 'He was on top of everything when he was in the job,' a detective said later, 'but it all went wrong when he got out. He ended up with the Midas touch: everything he touched turned to mufflers.'

However, the financial disasters and a marriage break-up didn't destroy McLean's confidence. He was a big picture man and he was convinced that if he persisted, his luck would turn. He moved into the electronic-security industry and, finally, his big break came in 1995.

In the global field of new technology, teenage computer experts were making fortunes overnight. If McLean could combine his knowledge of policing and security with state-of-the-art software, he calculated, he would be on his way.

Finally, he was in on the ground floor of a promising deal. He was going to invest in a mobile 'smart phone' designed to provide immediate access to a stream of security functions for the elderly. It was going to be manufactured in an Ararat factory, and it seemed set to make a millions.

McLean had the idea, the market, the contacts and the business plan. What he didn't have was the money. So Dick McLean, businessman and entrepreneur, turned back to what he really knew, crime and corruption. But, this time, from the other side.

It was time to talk to his old protege, Gary Whelan.

DOMENIC GISONDA was a police groupie, the sort who always buys the beers and hangs on every word of detectives' war stories. Too quick to laugh at a bad joke and too slow to go home at the end of the night, the former bouncer and painter was always present at any social event run by the St Kilda police.

'He was a smarmy user,' a St Kilda policeman said. 'He would always drop coppers' names when he got a speeding ticket or a parking ticket. Every station's got one.'

Many police were irked by his too-smooth approach but tolerated him as part of the social rat-pack. One detective with a short fuse and a quick trigger finger once took offence at Gisonda but the coat puller didn't know when to leave well enough alone. He kept asking why the policeman disliked him. The detective punched him to the ground in a car-park, then pulled out his gun and fired several shots over the bleeding victim. The drunken detective was ushered into a cab and the incident covered up.

McLean, however, was one of the minority of police who liked Gisonda. 'We warned Dick about him but he wouldn't listen,' a former colleague said. It was to Gisonda that McLean turned for help to set up a corrupt venture which would eventually cost the former police high-flyer his reputation, and his freedom.

In April 1995, a police task force from Heidelberg found a drug gang was using a Thomastown factory to grow a crop of potent 'skunk' cannabis hydroponically. Police formally requested a secret surveillance camera be set up to gather evidence.

Enter Gary Whelan, who joined the operation as the video expert. He checked the area and positioned a camera and recorder at a nearby building. The operation was expected to last three weeks.

Two days later, police from the task force were stunned when a local criminal was able to tell them about their investigations, including details of target premises in Preston, Coburg and Thomastown. The criminal matter-of-factly pinpointed the exact location of the camera and the drug factory being watched by police.

Local police found the criminal was connected to a notorious 'run-through' gang, a group that raided and ripped off drug crops. Marijuana plantations are the perfect target for such gangs because the product is easy to sell and the victims can hardly complain. The rip offs have become so regular that some cannabis growers build man traps near their crops and police fear it is only a matter of time before a bush walker is killed after stumbling on to a remote drug property.

Police were told that information on drug properties was being passed on by a former detective known only as 'Dick' to Domenic Gisonda, who then passed it on to the rip-off gang. The original leak was suspected of coming from the technical section. The was a potentially catastrophic blow, as the section was privy to every major crime investigation underway. Modern police rely on video and audio tapes as their predecessors relied on fingerprint dust as an essential tool of trade. The lives of undercover police and informers would be put at risk if the technical section leaked.

The then Assistant Commissioner (Ethical Standards Department) Neil O'Loughlin, said the local detectives immediately contacted internal investigators with their suspicions. 'When they believed they were being sold out, they took the appropriate action,' he said. 'It was police who discovered the leak, police who investigated it and police who found the offenders.'

The internal investigators set up Operation Filter, which soon established there were links between Whelan, McLean and Gisonda, who was connected to a stand-over group. They baited a trap, giving bogus information on a fabricated drug target to Whelan. When he went straight to McLean, the watchers knew they had found their leak.

At one point, Whelan gave McLean a status report on the hydroponic marijuana investigation. Telephone taps proved the gang planned to steal the drugs before police moved in to arrest the growers. Early on the morning of Friday, 2 June 1995, the Special Operations Group arrested two burglars as they were attempting to break into the factory.

Soon the phones were running hot among gang members as they queried whether they had been set up. Whelan soon learned the truth when, three days later, an internal investigator, Colin Farnsworth, arrested him in the old Russell Street police complex. In simultaneous raids, McLean and Gisonda were arrested. It was a textbook operation, the same text that McLean used to lecture police at the officer's course only a few years earlier.

'If we had not had the full co-operation of the technical branch where Whelan worked then we wouldn't have got anywhere near him,' Inspector Farnsworth said. 'It showed that police will not tolerate corruption where members sell out investigations.'

Police in the section knew that fake information was being fed to Whelan to see if he was the leak and no-one warned him. It was an integrity test both ways. The suspect cop failed it badly, but his colleagues passed brilliantly.

Late in 1996, McLean, then 45, was sentenced to two years jail with a minimum of 15 months over the attempted burglary. The man who could have been a commissioner was forced to spend his time with convicted public officials and child molesters. Whelan, 41, was sentenced to three years jail with a minimum of two years three months at the same jail. Gisonda was sentenced to 12 months jail.

However, many police believe the Thomastown job wasn't the first Whelan had sold out.

One group of drug growers believed they had found the perfect spot for a marijuana crop, and for seven years they had quietly been reaping millions of dollars in profits. The place was protected from the air by a canopy of 60-metre mountain ash trees and it was at least four hours' walk through the thick bush from the nearest road. But there is strong evidence that soon after police found it, criminals moved in and ripped off the plantation.

The question which almost certainly will never be properly answered is this: was the gang tipped off by crooked crops?

When police found the property, at Fumina South in the Tanjil state forest near Warragul, there were camouflaged tents, drying areas and a pump-driven watering system connected to nearby Good Hope Creek.

The area was so rugged that police had to be winched in from a helicopter. They counted about 10,000 seedlings planted in rows. Half would later be pulled out to let the healthiest grow to their maximum size. The estimated street value of the crop was $30 million.

A drug task force of Gippsland police started Operation Snow White, which involved the special operations group camping out in the area, waiting to catch cultivators when they returned to the property.

It was a four-hour march for the SOG to get into position and a nine-hour return trip. Local police also notified the technical branch of the bureau of criminal intelligence for a video recorder to film the offenders. Gary Whelan got the job.

In late 1994, Whelan was briefed three times on Operation Snow White. He videotaped the area from the police helicopter.

In February 1995, Whelan walked to the property with other police. They spent two days trying to find a 'hide' for a secret camera but decided it was impractical. Later, a suitable spot was found.

The leaders of Operation Snow White decided it was likely the cultivators would tend the crop at weekends, so the SOG would pack up and go home every Monday. Whelan knew their movements.

When police moved in on 30 March 1995 and arrested one man present, Zeljko Duricic, there were only 1600 plants left. The original crop was 5000 mature plants, each up to four metres tall.

'There were certain indications there had been a rip-off,' an investigating officer said.

Duricic pleaded guilty and was sentenced to 12 months jail. Police believe he knew more than he said and refused to implicate others.

Some detectives believe the profits from the drug crops were used to buy arms for an international conflict.

Police are still not sure how the cultivators managed to bring in several tonnes of machinery and equipment, including petrol- driven pumps, gas heaters, fertiliser and a rotary hoe.

After Duricic's arrest, police used a helicopter to air lift about 593 kilograms of cannabis to the Warragul police station, where it was stored in a shipping container.

An informer told police that a drug rip-off gang, known to have been tipped off by McLean and Whelan on other crops, received information on Operation Snow White. The gang was told the SOG was pulled out every Monday and it was promised a diagram of surveillance positions.

At a meeting in North Coburg, the go-between, Domenic Gisonda, told the rip-off crew the information was solid and came from a policeman involved in installing cameras at the property. The informer said the gang expected to make $140,000 profit after a payment of $60,000 for the corrupt police. Later, according to the informer, the plan was changed after Duricic's arrest.

This time, the gang plotted to raid the Warragul police station and steal the stored marijuana. They were told the exact location of the cannabis and when the least number of police would be on duty. The plan was to make a hoax call to the station, ensuring patrols were tied up and leaving only one officer in the building.

The plan was for the gang to raid the station, lock up the policeman and steal the drugs. It was abandoned because of fears about consequences if they harmed the police officer on duty.

CHAPTER 15

A fish that wandered
The tale of Neil Wilson

*'It was probably the most
bizarre case we have ever seen'*

NOBODY knows why Neil Gordon Wilson, 49, wanted to be a fish. When Wilson was found dead in a meticulously-made fish suit near his family's Toolondo holiday home, 390 kilometres west of Melbourne, it opened a case which police say remains one of the most baffling on record.

The Coroner, Graeme Johnstone, officially closed the file with a one and a half page report that could not get close to finding why a respectable, middle-aged bachelor chose to hop about in a vinyl fish suit in a deserted paddock.

Police believe Wilson spent at least four years developing prototypes of fish suit before he finally died wearing one. He even photographed himself in one of the early versions on the banks of the local lake, a year before his death.

Wilson was a quiet, gentle man, who suffered brain damage after a motorbike accident in the 1970s. He was placed on medication to control epilepsy but, according to his family, he would often fail to take it.

The people of Toolondo knew their neighbor was different, but they also knew he was harmless. They grew used to his strange ways and were rarely shocked by his behaviour.

He was often sighted in the area in the most bizarre circumstances but locals knew it was 'just Neil' and went about their business unconcerned.

He lived in a world populated by one. He was always appeared busy, but no-one knew exactly what he was doing. He foraged in the local tip, hanging many of the items he found in the tree at the front of his family's holiday house, where he had more-or-less taken up permanent residence.

One local, Graham Bedford, told police he remembered seeing Wilson near long grass in Toolondo swamplands in 1991. 'He was totally naked except for a number of Coke cans tied to a piece of hayband around his chest like a bandolier. He said good-day to me and then started to get dressed.

'Most of the people who lived in Toolondo knew what he was like, but after so many years of strange behaviour, Neil was accepted. There was never any incident where Neil posed a danger to anyone else that I know of,' he said.

A few months after Neil had been spotted in the swamplands, Bedford went duck hunting with some friends at the Toolondo lake. They found a strange, homemade body suit made of a green plastic material. 'We knew it was Neil's because it was in one of his spots he used to go regularly and there were items of clothing around it,' Bedford said.

'I have never seen Neil with the body suit actually on but when I first moved to Toolondo I remember an occasion when I first spotted a strange coloured object moving backwards in the rushes at the edge of the water in Toolondo Lake.

'I remember that we found a brightly coloured sleeping bag in that area shortly after. I didn't know Neil at this time, but looking back, his behaviour is entirely consistent with this incident. This incident was actually in the water,' he said.

'It was not usual to see items of Neil's clothing and other unrelated objects lying around areas of the lake where Neil frequented.'

Bedford lived four doors from the Wilson holiday house and knew Wilson better than most. 'It was impossible to hold any rational conversation with Neil. He would string unconnected ideas and sentences together for a short time, then he would break off and walk away. Over the years I formed the impression that Neil was harmless to others, but had a serious mental disorder.'

'Neil seemed to avoid people and go about his business. It was not uncommon for Neil to run and hide on the approach of anyone,' he said.

'I know that he didn't have any close friends. In general he was a loner who kept to himself.

'Another strange thing I saw him do regularly was sit in a chair inside a tank on its side at the rear of the property. He would do this for hours for no apparent reason.

'From what I know of Neil, I would be unable to say whether he suffered from depression as he was usually active and enthusiastic. I could not say whether he was capable of suicide or even forming that idea in his mind.

'He would often do things without any apparent explanation or reason. We all just accepted it as part of his strange behaviour.

'There were often signs that Neil was or had been about. I often saw glimpses of him heading somewhere unknown and I often suspected he was hiding behind a tree or similar as often he appeared that he didn't want to be seen.'

In 1974 a tourist told local police he had found Wilson in the Toolondo channel attached to a bridge railing by a rope. The amazed tourist had pulled him, naked, from the water, only to be told that the he was pretending to be 'a fish at the end of the line.'

In November, 1995, Wilson was driven from his parent's Melbourne home to Toolondo where he expected to stay three weeks. He was reported missing on 27 November. Police found his medication in the house and from the number of pills left police were able to deduce that he had stopped taking them ten days earlier.

Just after 4pm on 27 November the police helicopter spotted a body in a green fish suit in an open paddock about a kilometre from the lake.

Senior Constable Kerry Allen from nearby Natimuk pieced together what he thought had happened.

He believed Wilson had spent hours in the garage of the holiday house painstakingly fashioning together versions of the fish suit using plastic he recovered from a local tip, including a green vinyl waterbed mattress and a brown vinyl mattress protector.

Police found a sewing machine and plastic offcuts from the fish suit in the double garage of the home as well as an identical spare fish suit.

'On or after Monday 20 November, 1995, Wilson placed a bodysuit together with other items into a wheelbarrow and walked over 100 metres north into the paddock opposite the holiday house.

'He then stripped naked, placed a red flag marking his belongings, then pushed the wheelbarrow north for several hundred metres.'

Wilson covered himself with soap and water from a container in the wheelbarrow so that he could fit into the tight fitting fish suit.

He then used a padlock and wire to pull up the back zip of suit. 'It would seem that Wilson has then hopped 52 metres back south, where for some reason he collapsed,' the policeman said in a statement to the coroner.

The suits contained two separate vinyl layers separated by carpet underlay for insulation, four zips, a padlock, mittens, a headpiece with eyeholes, no mouth hole and mermaid type leggings made of an inner tube. It was carefully double stitched and waterproof.

Detective Sergeant Graeme Arthur, who oversaw the investigation for the homicide squad, said: 'It was probably the most bizarre case we have ever seen.'

Senior Constable Allen put forward two likely causes of death. The combination of lack of medication and the exertion of hopping about in the suit brought on a seizure and the subsequent lack of consciousness. Caught in an open paddock with the temperature in the low 30s the airtight fish suit would have turned into a death-sauna. He would have been killed by the heat.

'Alternatively, the design of the hood of the garment may have brought about suffocation,' he said.

The Coroner found there was no evidence that Wilson took his own life. But while no cause of death could be established, there were no signs of foul play. Strange as Neil Wilson's life was, there was nothing fishy about his death. Apart from the suit.

CHAPTER 16

A dishonourable society
The 'Mafia' in Australia

*'One of them had his ears sliced off
as a warning that he heard too much'*

IT was the proudest moment of Giuseppe Arena's life. It was a pleasant August evening in 1987 and he was moving contentedly among 450 guests at a big reception centre in the Melbourne northern suburb of Brunswick, graciously accepting their best wishes.

Arena's only daughter was being given the best traditional Italian wedding her father could provide. He had, in fact, wanted 900 guests but his family had persuaded him to halve the list.

It was a memorable night. Giuseppe, after all, was known as 'The Friendly Godfather' and was a popular and influential figure in the Italian community. As he circulated, people kept coming forward. Some shook his hand or patted him on the back. Some kissed him on the cheek.

The night went perfectly.

A year later Giuseppe Arena was dead. The father of three was shot from behind taking out the rubbish at his Bayswater home. It was a classic Italian organised-crime hit and has never been solved.

His widow, Maria, has no idea who killed her husband or why, but she now knows the power of Omerta — the code of silence. She says that, except for her immediate family, she has been abandoned by the guests who hugged and congratulated her husband at the wedding. 'They have all dropped off like flies,' she said.

'Since the funeral we have not heard or seen from any of them. They were our friends. Now they are too frightened even to pick up the phone and ring. They should be ashamed of themselves. It is as if when Joe was buried we were buried too. If that is the Calabrian way, they can have it. They used him, now they have discarded us.'

She knows one of the wedding guests might have already been considering ordering her husband's execution at the reception. But why? Joe Arena didn't appear to be a big shot. Ostensibly a retired insurance broker, to those in an inner circle he was much more. He was an associate of Liborio Benvenuto, the undisputed Godfather of Melbourne.

Benvenuto rose to prominence following the 1963-64 market murders, committed at the height of a struggle for control of Melbourne's Mafia. He was related through marriage to Vincenzo Muratore, who was murdered in 1964 and whose son, Alfonso Muratore, was murdered in 1992. It was during the power struggle in the markets that Australians learned that traditional Italian organised crime had become part and parcel of life in the lucky country. It began when Domenico Italiano died peacefully of old age in his West Melbourne home. His funeral, held at the nearby St Mary's Star of the Sea in December, 1962, gave an insight into the power of the man.

The funeral was more befitting a head of state than a little-known migrant. Thousands of people attended the church and thronged the grounds. The pallbearers, including Italiano's son-in-law, Michele Scriva, carried the body to its final resting place under an elaborate headstone in the Melbourne cemetery. In hindsight, it should have been no surprise that Italiano was accorded such respect. He was known as 'Il Papa' or 'The Pope' and was The Godfather of the Honoured Society, known in some circles as The Black Hand.

Police already knew of its existence, with reports of mob-related extortion going back to the cane fields of Queensland as early as the 1930s. But they were unaware that the organisation had become a powerful influence in the fruit and vegetable industry where Calabrian migrants were helped by the Society, but in return were indebted, often for life. Soon after Italiano's death another old Italian died. This was Antonio Barbara, known as 'The Toad.' He was Italiano's right hand man and his violent streak was well-known. He had served five years for killing a woman near the Queen Victoria Market in 1936. The loss of both men left a void at the top of the Society, and a dangerous power struggle erupted.

Their places were filled by Domenico Demarte, who took Italiano's position, and Vincenzo Muratore, who was the financial adviser. One man not happy with the easy succession was Vincenzo Angilletta, a gunman who had migrated to Australia in 1951. He became a producer of fruit and vegetables to the Society, but had bigger ideas. He wanted the Society to become the Australian version of the Sicilian-based Mafia in the United States. He wanted extortion rackets to be broadened to include non-Italians, a move rejected by Demarte and the elders.

Angilletta responded by refusing to sell his produce to designated wholesalers and going direct to the public. He was warned but refused to conform. He was stabbed once on Society orders but still refused to return to the fold. He was abducted and taken to Woodend where he was painted with human excrement as a ritualistic punishment called *il tartaro*. He vowed revenge and formed his own organisation called *la Bastarda* — 'The Bastard Society' and recruited 300 members. He sold his market garden in Kew to a Greek couple rather than to a designated Calabrian family. Demarte, Muratore and the elders decided Angilletta must die. The renegade knew he was a marked man and began to carry a small pistol for protection. It did him no good. In the early hours of 4 April, 1963, Angilletta was shot twice with a shotgun from behind. It is considered a dishonourable way to die, to not be allowed to see the killer's face. Forensic tests found he was killed with heavy lupara shot — the same sort of shot traditionally used to shoot wolves, and people, in Calabria.

Angilletta's friends vowed revenge. They blamed Demarte and Muratore for the hit. On 26 November, 1963, Demarte was shot at 3.30 am as he left his North Melbourne home on the way to the market. He survived, but immediately retired from his senior position in the Honoured Society. On 16 January, 1964, Muratore was shot dead as he left his Hampton home about 2.30 am.

The Victorian Government asked for international help and it arrived in the shape of John T. Cusack, one of the most respected investigators of organised crime. In 1957 he had managed to document a key Mafia meeting in New York and as a result, 60 major mob criminals were arrested.

After completing his investigations in Melbourne Cusack submitted to the government a 17-page report which was never officially released. He made it clear organised crime was already well entrenched.

'It is already engaged in extortion, prostitution, counterfeiting, sly grog, breaking and entering, illegal gambling and smuggling aliens and small arms. Its infiltration and effort to control the fruit and vegetable produce business has been exposed. Within the next 25 years, if unchecked, the Society is capable of diversification into all facets of organised crime and legitimate business,' he wrote.

Cusack established the five rules of the Society. Aid was to be extended to a member, no matter what the circumstances; there was to be absolute obedience to officers of the Society; an offence against an individual member was an attack on the Society and must be avenged; no members could turn to a government agency for justice. The final rule, which has frustrated countless police investigations, was Omerta, the code of silence. No member was to reveal the name of other members or reveal any of the organisation's secrets. 'They realise in silence there is security while testimony against a Society member can bring death,' Cusack said.

Police solved none of the murders and eventually peace returned.

A small, dapper fellow was largely responsible for bringing the Society back under control. Liborio Benvenuto was related through marriage to Vincenzo Muratore. Born on 15 December, 1927, in Reggio Calabria, he was allegedly the son of the boss of seven Italian villages. Benvenuto was in the fruit and vegetable industry.

His right hand man was Michele Scriva, who was married to one of the daughters of Domenico Italiano and related through marriage to Benvenuto. Scriva was born in Reggio Calabria, on 19 June, 1919, and migrated to Australia as a 17-year-old. In 1945 he was the main suspect in the killing of Giuseppe 'Fat Joe' Verscace, stabbed 91 times in Fitzroy.

Scriva was charged with two other men, Domencio Demarte and Domenico Pezzimenti. They were acquitted, but five years later Scriva was charged with murdering Frederick John Duffy, who had attempted to intervene in a fight and was stabbed to death. Scriva was sentenced to hang but this was commuted to life imprisonment. He served ten years.

Things seemed to settle but on 10 May, 1983, Benvenuto's four-wheel drive was blown up at the market, where he worked with Alfonse Muratore. When asked what was behind the attack he said; 'I have no enemies, only friends at the market. I don't know why anybody would do this. I have never done anybody harm.'

A year later, two close associates of Benvenuto were found murdered in the Murrumbidgee River in the Riverina. Rocco Medici and his brother in law, Giuseppe Furina, both from the Melbourne suburb of East Keilor, had been tortured and their bodies dumped in the river. One of them had his ears sliced off, a symbolic warning that he heard too much.

While drugs, particularly marijuana, have become a huge money maker for the society, its role in primary production has remained strong. In fact, society members have been able to use their agricultural knowledge to grow cannabis, then use their fruit and vegetable trucks to transport the product and launder funds through the vegetable markets in capital cities.

The families have long since moved from the Queen Victoria market to the Melbourne Wholesale Market at Footscray. The location may have changed, but the old ways of business remain.

The market has a turnover of $1.2 billion a year. It sells 6000 tonnes of produce a day and is reputed to be the biggest growers' market in the world. For years it was underpinned by a culture of corruption built on a cash economy, a fortress mentality backed with the constant threat of violence. To survive, you had to pay.

A registered casual grower at the market could pay a daily fee of about $30 for a stand to sell produce. If he didn't pay a bribe on top of that, his stall location at the market would be changed daily so that regular customers couldn't find him. The choice was simple: stand on your principles and watch your produce go rotten waiting for customers, or pay up.

Some officers had several schemes operating. One would walk into the coffee shop at the market and drop his hat on a table. Within minutes it was full of money. Some of the corrupt market officers called the bribe network 'insurance money' or the 'retirement fund'. The growers in the market called it 'the club'.

Buyers paid bribes to get into the market early to pick up produce, to park their truck undercover, to keep the fruit and vegetables out of the weather, and to leave the site before the 6.30 am exit time.

The sellers paid bribes to crib space for their stalls, to protect them from parking fines and to be given prime selling spots. Friday was collection day. Money was left on the seats of unlocked trucks or just collected from the stalls. It was no great secret.

Some market officers were netting $25,000 a year in tax-free bribes. One was ordered to pay $50,000 in back taxes. Three were found guilty of accepting secret commissions. One was sentenced to 16 months jail.

It wasn't just small greengrocers who were forced to pay bribes. No-one was immune. Even Australia's biggest retailing company, Coles Myer, had to pay. This meant that in real terms, every Australian was paying a secret tax to organised crime for the staple of life. Food.

'It was all about money and power,' said the then National Crime Authority chief investigator, Peter Fleming. 'That is why people were prepared to kill for it and others prepared to die for it.'

The schemes varied. Growers said one corrupt official would, for a price, condemn truck-loads of perfectly good fruit as unsuitable for human consumption. It would then be secretly transported to a market merchant who would then sell it to a supermarket chain for a huge profit.

The market is a huge, undercover city. There were more than 750 forklifts on the property, which were supposed to be left in a secure cage. There was a huge black market in the machines. When police raided a huge marijuana property in the Northern Territory they found expensive farm gear, including four special motorised produce trolleys, reported missing from the Melbourne market.

Because of the cash economy in the market, there was a spate of robberies. Veterans were resistant to change and would not deal in anything but cash. Some merchants used two sets of books. Tax was routinely avoided. Some merchants began demanding a tax of 20 to

50 cents for every case of produce sold. This, combined with a double invoicing scheme, cost Coles Myer about $6 million a year.

In 1989 Alan Williams, a senior executive with the Coles Myer produce section, realised the company was paying exorbitant rates for fruit and vegetables. When a glut of cauliflowers flooded the market, the price dropped, but Coles Myer was still paying an inflated price.

Williams ordered an internal inquiry, recruiting one of his own men, John Vasilopolous, to bring prices into line. He tried to report his concerns to police, but they were lukewarm about investigating.

Vasilopolous was a family man who had chosen a career in retailing. He could hardly be expected to put his life on the line over the price of onions. He started to send some produce back, claiming it was sub-standard. In reality, he believed the prices were too high.

Some buyers had been paid bribes to look the other way, but Vasilopolous would not. He was rocking a corrupt system that had been operating for years. He was costing the Honoured Society money.

From July, 1990, he began to receive death threats, but continued to offer fair prices for fruit and vegetables. He was reading at home in December, 1990, when the doorbell rang. He called out to ask who was there. A male voice replied: 'Open the door, John.'

He opened the door slightly, and was hit with a shotgun blast. Doctors later removed pellets from his legs, arms, stomach and chest.

Vasilopolous abandoned his promising career and Coles Myer brought in the produce wholesaler, Costas to try to insulate the company from the violence and corruption in the industry. But even then, while some of the obvious scams were closed, corruption continued.

In July, 1992, two well-known market identities, Alfonse Muratore and Orlando Luciano, met Coles Myer representatives in the Parkroyal Hotel on Little Collins Street to tell them of some of the schemes that had been costing them money. Coles Myer security men constantly checked the area, sweeping it electronically for bugs before the secret four-hour meeting.

Police believe the two men were pitching for business, claiming they could do the job cleaner and cheaper. Muratore had been out of the markets for two years and wanted to re-establish himself. But his reputation was tainted. He was married to Liborio Benvenuto's daughter, Angela. Shortly after the Godfather died in 1988, Muratore left his wife for another woman, Karen Mansfield. In the Honoured Society, this was not a wise move. About 1.30 am on 4 August, about two weeks after his secret meeting with Coles Myer, Muratore was shot dead outside his Hampton home, almost exactly as his own father had been killed 30 years earlier.

Things hadn't changed. One potential witness told police: 'You can put me in jail; they can give me the death sentence.' While detectives have not charged anyone over the killing they believe they know who was responsible. One was a member of the 'Big Three,' the men who ran Society business since Benvenuto died in 1988.

A three-year National Crime Authority investigation into Italian organised crime, code named Cerberus, found that the 'Mafia' was different in real life from the stereotype represented in films. It found that individual corrupt cells were involved in crime but there was no one 'Mr Big'. Individuals came together, motivated by profit and greed.

'Networks are used to facilitate organised criminal activity, particularly through the formation of temporary syndicates for the purpose of carrying out specific criminal ventures,' the report said.

'It is the family and extended family relationships that retain a significant role in Italo-Australia criminal organised crime at both the regional and national levels. There is a natural reluctance to inform on a family member or ... associates who share a ... town of origin.'

The study found that the syndicates had run extortion rackets from the 1930s to the 1970s, until drugs took over as the money-making business. The gangs became heavily involved in the cultivation and distribution of cannabis, importing marijuana, heroin and cocaine and the production and distribution of amphetamines.

Operation Cerberus also examined murders between 1974 and 1995 to see how many were connected to the Italian gangs. 'While it is apparent that some members of the Italo-Australian criminal community have utilised murder as a mean of discipline and suppression within this country, it is also apparent that the threat of such extreme violence to the innocent members of the community is minimal. In fact, considering the extent of the Italo-Australian community within Australia and the perceived extent of the criminal element of the same community, the use of murder is a relatively rare occurrence.'

This was of little solace to the family of Donald Mackay.

Australia's shame
Donald Mackay, 20 years on

'One school of thought is that people behind the (drug) trade have been incredibly stupid in acting against someone as prominent as Don Mackay. The other school says it was a master-stroke which has created enough fear to keep people's mouths shut for the next 10 years.'
– Bill Fisher, QC, counsel assisting the Woodward Royal Commission into Drug Trafficking, 1979.

IT is two decades since Donald Mackay disappeared and mouths are still shut. Despite thousands of hours and millions of dollars spent on investigation, the truth behind a crime that shames Australia is as elusive as it was the night he was killed. And justice is no closer to being done.

The known facts are bleak.

At 5.30pm on Friday, 15 July, 1977, the 43-year-old Mackay had closed the furniture store his family had run since the 1920s and driven his mini-van to the nearby Griffith Hotel. He had earlier told his wife, Barbara, he would be home by 7pm to look after the youngest of their four children while she went to a meeting.

At the hotel, he had a round of drinks and chatted with friends — largely about his efforts to draw attention to marijuana growing in the area — before buying a cask of white wine in the bottle shop and heading to the car park to go home. He was never seen again.

It was dark, the street almost deserted. Two people were working late in the office building on the other side of the car park. One was Mackay's solicitor and friend, Ian Salmon. The other was an accountant called Roy Binks. Salmon heard nothing, although he was later called from home to look for his missing client. Binks, however, later told police he'd heard a noise 'like someone being sick' and that he thought he'd heard a sound like 'whip cracks'.

Today, understandably, Binks's recollections are even vaguer. He obligingly points out his old office, and where Mackay's van was parked, but doesn't want to rake over the embers.

In fact, he seems faintly embarrassed and nervous, an attitude shared with many other honest Griffith citizens, who tend to start sentences warily with 'It's all such a long time ago'. The unspoken suggestion is that it's easier to let sleeping dogs lie.

Binks asks to be faxed a copy of anything he'll be quoted on. He doesn't want to stir up trouble, he explains apologetically.

Ian Salmon is not quite so shy. After 33 years in Griffith, he has moved interstate to retire and he sometimes thinks about what happened that Friday evening after a worried Barbara Mackay called to say Don hadn't come home.

Salmon agreed to drive around looking for him, as Mrs Mackay was reluctant to call the police immediately.

At first he didn't feel it was sinister, only that it was out of character for Mackay not to go home. But, by midnight, he was getting worried and contacted police. He kept looking and found the mini-van in the hotel car park.

First, he noticed the imprint of a man's hand on the driver's window. Then he swung his car around so the headlights lit the scene. That's when he saw pools of blood and three .22 bullet shells glinting on the ground ...

DON Mackay's body has never been found. No one has been convicted of his murder. No one is likely to be.

An old and dangerous man called James Bazley, career criminal and gunman, sits in a Victorian jail, convicted in 1986 for conspiring to kill Mackay and for another drug-related double murder, but he's not the talking type.

Neither is George Joseph, the one-time gun dealer who sold Bazley a rare French .22 pistol believed to be the murder weapon and recommended Bazley when approached on behalf of a marijuana syndicate keen to hire a killer. With the exception of the late Robert 'Aussie Bob' Trimbole, who died on the run in Spain in May, 1987, those who ordered Mackay's death — many of them publicly named by a royal commission — are still going about the business of turning illicit millions into 'legitimate' assets.

They do this with the best legal and financial help money can buy. The way, some say, they bought police and politicians when they needed them.

Mackay's family, friends and supporters see this but they are powerless where governments and police have pointedly failed. Some avoid certain shops in Griffith, or cross the street rather than share the footpath with certain people. None wants to be quoted.

It's hard to credit this nightmarish undercurrent in the bustling main street of an outwardly peaceful country town. But the Riverina, for all its Banjo Paterson red gums and sunlit plains, is in secret ways a little Calabria, stronghold of the so-called 'Honored Society'.

Sydney has a dark side, too, like Al Capone's Chicago, where corruption seeped to the top, like rising damp in a wall. Some people in Griffith still wonder why investigations went nowhere, about who tipped off Trimbole and why he was not arrested after Victorian police passed on his address to other authorities.

They recall the times that visiting political figures would go straight to the shop of a Calabrian identity, now dead, who was known locally as 'The Godfather'. It was known that this man — once charged with having unlicensed pistols — could deliver blocks of votes to politicians he could deal with.

It was speculated he could also deliver campaign funds. What isn't certain is whether he won any favors in return.

'Don't let anybody fool you,' one long-time Griffith businessman says in disgust. 'In this town crime pays. Crime is probably the biggest industry here.' By this he means drug money used to establish legitimate businesses.

It costs millions to buy and set up modern, irrigated vineyards and orchards but some families have no trouble finding the money, although neighbors on identical farms remember the same people battling to get by before the 1960s . . . before the marijuana boom.

The businessman points at a house nearby, owned by a family

whose common Italian surname, Sergi, figured prominently in the Woodward Royal Commission's report in 1979. He remembers former local member (and Whitlam Government Immigration Minister) Al Grassby's Commonwealth car, Australian flag fluttering on the bonnet, arriving as guest of honor at a family gathering.

Grassby, after 1974 the federal Commissioner for Human Rights, was derided at a public meeting in Griffith when he claimed to have heard nothing about marijuana growing. Local lore had it that you could arrive at Griffith Airport on certain days and smell what locals called 'Calabrese corn'.

This was long before Grassby was charged with criminal defamation for allegedly circulating a vicious document in 1980 that accused Barbara Mackay, her son and family solicitor Ian Salmon of conspiring to murder her husband. Grassby was found guilty in 1991 but was acquitted on appeal in 1992.

Investigators believed the document originated in one of the so-called 'grass castles' that members of certain families started to build in the early 1970s, and which are still being built today.

The Riverina has many such houses — eruptions of brick, tile and concrete so huge and so ugly that they're worth less the day they're finished than the total cost of construction. These are not built as an investment, but as a self-aggrandising way to soak up black money. There are always tradesmen who will work for cash.

Marijuana growing has ensured some words have entered the local language. When Riverina people talk of a 'crop', they mean marijuana, not wheat or rice.

They talk of 'crop sitters', minor players who specialise in the risky business of being gardener and guard to million-dollar marijuana plantations.

The accepted wisdom now is that the Griffith area is too close to home, too closely observed by agricultural pilots and local police keen to clean up the tarnished reputation of their predecessors, of whom three went to jail for corruption in the early 1980s.

These days, they say, the crops are grown much further afield — as far as Queensland and the Northern Territory. But, even so, if there is a police raid it's odd how often a Griffith connection is made: trickle irrigation equipment from a Griffith supplier; bags stamped with

Griffith producers' names; crop sitters from Griffith families. The younger members of such families disappear from town for a few days or weeks, then return flush with cash. 'They've got a crop off somewhere,' locals mutter to each other. But not too loud, and never on the record.

Meanwhile, money keeps pouring into an already prosperous district. The town where tax investigators in the 1970s estimated half the banks' cashflow was from marijuana is still remarkably recession-free.

DONALD Bruce Mackay was, according to Ian Salmon, more than a decent man. He was a good bloke, as well. Like Mackay's widow and (now adult) children, Salmon resents the headline argot that has labelled Mackay an 'anti-drug crusader'.

It's a tag that ignores the warmth, intelligence, humor and strong physical presence of a husband and father, businessman and sportsman. It leaves a patronising suggestion that he was a naive, wowserish zealot who blundered into trouble.

The truth, says Salmon, is that Mackay was big — in size, intellect and heart — and brave enough to stand by his principles when lesser people shuffled their feet and looked the other way. Two days after he disappeared, Barbara Mackay told reporters her husband believed if people 'didn't do anything, then evil won'.

A tendency to blame the victim has crept into references to Mackay by some who didn't know him, which suits the ends of those responsible for his death. It has also suited them to suggest that support for Mackay and demands for a full investigation are somehow detrimental to the harmonious relations of an area that is more than 50 per cent Italian, mainly Calabrian.

For 20 years it has been repeatedly asserted that '98 per cent' of Griffith people are law-abiding citizens, which is undoubtedly true. What some find galling is that the other two per cent — representing organised crime — have much to gain by repeating that assertion.

The feeling is that the corrupt few can hide among the law-abiding majority, at the same time leading a righteous refrain that it's unfair to brand all Calabrians as crooks. Unfair, but none the less convenient, for the people who plotted murder.

Ten days after Don Mackay disappeared, 5000 people crowded the lawns of the local hospital for an ecumenical memorial service. Shops closed. Many people openly wept.

Two weeks later, 2000 people jammed a local club to take part in a television special hosted by famed British interviewer David Frost, who flew in for the event. Al Grassby was jeered off stage at the same event when he claimed he'd had only one complaint of marijuana growing.

Meanwhile, a reward of $25,000 soon leapt to $100,000 with pledges from local business people — and there were predictions it would reach the then staggering sum of a million dollars.

Members of Concerned Citizens of Griffith were widely quoted about the need to investigate and clean up drug trafficking and corruption.

But former members of the now defunct group rarely meet and few are willing to be quoted. Time has dulled the outrage and the determination, but not the fear.

Compare the response in Australia with the death of a whistle blower with a similar case half a world away in America.

On 2 June, 1976, a little known reporter, Dan Bolles, was critically injured when his car was bombed. He died eleven days later. Bolles was killed on the orders of an organised crime figure to stop his investigations, published in the *Arizona Republic* newspaper.

In response to the death 40 reporters from 26 papers around the US arrived in Arizona. They decided to continue the dead reporter's work to show that killing the messenger doesn't kill the truth. Many of the reporters took leave to work on what became known as the 'Arizona Project.' Some turned up and worked for nothing.

After a seven-month investigation the team published 23 major articles around the country, exposing more than 200 people with organised crime connections, many with state and federal political links.

Years later, a mobster, Tony Spilotro, later to be murdered himself, was picked up on police phone taps, talking of killing a reporter who was investigating organised crime. He dismissed the idea. 'I want nothing to do with another Arizona project,' he said.

In America, creative minds tried to finish the work of the man killed by organised crime. In Australia one 'creative' mind wrote the song,

I Ate The Yabby That Ate Donald Mackay. Many arms of the media in Australia were happy to run palpably false stories about Mackay. Such stories, shamefully, could usually be traced to people connected with those who had most to gain by discrediting Mackay and muddying the truth about his death.

For the locals anger can swiftly turn to apathy when the trail goes cold.

The Concerned Citizens of Griffith wanted Mackay to be awarded a posthumous Order Of Australia, which was found to be impossible. Instead funds were raised around the country for a permanent Churchill Fellowship to be awarded in his name to study anti-corruption issues around the world.

Robert Trimbole was able to escape from Australia after he was tipped off by police and a lawyer that he should leave before the Stewart Royal Commission was able to call him as a witness. He died a free man. Trimbole was an example of the sort of money — and influence — to be made in the marijuana industry.

In 1959 he ran a garage in Griffith — badly — and nine years later he was declared a bankrupt, owing $10,968,63 to the Tax Department. Two years later he moved into the marijuana business. He went on to own a butcher's shop, a supermarket, a restaurant, a clothing store and a panel beating business. He had a string a luxury cars and showered friends and family with expensive gifts. He would often place bets of $20,000 on horse races. To his grass growing friends, Trimbole was the Mr Fixit, the man who could get things done. They turned to Trimbole when they wanted Mackay killed. He didn't let them down.

His associates included police, local businessmen, politicians, journalists, jockeys and heavy criminals. His phone was illegally tapped and some prominent people were embarrassed when their relationships with 'Aussie Bob' became public.

Many of those who ordered the death have been called before inquiries where they have parroted their carefully scripted denials. They have now been left to enjoy the fruits of their labors.

The NSW police who actively hid evidence from their Victorian counterparts because they didn't want another force to solve the case, have been allowed to retire with their reputations largely intact.

EVEN Barbara Mackay, the most articulate and fearless of women, feels there's little to be gained by repeating herself. She will talk off the record, but sees no point in spoiling the harmony of her life by appearing bitter.

Now a grandmother, she lives in a pleasant unit overlooking a park in a quiet street in one of Griffith's better areas. She is gracious, almost serene, given what she has suffered. She has faith in both God and in Griffith, but not so much in the system.

She has written a book that has been shelved by her publishers because of fears of defamation writs, but she plans to revive the project.

Meanwhile, her eldest son, Paul, still runs the family furniture store his grandfather started. But the youth who was outspoken and angry in the first years after his father's death is gruff and suspicious when the subject is brought up. He has seen his family hurt too often by new stories circulated by reporters who were children when his father disappeared.

But the facts speak in favor of the Mackays. They have been accused of being 'anti-Italian' and 'anti-Griffith' yet Barbara has never considered moving and Paul is married to a woman called Maria Minato, whose mother's family is from Plati in Calabria, a stronghold of the 'Honored Society' and birthplace of many Griffith Calabrians.

Barbara Mackay has been tortured by speculation about what happened to her husband's body. The reality couldn't be worse than all the rumors, she has told friends.

One story is that the body was put through a petfood grinder, another that it was burned in a hospital incinerator or an old brick kiln, another that it was weighed down and dumped in a river, or set in concrete underneath a building.

It is unlikely she will ever know the truth about his death. What she has, however, is the truth about his life.

Three days before he died, there was an attempt to lure him to Jerilderie, 160 kilometres away, to meet a mysterious 'Mr Adams', who claimed he was a lottery winner who wanted to furnish an entire house. It was soon to become clear that it was hitman James Bazley.

Mackay missed the appointment, instead sending an employee,

Bruce Pursehouse. The reason? He was arranging the funeral of a poor man called Harold Craig, one of many people he had helped in Griffith. 'If the truth's known,' recalls Pursehouse, 'Don probably paid for the funeral as well as doing everything else.'

He was like that. Three days later, he paid for his social conscience with his life. Was it in vain?

Three decades of violence in Victoria

1) 4 April 1963. Vincenzo Angilletta, cleaner and former produce grower, shot dead with a shotgun while parking his car in garage at home in Stafford Street, Northcote at 2.30 am.

MOTIVE: Allegedly shot when he rebelled against instructions of the Honoured Society to sell his farm to another member of the group. Killed on the instructions of Domenico Demarte and Vincenzo Muratore.

2) 26 November, 1963. Domenico Demarte, market commission agent wounded by shotgun blast while leaving his Chapman Street, North Melbourne, home for the market at 3.30 am.

MOTIVE: Allegedly shot as a payback for the killing of Angilletta. The shooters were believed to be two relatives of Angilletta.

3) 16 January 1964. Vincenzo Muratore, market merchant and commission agent, killed with a shotgun while leaving for the Victoria Market from his Avondale Street, Hampton home about 2.30 am.

MOTIVE: Payback for Angilletta murder. He was allegedly killed by two male relatives of Angilletta, one who escaped to Italy after the killing.

4) 18 January 1964. Antonio Monaco, a market seller was wounded when he was shot with a shotgun while leaving his home in Dandenong Road, Braeside, about 2.30am.

MOTIVE: Attack involved three men as a payback over domestic dispute.

5) 6 February, 1964. Domenico Cirillo, a fruit and vegetable retailer, was wounded with a shotgun blast when leaving his Ardmillan Road, Moonee Ponds, home on his way to the market about 4.30am.

MOTIVE: Two people involved in attack based on domestic and financial dispute.

6) 10 May, 1983. Toyota Landcruiser owned by Melbourne Godfather Liborio Benvenuto was blown up at the Melbourne Wholesale Fruit and Vegetable Market. No-one injured.

MOTIVE: Attempted murder or warning to Benvenuto as part of a power struggle in the Honored Society.

7) 6 May, 1984. Murders of Melbourne men, Rocco Medici and Giuseppe Furina. Their mutilated bodies were found weighted down in the Murrumbidgee River near Griffith.

MOTIVE: Punishment for the bombing of Benvenuto's car or the removal of rivals for senior positions in Honored Society.

8) 19 June, 1985. Greengrocer Giuseppe Sofra shot three times in the legs at the back of his Springvale Road fruitshop. The shop was owned by Antonio Madafferi.

MOTIVE: Related to price cutting war in green grocer trade in the area. Possible warning to Sofra. Possible warning to Madafferi.

9) 1 August, 1988. Giuseppe Arena, a popular insurance broker known as 'The Friendly Godfather', murdered in the backyard of his Bayswater home.

MOTIVE: Killed on the instructions of a rival as he was seen as a possible successor as Honored Society leader. He was killed six weeks after Liborio Benvenuto died of natural causes.

10) 18 June, 1990. Coles manager Robert Desfosses seriously assaulted by two men in the carpark of the Sunshine Fruit and Vegetable Distribution Centre.

11) June, 1990. The wife of Coles fruit and vegetable buyer Terry Hoskin received call at home claiming she would be going to her husband's funeral within a week.

12) August, 1990. Coles buyer Paul Rizza received an STD call at home warning him, 'You better watch your back.'

MOTIVE: Backlash at attempts to clean up corrupt practices at the market.

13) November, 1990. Coles State Fruit and Vegetable Manager, John Vasilopolous, received a number of threatening phone calls.

MOTIVE: Believed to be connected with Mr Vasilopolous investigations into overpricing of produce from the wholesale market.

14) Early December, 1990. Paul Rizza's wife receives a series of phone calls. No answer at the other end of the line.

15) Early December, 1990. Coles buyer, Charlie Raco, receives an anonymous call late at night. A male states: 'Damage has been done, someone has to pay.'

MOTIVE: Connected with power struggle at the market.

16) 19 December, 1990. Coles State Fruit and Vegetable Manager, John Vasilopolous, opened the front door of his Ivanhoe home. A man with an Australian voice who claimed to be 'Tony' shot him in the stomach.

MOTIVE: Connected with Vasilopolous' investigation into possible corrupt practices in the purchase of produce from the wholesale market.

17) 26 March, 1991. Ambush and $4000 robbery of Cheltenham fruiterer, Armedeo Di Gregorio.

18) 16 May, 1991. Cheltenham fruiterer, Jack Degillio ambushed and robbed of $1000 outside his home.

MOTIVE: Robbery.

19) 8 June, 1991. Arson caused $100,000 damage to Central Fruit Market in Bentleigh. Premises doused with kerosene and set alight.

MOTIVE: Unknown.

20) 11 June, 1991. Glen Waverley fruiterer, Antonio Peluso, ambushed and shot several times as he left his home on the way to the market. Robbed of $4000 but believed to be carrying $7000. Died on the verandah of his own home.

MOTIVE: Robbery.

21) 27 June, 1991. East Doncaster fruiterer, Tabaret Louey, bashed by two men and robbed of $2000 on his way to the market.

MOTIVE: Robbery.

22) 3 July, 1991. Ambush and $5000 robbery of Wantirna South fruiterer, Phillip Strati, outside his home.

MOTIVE: Robbery.

23) 5 August, 1991. Attempt to blow up the Central Fruit Market after explosives planted on the roof. Petrol was also poured onto the roof but it failed to ignite.

MOTIVE: Part of price cutting war involving local fruit and vegetable shops.

24) 20 November, 1991. Another attempt to burn down the Central Fruit Market. Petrol failed to ignite.

25) 29 February, 1992. Melbourne market fruiterer and his wife pistol whipped and robbed of $5000 at their Wandin home by two masked men.

26) 2 March, 1992. Robert Nancarrow, the founder of the Nancarrow supermarket chain, beaten to death in his Northcote shop. Drowned in his own blood.

MOTIVE: Robbery.

27) 4 August, 1992. Melbourne Wholesale Fruit and Vegetable Market wholesaler, Alfonso Muratore, shot to death outside his Hampton home.

MOTIVES: Dispute over money owed to the family business. Punishment for leaving his wife and family. Honoured Society power struggle. Involvement in attempts in bid to take major fruit and vegetable contracts from other market figures.

CHAPTER 17

Dummy run
'Mr Laundry' gets washed up

'Well, I want to stop him breathing'

IT was just after midnight in a seedy, dead-end lane in St Kilda. A man's body, trussed with black electric tape and with a hood over his head, was wedged into the back of a white van. The portly, middle-aged man who had ordered the abduction approached quietly. He was smiling, eyes sparkling with anticipation.

For months Philip Peters had planned this moment. The crooked lawyer who specialised in laundering cash had branched out. He was in the big-time now. He was about to turn killer.

Peters had planned it carefully. He was going to drug and abduct the man he believed responsible for losing him $200,000, then kill him. It was payback time.

Peters, known in the underworld as 'Mr Laundry', was going to take his victim to a remote farmhouse in St Arnaud in central Victoria, where he would be dismembered and buried in pieces by a butcher recruited for the job. 'Where do we kill him?' asked the former butcher.

'Put a bag over his head,' said Peters.

'I've already done that, I've got him trussed up, hands and ...' said the accomplice.

'Can he breathe? ... Well, I want to stop him breathing ... Put a plastic bag over his head,' ordered Peters.

But, apparently just in the nick of time, police arrived after a concerned neighbor yelled out. Frantically, they worked on the victim with mouth to mouth and heart massage, but the body remained deathly still. There was no flicker of life.

The police's apparently desperate actions were the final movements in an elaborate, three-month masquerade designed to snare Peters, the lawyer turned gangster, who had been determined to become a millionaire in six months – and was prepared to kill to get there.

As Peters was secretly taped in the back of a police car working out his alibi, police crowded around the lifeless body. It was lifeless because it was not the victim Peters had ordered killed. It was the dummy from Channel Seven's television series, *Full Frontal.*

The producers had agreed to lend the police the dummy* as part of Operation Soli, a sting to catch Peters, who had been taped for months planning the abduction, torture and murder of his enemy. He had provided the drugs to dope his victim and found a stooge to do the actual killing – or so he thought.

In 1997, Peters, a former lawyer for the Crown Solicitor's office and State Treasury, was jailed for attempted abduction, perjury and cultivating marijuana.

He was released just 22 days after being sentenced because of a deal where his original, more serious charges, including conspiracy to murder, were dropped in exchange for his guilty plea.

It seemed a tiny sentence for an ongoing conspiracy where a man could have died, but the deal was cut outside the court. The pressure is on to save money by avoiding long trials. A deal is a deal and Peters, having worked for the Crown and the other side, knew the unspoken rule that much of modern law enforcement is budget driven. Justice is

---

* Peters was not the only one fooled by the dummy. A senior policeman nearly collapsed when he saw what he thought was a suspect fall past his window after being thrown from an upper-storey interview room at the St Kilda police station. It was the dummy.

not only blind, but broke as well. According to police, Peters was a brilliant thinker, but gripped by greed and vindictiveness, who planned to torture a man he believed had contributed to his financial ruin.

Peters knew from personal experience that in his circles the loss of money could prove fatal. At one point there was $30,000 contract taken out on his life by an amphetamines dealer over a 'misunderstanding' involving between $450,000 and $600,000.

Police believe the drug dealer organised four men to beat an elderly member of Peters' family as a warning. Peters took the hint and changed his appearance, dyeing his hair and eyebrows, and carrying a gun.

Peters had taken possession of huge amounts of dirty money from the drug dealer and promised to launder it through a Melbourne computer firm and a property development in the Whitsunday Islands. The money went missing – and Peters would have too, but for a bizarre legal twist. The drug dealer took his case to the Solicitors' Guarantee Fund and was repaid around $500,000 in compensation and legal costs, even though it was known the money was drug profits.

A former client of Peters said he was 'known as Mr Laundry because he can launder millions for you.'

Peters, who was educated at Trinity Grammar and Melbourne University, spent ten years working for government departments before he started private practice in Essendon.

He soon earned the reputation as a 'no-questions asked' type who cleaned dirty money. He engineered property developments using a string of shelf companies and false names. He used his secretary's name without her knowledge in one development. She knew there was a problem only when she started receiving funeral wreaths as a threat.

A New Zealand family asked Peters to wind up the affairs of a relative, Michael Joseph Smith, who had died in Melbourne. Smith, an oil rig worker, died in January 1989, aged 33. His brother, sister and their spouses flew from New Zealand to tidy up his affairs and arrange the funeral. They needed a solicitor and, as they didn't have a car, they picked the closest lawyer to the motel they were staying in at Essendon. It was Peters. The family asked him to complete all legal details. He agreed to do so for a substantial fee, but later decided that wasn't enough.

Peters assumed the dead man's identity, taking out a licence, opening bank accounts, registering his car and working as a financier under Smith's name. In fact, Peters became Michael Smith in all his business dealings after his legal practising certificate was cancelled in 1989.

The Law Institute of Victoria moved on Peters late that year. It found money missing from his trust account. In each discrepancy the money was found to have been redirected to companies controlled by two drug dealers.

One witness described being in the office when a drug dealer arrived with money he wanted laundered. The man said the dealer produced $50,000 in cash from a paper bag to set up a bogus mortgage on an historic property in Essendon. The cash had previously been hidden from police in the ceiling of a house in Moonee Ponds.

Peter Kelly, a St Kilda solicitor, said Peters worked for him in the early 1990s using the name Michael Smith. He was supposed to help organise commercial and home loans. 'He said he had a legal degree from New Zealand, but had never practised. What I remember most about him was his eyes, which looked straight through you. It was like he was from another planet.' Peters did not conclude any loans, Kelly said. 'I think, looking back, he was trying to set me up as another front for him.'

In 1994 Peters manipulated a client to perform minor criminal acts for him. In the end he asked the man, John, to help him kill someone he believed was responsible for a loss of $200,000 in an insurance fraud gone wrong.

The proposed victim allegedly 'stole' computer equipment from Peters' company so the loss could be claimed, but the brilliant lawyer had made an unbelievable blunder. The insurance cover on the business had lapsed and the burglar with the green light would not return the gear or cough up the money he'd made.

Peters' planned revenge was to organise a drug deal and then rip the man off for the money. He planned to take the man to a pit under a farmhouse in St Arnaud and torture him until the victim provided the cash. To do this, he wanted John, a butcher, to help abduct 'Peter' and ultimately to chop up his body so it would never be found.

John had been running two businesses when he was introduced to Peters, but both had failed after he was effectively manipulated into signing over his interests to Peters.

John said Peters used his legal experience to plan crimes. 'He said he read files to see how criminals had worked. He read legal transcripts and his notes to see where they went wrong.'

Once Peters had effectively taken over John's firms, the once successful businessman was at the mercy of the master manipulator.

John became involved with Peters at the lower end of crime. 'We had no money and were in debt. We had to go with them. I was going to lose my house. They had me.' He grew marijuana seedlings for the bent lawyer's Sunbury property. It was not a great success. 'The sheep ate the plants. They ended up stoned,' John said.

Each crime was the same. Peters did the planning and John did the dirty work. Peters was almost never there when there were any risks.

He planned several major frauds, but when the plans turned to a murder plot, John went to the police with three boxes of documents to prove his claims. Police turned John into an undercover agent in early 1994. More than 4000 pages of conversations between the two men were taped, including plans to drug and kill the proposed victim. John had no doubt Peters wanted his enemy dead. 'He was going to kill him for sure.'

The policeman in charge of Operation Soli, acting Detective Sergeant Jeremy Oliver, said Peters always used middle men as fall guys to try to protect himself from prosecution. 'He always wanted someone else to do the dirty work.' There was no doubting Peters' intelligence. 'He would just make up a story as he went along which would sound quite credible. He was able to think on his feet,' Oliver was to recall.

Another policeman who had dealt with Peters made a blunter assessment. 'His looks were deceiving. He looked like a fat idiot, but he had an incredibly quick mind.'

At one point Peters developed a plan to rip-off the Solicitors' Guarantee Fund. He set up a false investment portfolio under the fictitious name of Giovanni Sanetti. The file said that Sanetti invested $60,000 which would eventually mature to $100,000. Police said that in 1993 Peters approached John and asked him to pretend to be 'Sanetti'. The plan was to apply to the Guarantee Fund for the investment money which had allegedly been lost or stolen by Peters.

According to police tapes, Peters also planned an insurance fraud by buying a fish and chip shop in Gordon, near Ballarat, and burning it down three months later.

Peter's plans to be a crime boss folded when he was arrested in the culmination of the sting. Peters forgot his golden rule: don't get your hands dirty and always use a patsy. As agreed with police, John rang Peters to say he had drugged the target, who was in the freezer in the back of his St Kilda shop. Peters wanted John to put the body in the van and drive to the St Arnaud farm. Peters, naturally, would be in another car, away from any problems.

As part of the police plan, John persuaded Peters to come to the shop. When he arrived he was told the man was still alive. It was then that Peters showed himself to be a would-be killer.

Even when police arrived he remained cool, discussing possible legal defences with his partner, still unaware that the victim was a television dummy. As police 'worked' to save the alleged victim, Peters was plotting a plan that would put him in the clear, but leave his mate John out in the cold.

PETERS: 'Just don't worry about him, John.'

JOHN: 'So, who – who – drugged him, what – what if they ask me questions like that? Hey?'

PETERS: 'Well, we're gonna have to say you did, John.'

Peters was originally charged with 13 major criminal charges including incitement and conspiracy to murder. The charges were later amended after he agreed to plead guilty to incitement to kidnap, cultivate marijuana and perjury.

County Court Judge Byrne sentenced him to three years and six months' jail with a minimum of five months. When pre-trial detention was taken into account he was freed 22 days after he was sentenced.

John was handed a two-year suspended sentence for his activities with Peters and on his release worked 18 hours a day in two jobs to recover financially. 'I always knew he would get away with it. It's a joke what he got.'

FOLLOWING is an edited transcript from 4000 pages of secretly-taped conversations between 'John' and corrupt lawyer, Philip Peters, in which they discuss the plot to abduct and torture a man before butchering him to dispose of the body.

Tullamarine, 11 February, 1994:

JOHN : '... You and Phillip were gonna take him up to St Arnaud and stick him in a f...... pit and things like that, now I've been trembling, you know for a f...... week.'

PETERS: 'Well, that's what I was gonna do. I really was. Because the bastard had pinched $200,000 worth of stock.'

JOHN: 'Yeah, and what would have happened if he got out of the pit?'

PETERS: 'Well, he wasn't gonna get out. He wasn't gonna get out, ever. We were gonna get the stock and then he was gonna vanish. He was gonna vanish, John, believe me.'

JOHN: 'All I could think was my wife, my kids, you know, things like that – nothing else.'

PETERS: 'No, I would never, ever have let it get to a situation where there could be any risk at all. He was going to vanish totally.'

JOHN: 'As in totally dead, dead.'

PETERS: 'Dead, dead. Well, he – he has pinched so much from so many people that the world – you would get a medal. Apart from the stuff he pinched from Phillip, he pinched a car from me and sold it and then told the coppers that I told him to do it.'

PETERS: 'Yeah, well, Danny has I believe – no, not has – had put a contract out on him.'

JOHN: 'That'd explain the way sort of you know he rang, yeah.'

PETERS: 'Yeah, yeah. No, that's why he's got seven around with him ... I made some inquires and Danny had apparently put a contract out on him two years ago.'

JOHN: 'Yeah.'

PETERS: 'The bloke took Danny's money then told K .... .'

JOHN: 'Like I said to you believe ... with the pit, it's the wife and kids, I'm not worried about anything else.'

PETERS: 'No, well look, don't worry about that, there is no way on earth I would let that sort of thing happen. No, he was never gonna get out of the pit. I was gonna get as much as we could, because he owes me ... he took $200,000 worth of stock ... the business went down.'

PETERS: 'When you're talking on the telephone be very cautious because I just don't trust telephones.'

Tullamarine, 16 February, 1994:

JOHN: 'Well if there's money to be made, I'll – I'll go along with the original idea, mate.'

PETERS: 'Right. Well, if he turns up with the cash.'

JOHN : 'Yeah.'

PETERS: 'Then as long as we can get him away, where we can see what the hell is going on.'

JOHN: 'Yeah.'

PETERS: 'You know, if he brings the cash up the bush or whatever, then we can do it ... providing things go right we can, but, you know, we're – step number one is protection.'

JOHN : 'Yeah.'

PETERS: 'Step number two is the money. You know, money's no use at all, if you're not protected. It's something to think about.'

JOHN: 'I think he's – he's greedy enough to fall for it ... If he smelt the dollar, yeah.'

PETERS: 'He is, but the one thing you've got to be careful of ... is that you're not followed. You know, you're going to need back roads and all sorts of things.'

A St Kilda pizza parlour, 17 February, 1994:

PETERS: 'This is getting beyond me, but I – I want to get this bastard.'

JOHN: 'Yeah.'

PETERS: 'You know, that – Theo had already indicated that he's quite prepared to run him up and then knock him over. Now he's gonna be even happier to do it ... Look, if his money goes – he's got to be put away, otherwise, you know, it's, it's exposing everybody to too much risk ... We'll do – we'll do the community a service.'

(Peters then goes on to explain that the man he wants dead will try to cut John out of any major cannabis crop and deal directly with the drug dealers.)

PETERS: 'Yeah, well he's a lying, thieving, nasty little bastard.'

JOHN: 'Yeah'

PETERS: Once that's happened, you're free, and then we can hit him with impunity.'

Happier times … policeman Denis Tanner signs his brother's marriage certificate in 1981.

In the frame … Tanner (middle) at detective training school. Ron Iddles is behind Tanner's right shoulder.

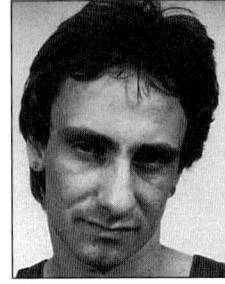

ABOVE:
ATTILA ERDEI
A millionaire drug
dealer and killer
who was unknown
before Operation
Pipeline.
Sentenced:
22 years.

BELLA
BERNATH
Head of an elusive
and established
group supplying
many substantial
street dealers.
Sentenced: Four
years.

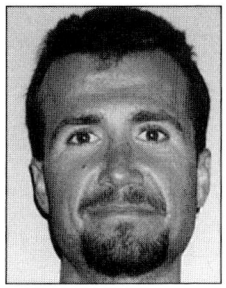

MANUEL
VENERIS
Assets exceeding
$800,000. Sold
drugs valued at
$1.2 million during
the operation.
Sentenced: Four
years.

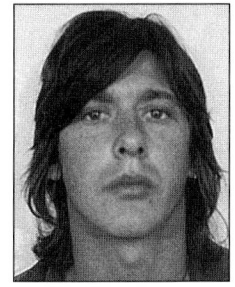

PAUL WOOLES
Involved in the
distribution of
heroin and ampheta-
mines in Victorian
and WA prisons.
Sentenced: Six
years with a
minimum of two.

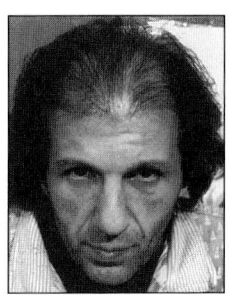

PETER BABES
An associate of
Leimonitis.
Bragged of his
ability to supply
pistols and machine
guns.
Sentenced: Two
years.

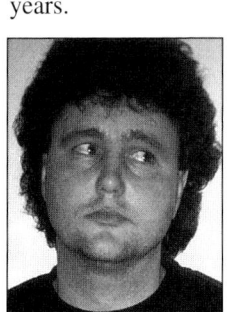

ANTHONY
HICKEY
Primary source of
amphetamines.
Second in charge to
Veneris. Career
criminal. Sentenced:
Six years, minimum
of three.

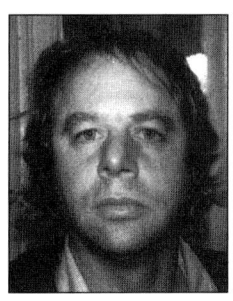

JOHN FALZON
A millionaire from
Laverton who
trafficked in heroin,
amphetamines and
hashish.
Sentenced: Seven
years with a
minimum of five.

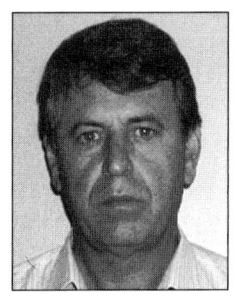

THEODORE
LEIMONITIS
His syndicate was
linked directly to an
amphetamines
laboratory; a major
hashish importer.
Sentenced: Four
years.

 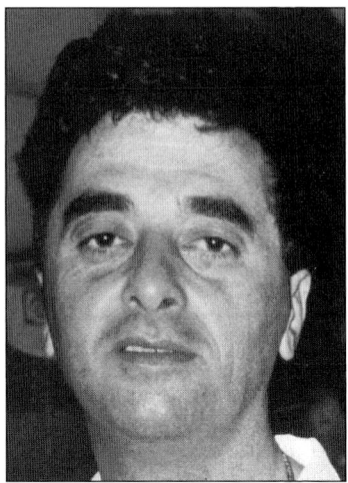

Father and son ... Vincenzo and Alfonso Muratore. Both gunned down in Hampton 28 years apart.

Rocco Medici and his brother-in-law Giuseppe Furina ... found tortured and murdered in the Murrumbidgee River.

The only picture of US mafia hunter John T Cusack (circled) in Australia, at a gathering of Victorian investigators in 1964.

Anti-drugs campaigner Donald Mackay … murder unsolved.

The 'Friendly Godfather' Joe Arena … murder unsolved.

Police needed to fly in to destroy this remote bushland
marijuana plantation … but was the job sold out from within?

Respected senior policeman Dick McLean (above, centre front row, and below in cap) … turned bad when he left the job. LEFT: Policeman Gary Whelan … was given a second chance, and blew it.

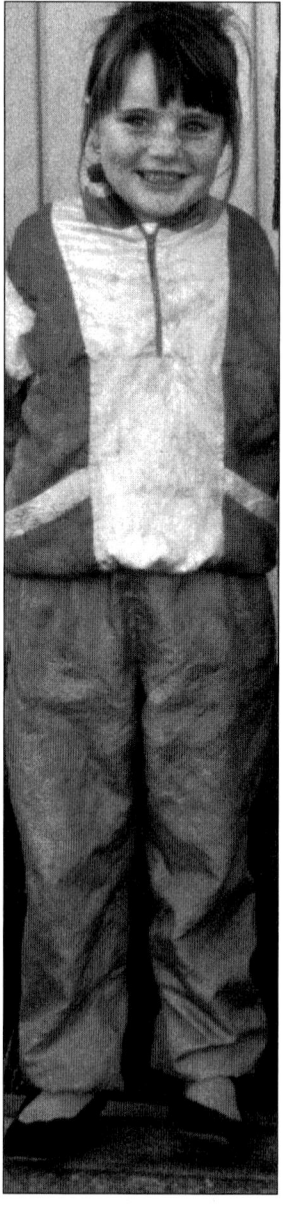

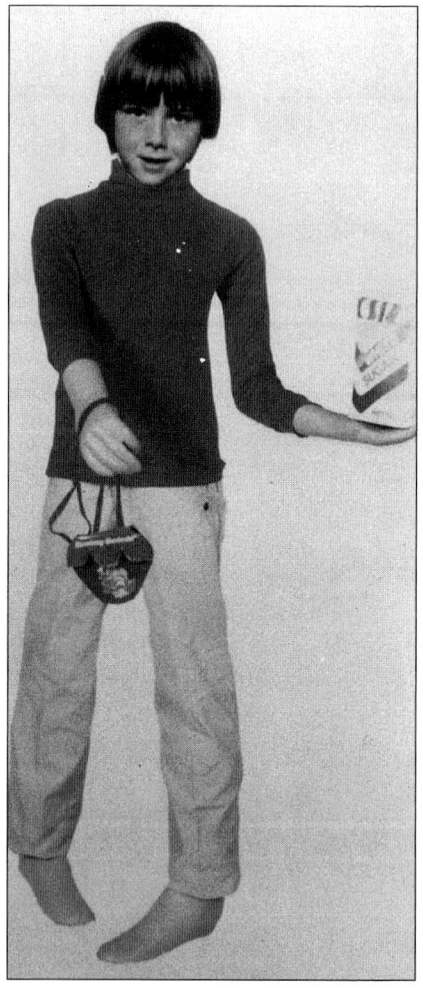

Robert Arthur Selby Lowe was convicted of the 1991 murder of Sheree Beasley (left). He remains the prime suspect in the disturbingly similar case of Kylie Maybury in 1984.

Tullamarine, 24 February, 1994:

Peters talks of buying a fish and chip shop and then burning it down for the insurance.

PETERS: 'What's gonna happen, gonna buy this fish and chip shop and go into ... three months or whatever and then there's gonna be a fire in the place and that's gonna be .... Fish and chip shops go all the time.'

JOHN: 'What exactly is going to happen to him eventually? Is he –?'

PETERS: 'He's going to vanish. You don't need to know about that ... I want to get some money out of him first.'

18 February, 1994:

JOHN : 'I mean, are we really going to kill him? What are we going to do?'

PETERS: 'Well, look, that's up to them. I don't give a stuff.'

JOHN: 'Yeah.'

PETERS: 'All I want is – is my money back and Phillip's money back.'

JOHN: 'Yeah.'

PETERS: 'I don't give a stuff what they do with him. But obviously, if he vanishes, it's going to be better for you.'

(They talk of the marijuana John grew for Peters, later eaten by sheep.)

JOHN: 'The sheep ate them, Philip. Go outside and see if there's any stoned sheep running around the paddock.'

PETERS: 'There's dead sheep all over the place, they probably suicided.'

(They discuss getting drugs to knock out the man Peters wants abducted.)

JOHN: 'And make sure you bring it down to the shop and I've got it there.'

PETERS: 'Yeah, yeah.'

JOHN : 'I'm not running around for three days like we did with the bloody sample.'

PETERS: 'No. It's got to be there first.'

(He returns to the subject of the fish and chip shop).

'But basically what it is, we run the fish shop for three months or something and then the fat boils over ... you've seen it happen.'

At a St Kilda pizza parlour, 2 March, 1994.

JOHN: 'And with (the name of the target), what's going to be the outcome with him, mate?'

PETERS: 'Well.'

JOHN: 'Is he still goin' up to St Arnaud, or what?'

PETERS: 'Yeah, providing we can get him up to a big enough deal.'

JOHN: 'All right.'

PETERS: 'I'm not interested in knocking him off – over four, five grand or ten grand, but if we can get up – get him up to fifty or a hundred grand, yes, it's worth it, to get my money back.

JOHN: 'All right.'

PETERS: 'Bloody rotten little shit, he is. He – look, John, you've got no idea of what a bloody, lying, devious, dishonest, nasty little shit he is.'

JOHN: 'He – he looks like that, that's why he – he – just like a little ferret.'

PETERS: 'What I'm trying to do is build the bank – the bank roll … for other operations. I've got to find a million dollars within the next six months.'

JOHN: 'That's – that's a small order.'

PETERS: 'Well, I'm gonna do it, John.'

Tullamarine, 23 March, 1994:

JOHN: 'Is there really a pit, up at St Arnaud, or what?'

PETERS: 'Yeah, there's a cellar in the house.'

JOHN: 'Right.'

PETERS: 'Brick, you know, with a very narrow staircase, so, you know.'

JOHN: 'I just hope he doesn't get out of there mate.'

PETERS: 'Well, that's why I'm thinking we might need a third person, we might need a third person, we might need someone to go and sit up there.'

JOHN: 'And how long do you think you're going to need to set up somebody to sit up with him?'

PETERS: 'I would think only a day or two, he's going to give us the information. If he doesn't then, he vanishes, which he's gonna do anyway.'

McDonald's car park, Tullamarine, April, 1994:
PETERS: 'Well, I think he's got to vanish anyway.'
JOHN: 'Yeah.'
PETERS: 'The minute we do that, for your, our, for your sake, he's got to vanish.'
JOHN: 'Yeah.'
PETERS: 'But what I was – what I had originally intended to do, was either get the two hundred, or get some satisfaction.'
(The two men talk about how that will be able to get the victim to St Arnaud.)
PETERS: 'It'll be something like an old-fashioned Mickey Finn.'
JOHN : 'We, the other thing, if he was – who is gonna kill (the man), up at St Arnaud, then?'
PETERS: 'If necessary, I will, but I – I think we've now got to the stage, where – you know, it's got to be you and me and no-one else, John.'
JOHN: 'All right.'
PETERS: 'I don't nee-, I don't want a third person involved, either.'
JOHN: 'Fine with me, mate.'
PETERS: 'That way, if something goes wrong, we know there's only two people to blame.'
PETERS: 'You'd take him out and bury him.'

Tullamarine. McDonald's carpark, 14 April, 1994:
(The two men discuss how they will drug the target.)
PETERS: 'But it's basically knock-out drops.'
JOHN: 'Yeah. Where do you get 'em?'
PETERS: 'They used to be all over the place. I'm finding it very difficult – I've got a half a dozen people looking for them.'
JOHN: 'It must be the signs of the times, mate.'
JOHN: 'But can you use anything else.'
PETERS: 'Look, I'm sure you can, but I don't know – you know, I've got no idea what three or four moggies tastes like.'
JOHN: 'What are moggies?'
PETERS: 'Mogadons.'
JOHN: 'Oh.'
PETERS: 'Sleeping pills – but you know, presumably, that'd be the

same … I've got a couple of blokes having a hunt around for me, so we'll see what they come up with. There was a woman, Poison Ivy, convicted a couple of years ago, and if I could find a copy of the court transcript, I'd know how to make the stuff, even, because she was using it, but it – it's around.'

(The two men discuss disguising the taste of the Mogadons.)

PETERS: 'What does (the victim) drink?'

JOHN: 'Coffee.'

PETERS: 'They tell me it (the drug) is fairly bitter, so it'll have to be coffee with sugar, or something – anyway, you can do some tests on it, John, try it on the girls.'

(By 19 April, as they are getting close to abducting the target, Peters also considers killing a woman.

PETERS: 'You said you wanted to kill her … There is no way on earth I'm going to do business with her, but have a think about it – what we should be able to do, is set her up in the same way we've set up (the target) and do the same thing. I'm getting enough – and for Christ sake, don't call them 'Mickeys' on the phone … you never know who's listening.'

PETERS: 'But if we set her up in the same way, we can achieve the same result, and pick up a substantial quantity of material.'

(Peters said he would like to experiment with the drugs to get the dose accurate.) 'The bloody things have turned out expensive. It's costing a hundred bucks for the what, three doses I'm getting. I'm picking them up tonight.'

JOHN: 'All right and (the target is) gonna be done this week?'

PETERS: 'Mm, I think you should give this stuff a test. If it doesn't work, then we review everything, but you know, if you give Ben or someone.'

On 20 April Peters hands the drugs to John.

JOHN: 'So, how do – how many of these do we have – do – do I use?'

PETERS: 'I would put – I'd give him four, two and two.'

JOHN: 'Well, after he's asleep, what'll I do with him?'

PETERS: 'You're going to have to secure him reasonably – very, very well.'

JOHN: 'What, so he's gonna be slapped about?'

PETERS: 'Mm, as long as he's properly secured – that's gonna be the – real trick … A tape around the mouth, cuffs on the hands and ankles, and you haven't got a problem … Make sure you've got some heavy, sticky bandage, or whatever, we may need to wrap that round his mouth.'

JOHN: 'Right. They're not gonna find him, up at St Arnaud, then?'

PETERS: 'No.'

JOHN: 'They're not gonna find the body, are they?'

PETERS: 'Nuh, nuh, they're not going to find anything.'

21 April, 1994:

(John rings Peters and tells him he has drugged the victim. Peters drives to a shop in St Kilda where, he believes, the unconscious man is trussed in a van outside. But it is the dummy in the van, and police hidden nearby.)

JOHN: 'Well, the moggies you gave me, mate, worked beautifully.'

PETERS: 'Good.'

JOHN: 'Where do we kill him.'

PETERS: 'Put a bag over his head.'

JOHN: 'I've already done that, I've got him trussed up, hands and.'

PETERS: 'Yeah, but.'

JOHN: 'I'll show you.'

PETERS: 'Can he breathe?'

JOHN: 'Yeah, come on, I'll show you.'

PETERS: 'Well, I want to stop him breathing.'

JOHN: 'Well, come and have a look.'

PETERS: 'Put a plastic bag over his head.'

UNIDENTIFIED SPEAKER: 'Hey, what are you doing there? Hey, what are you doing there? Police, call the police.'

POLICE OFFICER: 'Police, don't do anything, get on the ground.'

POLICE OFFICER: 'Get on the ground, go on. Get on the ground.'

POLICE OFFICER: 'Put your hands behind your back. Hands behind your back.'

The police then pretend to find the 'victim' in the car.

John and Peters are put in a police car. Peters sets out to concoct a legal defence, unaware he is being taped.

POLICE OFFICER: 'Who's gettin' the ambulance?'

POLICE OFFICER: 'They didn't – they didn't call an ambulance.'

POLICE OFFICER: 'Well, arrange an ambulance now.'

JOHN: 'What do we do now, Phil?'

PETERS: 'No conspiracy to murder.'

JOHN: 'You're f ...... ' kidding me.'

PETERS: 'Well, all we were trying to do, is get some money out of this bloke that owes me and Phillip some money.'

JOHN: 'What do I tell 'em?'

PETERS: 'Just that.'

JOHN: 'So what did we do to him?'

PETERS: 'Nothing.'

JOHN: 'How did he get in the back of the van?'

PETERS: 'Just don't worry about him, John.'

JOHN: 'So, who – who – drugged him, what – what if they ask me questions like that? Hey?'

PETERS: 'Well, we're gonna have to say you did, John.'

JOHN: 'With what. What did I use?'

PETERS: 'Just a couple of Mogadons.'

JOHN : 'And where'd I get 'em? Who am I – you gave me the shits, mate.'

PETERS: 'Yeah.'

JOHN: 'Come on, what do I say, Phil.'

PETERS: 'I gave you a couple of moggies, that's all.'

JOHN: 'If they ask me, how many'd you give me, how many?'

PETERS: 'Two. Two.'

JOHN: 'If they ask me when you gave them to me, what, what do I say?'

PETERS: 'A couple of days ago.'

JOHN: 'All right. How much shit are we in?'

PETERS: 'Oh, a bit.'

CHAPTER 18

The finger of suspicion
The abduction of Kerry Whelan

*Bruce Burrell was good at
keeping up appearances*

THERE'S a Raymond Chandler feel to Maroubra. Its sunbaked streets of ageing stucco and tile houses, sprawled next to Coogee on Sydney's eastern beaches, suggest Chandler's between-the-wars Los Angeles. So do some of the goings-on there.

It was here, in a street with a million-dollar view of the Pacific, that a little old lady with a big bank balance went for a walk and never came back.

Chandler himself couldn't have plotted the last-known movements of Mrs Dottie Davis more bleakly, or have left fewer clues.

Late on a Tuesday morning in May 1995, the 74-year-old widow came home to her ugly double-storey brick house at 9 Undine Street, after an appointment with her doctor.

About an hour later, according to a builder working on an awning at the back of the house, the old woman said she was going to visit a sick friend. The builder wasn't wearing a watch, and could later offer only vague estimates of crucial times, a fact that was to earn him the undivided attention of detectives who considered him, briefly, the best suspect they had.

What the unfortunate tradesman could tell police was that Mrs Davis did not drive her Mercedes. The signs were that she didn't intend to go far, or to stay long. Though she suffered badly from arthritis, she walked. She left meat out to defrost, and the prescription her doctor had just written was on the kitchen table.

The old lady walked down the drive, past the fake antique gaslight and the rickety letterbox, and was never seen again.

UNDINE Street is only a dozen houses long and slopes down towards the bay. At the bottom of the street, probably 60 metres from Mrs Davis's house, a walker can turn right into a footpath that skirts the shore in front of a few houses.

The last of these buildings, on the next corner, is a stylish duplex pair. One of the pair, 34 Marine Parade, was in 1995 the home of a close family friend of Mrs Davis. This was Dallas Burrell, who'd known Mrs Davis all her life, and called her 'Auntie Dot'.

In May 1995, Mrs Burrell had just been diagnosed with cancer. Police now consider it highly likely she was the sick friend Mrs Davis intended to visit. As far as they can tell, no one else fitting that description lived within walking distance. In 1995, the Burrell connection was only one of many possibilities for puzzled police. That has changed.

When Mrs Davis vanished, police spoke to Dallas Burrell, and to her husband Bruce. It was a routine inquiry. The Burrells, after all, were a respectable professional couple. Dallas Burrell was an advertising art director, and her husband worked for a Sydney advertising agency, Peter Grace and Associates.

Not only was there nothing to link either of the Burrells with the disappearance of a dear family friend, but both seemed understandably distressed.

What police didn't know, nor would they have cared then, was that Bruce Burrell had been retrenched five years before by the Australian arm of the international forklift firm, Crown Equipment, which has its national headquarters in Smithfield in Sydney.

Business had been tough for Crown in 1990. The company liked to think of itself as a big family, but when the crunch came, heads had to roll to cut costs. One of them belonged to Bruce Burrell, the advertising manager, until then one of the close-knit management team. He was called into the executive offices on the top floor of the Smithfield address. There, he faced the man who had been chief executive of the company since 1974, and had become its Asia-Pacific vice-president. A man who had known Burrell through work, tennis days and shooting trips for more than ten years, and who thought it his duty to wield the axe personally. His name was Bernie Whelan.

BRUCE Burrell was good at keeping up appearances. He always had cash to spend, according to workmates, but privately he was doing it hard. Friends later told police they suspected he was largely supported by his wife, and that his 'advertising' job was as a contract salesman, a hand-to-mouth existence compared with his days as a high-flying marketing executive.

Coincidentally, after Dorothy Davis's disappearance, the Burrells' marriage broke up. Dallas Burrell moved from the smart duplex at 34 Marine Parade just up the road to number 44, a big block of flats – luxurious by 1960s standards – sitting on a headland overlooking the ocean. Her estranged husband, meanwhile, moved to the 192-hectare property he had bought some years before at Bungonia, near Goulburn, in the southern tablelands.

Burrell's property is the last on a quiet track beyond Bungonia township, which comprises only a dozen houses and no shops. There, according to locals, he lived alone after his marriage breakdown and mostly kept out of people's way. One neighbor says he 'enjoys a beer and a talk', but not many have had the chance to find out even that much about the bloke from Sydney.

In Goulburn, 30 kilometres away, few remember that Bruce Burrell was once a local. In fact, according to a local optometrist, on at least one occasion Burrell wasn't keen to remember it himself.

It happened some time in 1996, when Mr Burrell stepped into the optometrist's shop. He wears glasses, and might have wanted to look at a new pair or have his eyes tested, the proprietor can't remember which. What he does recall is Burrell's reaction when the optometrist remarked that he'd known him as a child because his father, Alan Burrell, had once worked for the family as a wool classer.

To his surprise, Burrell bluntly contradicted him. 'He said, 'Oh, no.

That's not right',' the optometrist was to recall. Several other people in Goulburn remember Alan 'Splinter' Burrell, who lived at West Goulburn with his family, including a son called Bruce, before moving to Sydney in the 1960s. They have no doubt it is the same Bruce Burrell.

The optometrist had no reason to dwell on this trifling exchange until May this year. That was when the wife of the man who had sacked Bruce Burrell seven years before, vanished without trace.

THE facts of Kerry Whelan's last-known movements are few and worn with retelling. But when the 39-year-old mother of three went missing on Tuesday, 6 May, 1997, only her family, close friends and police knew. It was kept secret for the next ten days. Then the media were told, but police negotiated a news blackout for another six days.

So it wasn't until 21 May that the rest of Australia heard the news that had crushed Bernie Whelan and his children, Sarah, 15, Mathew, 13, and James, 11.

After breakfast on 6 May, Kerry Whelan drove her new silver Land Rover Discovery from the family's lush property at Kurrajong, in the foothills of the Blue Mountains, to Parramatta, where it was due for its first service. And where, she had told her family, she was to have beauty treatment before accompanying her husband to Adelaide on a business trip that afternoon.

The secretary who'd married her much-older boss after an office romance 16 years before, retained a business-like habit of keeping a meticulous daily appointment diary. But for that Tuesday she had made only one cryptic entry: 'Parramatta 9.30.'

She had been running late. The security film recovered from the car park underneath the Parkroyal Hotel in Parramatta shows that she drove in at 9.36 am.

After speaking to attendants at the boom gate, she parked near the entrance. Leaving the keys in the ignition so an attendant could later move it to another spot, she took her bag and walked quickly out to the street, as if late for something. She hasn't been seen since.

When she didn't meet her husband at 3.45 pm, ready for the Adelaide flight, he went searching. When he found the Land Rover in the car park with the keys still in it, he called the police.

From the start, it was a frustrating and delicate investigation. At first, as in most missing persons cases, police were sceptical. The odds were that the young wife of the wealthy, busy executive would turn up within hours or days, as 95 per cent of missing people do.

Next day, the ransom note turned up, and all bets that it was just an embarrassing domestic drama were off. This was life or death.

The note was typed, and postmarked in central Sydney. It demanded a $1 million ransom, which happened to be the exact amount of kidnap insurance Crown offers its executives and their families. This raised speculation that the kidnapper had inside information.

The note made conditions that baffled police. Contact would be made in ten days, through newspaper advertisements. And, it demanded that police not be told. Here, the kidnapper had miscalculated badly, because the note hadn't arrived until after the rattled husband raised the alarm.

Meanwhile, detectives combed through the Whelans' social and business contacts, looking for the classic suspect: someone with an opportunity and a motive. The common motives are greed, revenge or lust, sometimes all three.

Bruce Burrell's name came up quickly. Two reasons for this have been made public; if there are more links, the police aren't saying.

One is that Burrell telephoned Bernie Whelan out of the blue, the month before the abduction. If a coincidence, it was lousy timing. The other was the discovery that Burrell had visited the Whelans' place while Bernie Whelan was away, only days before the abduction. He had no good reason to go there.

There was no clue in Kerry Whelan's behavior that anything was amiss in her life as a wealthy wife and devoted mother.

The days leading to her disappearance were filled with family engagements and meeting friends. Sunday 4 May was the 11th birthday of her youngest child, James. Her husband had arrived home the day before from one of his frequent overseas business trips.

On Monday, after dropping the children at school, Kerry went to a hairdresser and had a color rinse put through her hair. That night the Whelans entertained neighbors.

Next morning she set off for Parramatta. On the way she dropped in on a friend, Marj Taylor, for coffee. She seemed normal and happy.

BY 11 May, just five days after the abduction and more than a week before the story broke publicly, there were strange sights in the tiny hamlet of Bungonia, 200 kilometres and more than two hours' drive from Parramatta.

At first the tightlipped strangers were coy about what they were doing, or as coy as you can be when hitting a township of a dozen houses in a fleet of shiny new cars with tinted glass and bristling with aerials, taking over two churches as temporary headquarters.

They could hardly deny being police, but they told curious locals that they were doing 'an exercise'. It didn't take people long to realise that they were watching Bruce Burrell's property, although no-one could have imagined why until after the kidnap became headlines on 21 May.

By then Bernie Whelan was begging for his wife's life. He was prepared to pay the ransom, but there were no takers.

In a videotaped appeal released on 23 May, the stricken man urged the 'kidnappers' to contact him, to let him know his wife was all right. 'For ten days we have tried to comply … with their ransom demands. For reasons unknown to us, the kidnappers have stopped contact. I would do whatever they asked, and I would go anywhere to get the safety of my wife.'

Detective Inspector Mick Howe, head of the kidnap taskforce, codenamed Operation Bellaire, said police supported Mr Whelan and his company paying the ransom if it would ensure her safety.

There was no reply.

Asked on 25 May what had led police to Bungonia, Detective Sergeant Dennis Bray played the regulation straight bat, talking about following all leads and searching other properties. Asked if the man police were looking at had once worked for Crown, he intoned dutifully: 'I don't believe this has any consequence to this inquiry.'

But, in murder inquiries, the rule of thumb is that no confession and no body means no case. After days of searching, surveillance and interviews had produced neither, police were not so keen to protect the identity or feelings of the man they rather quaintly termed 'a person of interest'. They pitched tents near his house, and for five days in late May combed the property, dragged dams and went through every inch of his home and sheds.

They found two suspected stolen cars, a Jaguar reportedly worth $150,000 and a Mitsubishi Pajero. Police also allegedly found weapons, including a .44 calibre Ruger semi-automatic rifle, allegedly stolen from Mr Whelan, as well as a pistol and a prohibited crossbow.

It seemed that the jowly 44-year-old with glasses and a walrus moustache might look like a country bank manager, but he had some interesting hobbies. He became front-page news, the mystery man at the centre of the hunt for the millionaire's missing wife.

The publicity gave the task force what looked like its biggest break. That was when Sue Whitfield, a police officer at Maroubra, recognised Mr Burrell as someone local detectives had interviewed about the disappearance of Mrs Dorothy Davis almost exactly two years earlier. The odds seemed long against one man knowing two wealthy women who'd vanished.

The police turned the screw, sending dozens more searchers to comb hundreds of mineshafts and caves in rough country next to the Burrell farm. One reason was to try to find usable evidence. Another was to apply pressure.

More than three months after Kerry Whelan disappeared, little had changed. Except, perhaps, that Bruce Burrell voluntarily crossed the line that separates 'a person of interest' from a 'suspect' when he appeared on Channel Nine's tabloid current affairs show, *Sixty Minutes*.

While it's likely Mr Burrell had many thousands of good reasons to submit himself to the theatrical inquisition by Richard Carleton, it didn't look as if he was enjoying the chance to clear his name.

He confirmed that he had borrowed or 'minded' $100,000 for Dorothy Davis – but said he had paid her back in cash some time before her disappearance. There were, sadly, no witnesses to this transaction, which he admitted was 'bizarre'.

He said he was amazed about the chances of him knowing both Dorothy Davis and Kerry Whelan. 'It's freakish, he said, shrugging. That's his story and he's sticking to it.

CHAPTER 19

The stink, the fink and the missing link ...

Nazi madness

'I've got a hammer in my head, you bastard'

DANE Sweetman was a smalltime criminal and fulltime loser when he embraced the ultra-right, racist world of the neo-Nazis while serving a two-year term for armed robbery.

His love or violence was already ingrained. The skinhead bovver boy who had left school in year eight had been found guilty of attempted murder by the time he was 16 years old.

While in jail in the late 1980s Sweetman found a violent cause to match his vicious nature. In his eyes, he was no longer just another violent head case, but a political freedom fighter.

He covered himself in tattoos which included swastikas and the words 'Nazi Skinheads', 'KKK' and 'Native White Protestants Supreme'. From inside jail, Sweetman wrote to colleagues, urging them to violence and providing plans on how to build bombs.

In one letter, Sweetman told a Nazi sympathiser how a group of right-wing fanatics formed a secret organisation called 'The Guard' in Pentridge Prison in 1987. 'Give the dogs what they deserve, full on racial warfare. There is no stopping us when we've started,' he warned.

Sweetman provided detailed plans of a car bomb and how to build it. He instructed an associate that the device was 'very effective and causes major damages to the car and (could) blow it and its miserable contents to Hell!'

'I've seen them blow the entire back end off a Commodore,' he wrote.

In his rambling jail diary, *Dance of the Skin, Reflections of a Neo Nazi Skinhead*, Sweetman gives an insight into the mind of a dangerously disturbed racist.

Sweetman said that while in prison in the 1980s he developed his 'Manifesto for Racial Warfare.' He declared he wanted to kill drug users, pushers, homosexuals, doctors, teachers, police, child molesters, priests and pornographers.

'All would and will one day face the rope,' he frothed, sounding like a talk-back radio host. We recruited men within the jail and even some in blue for the purpose of information. There are many screws (prison officers) who espouse our Guard philosophy, some are Klan (Ku Klux Klan),' he wrote.

In his diary Sweetman claims to have been responsible for a secret race war carried out in the streets of Melbourne. He admitted to a series of violent crimes, including murder, arson, stabbings, bashings and street assaults. 'The day after my release (in December, 1989) we set about and thus firebombed the St Kilda Road Synagogue. The Yids were furious,' he gloated. His group returned the following day and daubed the synagogue with racist taunts and Nazi slogans before throwing more firebombs. 'We then made our petrol bombs right there on the street. It was a job well done.'

He described the people he saw around the city in these terms: 'The place was awash with yellow, black and mongrel brown faces.' He gave brutal details of his gang attacking two Asian men in the city, in which one had his throat slashed with a razor.

He wrote about attacking another man because he suspected he was a homosexual. Sweetman said he brought gloves and balaclavas at an army disposals shop in the city just for the job.

His gang wrapped the man's head in a sheet and beat his genitals with a baton. 'Before leaving, I leaped off the couch and landed my full weight on ... ribs, crushing five of them, as I later found.' (Sweetman was later convicted of the assault.)

As a payback against the man who informed police of the assault, Sweetman wrote, he built another bomb. 'I sat the bomb at the base of the front door, I lit the fuse and ran.

'Later that night we drove back to the scene. The house was a scene of utter destruction. The front door was nowhere to be seen, the veranda had a huge gaping whole in it and the brickwork surrounding the door was blackened and ruined. The paper said no-one was hurt, which was unfortunate as we wanted to see as many hurt and maimed as possible.'

He wrote proudly of attacking and kicking a young woman in the street in Fitzroy because she had an Asian boyfriend. 'Her faced washed in gore, I delivered this ... a kicking she would never forget. I would take her to the very brink of death. A few more decent kicks to the gooks and their dog of a woman race traitor and we were on our way.'

Sweetman's criminal record shows that by the time he was 22 he had been charged with sexual penetration of a male under 16, attempted murder, malicious wounding, intentionally causing serious injury, possession of a pistol, assault with a weapon, armed robbery, assault by kicking and murder.

When police arrested him as a teenager, they found the walls of his bedroom covered with posters from horror movies, and kit 'creatures' from horror movies and violent films. These alone were not a problem. The two sawn-off shotguns and the canister of cyanide were.

A policeman who wrote a report on Sweetman in the early days, noted with typical bureaucratic understatement: 'The defendant appears to be pre-occupied with violence'.

Sweetman readily admitted trying to kill another man. 'He was a race traitor and a traitor to his people,' he boasted. He said he put a gun to the victim's head, then 'pulled the trigger but it jammed. I cocked it and reloaded, pulled the trigger, but it misfired. We belted him.'

On his birthday, on 19 December, 1991, he was sentenced to 20 years with a minimum of 15 for the murder of David Noble. He expected a longer sentence. Sweetman murdered Noble with an axe at a party to celebrate Hitler's birthday on 20 April, 1990, and then cut the legs off the body before dumping the remains in Kew Boulevard.

'I took him into the darker area of the yard nearer the shed. I saw tools lying around the table near the shed. I did not need a weapon to take this drunk, but I could not let the opportunity pass without grasping it and harnessing it fully. Dave's last ever words were: "I've got a hammer in my head you bastard." I'd picked up a pick axe and swung it arch ways. It entered his head at the cerebellum. He staggered back and pulled the tool from his head. Dave lay on the ground I gave him several more smashes to the head with the blade edge of the axe. He was gargling, blood bubbles of gore erupting from his wounds. He was not yet dead so I picked up a garden edger. I stood over him, I could not turn back now. Dave was mine for the taking. I embedded the edger in his back, the second time it got stuck. I had to lever it out. White Power was in existence and we were its accelerant, its maker!'

He stunned the court when he produced a prison shiv and slammed it into the bench in front of him. 'I had a home-made knife given to me by one of my compatriots in blue for the sole purpose of murdering Sean Shilling (a police witness),' he boasted. He said he was unable to carry out the crime because Shilling did not attend. 'It was my chance to take another bastard and it slipped though my fingers.'

Sweetman is due out of jail on 8 November, 2005. He has a written hit list of eleven witnesses and police he intends to attack. 'Your day is coming,' he wrote.

But while Sweetman has vowed war against the world, mainstream prisoners have tired of his activities. For a man who says he despises homosexuality, Sweetman's predatory sexual behaviour in jail has made him an outcast. On 30 December, 1994, five of Australia's toughest prisoners went to see Sweetman. The informal committee was made up of a murderer, a major drug dealer, an armed robber and two brothers with violent criminal records.

'They told Sweetman that he was a boy raper and a dog. They said they knew he was providing sweets and canteen goods to a group of younger prisoners in return for sexual favours,' a prison source said.

'He was told he was to be put off (murdered).'

The following day he put himself into protection in Barwon prison, but seven times notes were shoved under his cell door telling him he would be killed.

In March 1995, Sweetman was moved to the protection unit in K Division in Pentridge. His fellow inmates included Paul Denyer, the

Frankston triple murderer, the multiple rapist and double killer Raymond 'Mr Stinky' Edmunds, and Hoddle street mass murderer Julian Knight. He has become particularly close to Knight.

Sweetman wrote in his diary about Nazi band *No Remorse,* and of listening to the band before bashing a man with a bottle. He has the name of another hate band, *Screwdriver,* tattooed on his neck.

The federal race discrimination commissioner, Zita Antonios, warned that people possessing imported neo-Nazi rock music could be prosecuted under racial hatred laws.

'In my view it incites violence and hatred and could incite murder,' she said. Anyone singing the lyrics or selling compact discs could be dealt with by the commission.

The warning was made after information from a Melbourne Jewish group that ultra-right organisations were promoting racist rock bands to encourage young people to embrace their philosophies.

The executive director of the B'nai B'rith Anti Defamation Commission, Danny Ben-Moshe, said a group of Australians was involved in forming the neo-Nazi band *No Remorse* in Britain. He said there was a trend in Europe to use music to recruit new members to Nazi groups. 'We believe the same methods will be used here,' he said. 'It is seen to attract disaffiliated youth to the extreme groups.'

Some of the music, which is illegal in Britain, is available in Australia through a post office box in Ashburton and through imports at some music shops.

Ben-Moshe said public anti-Semitic attacks continued to worry the Jewish community. An elderly woman out for a Sunday walk in Kew had recently accepted a newsletter thrust towards her by a young couple, he said. The Holocaust survivor looked down and read the same hate propaganda she had seen in Germany 60 years ago.

'It deeply distressed her. This is Melbourne, Australia, not Nazi Germany.' He said a hard-core minority of right-wing fanatics persisted with a terror campaign against Jews in Melbourne. 'There is an incident at least once a week, sometimes more.'

In 1996, the Jewish community organised a golf competition. When the competitors arrived at the course, they found a gang had broken in and mowed swastikas into the fairways.

The most feared man behind bars

*'I look forward to doing battle
with the Homicide Squad'*

OF the hundreds of prisoners in Victoria's jails, Gregory John 'Bluey' Brazel is considered the worst. The convicted double murderer was sentenced in effect to an extra three years in the County Court in 1994 on charges of holding a prison officer hostage.

This means that Brazel will serve at least 28 years, taking into account his murder sentences. Brazel is considered by the Office of Corrections the most dangerous man in the prison system. The court was told that Brazel held a Melbourne Remand Centre staff member hostage with a knife to his throat in November 1991.

Brazel held Gunther Krohn hostage and threatened to kill him because of a decision to transfer the prisoner from the Remand Centre to Pentridge. He surrendered after a three-hour seige.

A prisoner with 78 previous convictions, he has proved to be virtually uncontrollable in custody. He has a history of appearing to reform and returning to the mainstream prison population, only to attack staff or fellow inmates.

His prison record shows he has been involved in at least 25 violent incidents, including stabbing three prisoners in separate attacks, breaking the noses of two prison officers, assaulting police, setting fire to his cell, cutting off the tip of his left ear, going on a hunger strike, threatening to kill staff, pushing a governor's head through a plate-glass window and using jail phones to intimidate witnesses.

He has often stabbed inmates who then refuse to give evidence against him. In one of his brief periods of freedom he killed two woman near Colac.

Police believe he knew he was under investigation for the first murder and killed his second victim purely to taunt them. He was found guilty of murdering Sharon Taylor and Roslyn Hayward, whose bodies were found in shallow graves in 1990.

In his trial over the Remand Centre kidnap, Brazel handled his own defence. His legal tactics were unorthodox. In his final submission he read the jury a poem, then told them the story of Jack and the Beanstalk, and referred to the appearance of Judge Lewis in his wig and gown. 'I must say His Honor looks magnificent.'

The flattery didn't help. He was still found guilty.

Medical tests showed that Brazel had brain damage that affected his self-control. Brazel can be charming and friendly, but when he turns nasty he plays for keeps. One of his best friends in jail was standover man Mark 'Chopper' Read. In 1979 he attacked Read with a knife, stabbing him repeatedly.

Read, who complimented Brazel for the sneak attack, was taken to hospital for emergency surgery involving dozens of stitches. The next day he was found doing push-ups in the hospital with his stitches split and his intestines hanging out. He explained he was trying to get fit, ready to get his revenge against Brazel.

Brazel had a habit of ringing police in their offices for a chat and then dropping private details about the detective's family as a subtle form of intimidation.

He has a history of setting fire to his cells. Once he set his mattress on fire, but prison officers kept him in the cell until he gave in to their demands to stand away from the door. Only then did an emergency crew with breathing apparatus storm in to grab him and put out the fire.

In another incident police had to immobilise Brazel when he tried to fight them in a cell. He was overpowered but lay on the floor laughing as he was manhandled, exhorting the group to do their worst.

Brazel was born in Blacktown, a western suburb of Sydney, the son of a New South Wales detective. In 1976, while in the army medical corps, he took five privates hostage during an exercise in Healesville. He fired shots during the siege before a captain persuaded him to give up. He was dishonorably discharged.

A confidential police report on Brazel said: 'He is cunning and sly and could never be trusted.' Detective Senior Sergeant Graeme Collins, who arrested Brazel for the Taylor murder, said Brazel simply smiled and said: 'I look forward to doing battle with the Homicide Squad.'

Inside the evil mind of a mass murderer

*'He is clever and articulate and you would
never know he was a killer by talking to him'*

BALDING, slight, with a sharp wit and an engaging personality,
Alistair Farquhar MacRae hardly fits the image of a cold-blooded,
multiple murderer.

But, according to police, he is probably Australia's most prolific
killer, having been implicated in at least 20 suspicious deaths and
disappearances and convicted of four murders in two states.

He was convicted in the Supreme Court of the murder of Albert
Edwin Gerald O'Hara, shot during a drug sting in Mildura. Police are
convinced MacRae has killed nine people, and suspect that he could
have been involved in up to 15 more deaths.

'I would have to say that he would be Australia's worst known
multiple murderer and perhaps we will never know how many people
he has killed,' says Detective Senior Sergeant Paul Hollowood, of the
homicide squad.

'Sandy' MacRae made his name as a massage parlour standover
man, a briber of police, an informer and, last of all, a killer who
thought of murder as a legitimate tool of his business.

But MacRae is no crazed killer. He didn't kill for pleasure, or out of
anger, or because of some deep-seated psychological problem. He
killed to maintain his position in the underworld, or for cash.

Police still don't know how many bodies are buried at his 10-
hectare property at Merbein, near Mildura, but he joked with friends
that the small vineyard would never need fertiliser 'because there's
plenty of blood and bone out there.'

Detectives have exhumed two bodies, and believe at least one other
is buried there. The property is too big to dig up without knowing
exactly where the bodies were allegedly buried.

Police found the body of Domenic Marafiote buried under the
chicken coop in 1987. Police alleged MacRae shot and killed
Marafiote on 18 July, 1985. He lured the man to the property to buy
marijuana, but had already dug the grave.

A Supreme Court jury was told that MacRae then drove to Adelaide where he killed Marafiote's parents, Carmelo, 69, and Rosa, 70. He was allegedly desperate to find the money that Marafiote was to use for the marijuana deal. It is believed a large amount of cash was found sewn into Rosa's clothing.

Detectives say MacRae was so cold-blooded that before he buried Domenic Marafiote he repeatedly stabbed the body 'for practice'. He was sentenced to a minimum of 18 years for the killing, and pleaded guilty to the Adelaide double murder.

MacRae told friends he had killed a woman and buried her on the property, only to later exhume the remains, pulverise the bones in a concrete mixer and then pour the mix into a concrete garden roller, which has never been found.

MacRae moved to Mildura from Melbourne in 1983. He had been the second in charge to the massage parlour boss Geoffrey Lamb, who allegedly controlled a large slice of the illegal vice industry with the help of a group of corrupt police. But MacRae moved on after Lamb became addicted to heroin and began to lose control. Police say MacRae later chained the hopelessly addicted Lamb to a bungalow on the Mildura property in a bid to help his former boss beat the heroin problem.

In 1984 MacRae failed in a bid to establish a massage parlour in Mildura. He then met and befriended Albert O'Hara, who was planning to buy a houseboat-building business in the area. He convinced the 59-year-old O'Hara he could make a quick profit from buying and selling marijuana. On 21 December 1984, O'Hara came to MacRae's property with $10,000 to buy drugs.

Police said MacRae shot him in the back of the head and buried him on the property. He then used oxy welding gear to cut up the dead man's car so it could be dropped, piece by piece, at the Merbein tip.

'He was like a scavenging vulture who made sure there was nothing left after a kill,' Hollowood was to say.

After the success of the O'Hara killing, MacRae invited a massage parlour contact, Johnny Selim, to visit him at the property in early 1985. He put forward a proposition they form a local version of Murder Inc, luring people to the vineyard on the promise of buying marijuana, killing them and keeping the money.

'He always said the people he killed didn't matter as they were outside the law. To him it was all business, there was no hate involved,' Hollowood notes.

Selim declined the offer and returned to Melbourne.

Police believe MacRae killed a rival underworld standover man, Michael Ebert, who was gunned down outside a Carlton brothel in April, 1980. Ebert had bashed MacRae two weeks earlier and the beaten man had vowed revenge. The murder remains unsolved.

Police also suspect he killed his drug-addicted girlfriend, Deborah Joy Faher, 22, who was found dead of a drug overdose in a St Kilda motel in August,1981. Police believe MacRae may have given her near-pure heroin. He is also suspected of killing a prostitute known only as 'Little Lisa', in 1984.

In July, 1990, police found the remains of a woman buried in the backyard of a Kensington home that had once been owned by the mother of an underworld figure. Police believe the woman may have been an unidentified South Australian prostitute killed by MacRae.

In the early 1980s police became concerned at the number of unexplained deaths of drug-addicted prostitutes who died from overdoses. A homicide group, led by then Detective Sergeant Gary Landy, investigated about 15 of the cases. He said one of the common denominators was that the victims all knew MacRae.

'Certainly, some of them well could have been murders but there was not the evidence to justify charges,' says Landy.

Hollowood had no doubt MacRae still knew more about killings than he would admit. 'He is clever, articulate, and you would never know he was a killer by talking to him,' he said. 'He was a conman killer who talked his victims into a position where he could move on them. He was prepared to try and manipulate the system while he went on killing. He had no conscience at all.'

While MacRae was under investigation for murder he was also informing to the police anti-corruption investigation, Operation Cobra. He gave evidence that he helped in paying off police to protect Lamb's massage parlour empire in the late 1970s and early 1980s.

One of the accused police, former Senior Sergeant Paul William Higgins, was sentenced to seven years' jail last year. Higgins is bitter that a multiple murderer was largely responsible for his conviction.

While in witness protection MacRae made a bad blunder, confessing to another witness that he had killed the Marafiotes. He said that he had used a doona to try to muffle the noise. He complained that when he tried to fire one shot the hammer of the weapon caught the webbing between his thumb and forefinger.

When Victorian police checked with their Adelaide counterparts, they confirmed there was a small, unexplained, spider-web blood stain at the scene of the Marafiote murder. MacRae had unintentionally solved the mystery.

While MacRae was in Barwon prison his ex-wife was surprised when she received a phone-call from Barwon jail from him well after lock-up time.

He told her his cell had been left open and he feared he was being set up to be murdered by other inmates.

The prison governor was most surprised when he received a call from the former wife to inform him the cells were still open. It is believed prison officers found several inmates in the yard sunbaking, but no attempt was made on MacRae's life.

He was later extradited to Adelaide to stand trial on the Marafiote double murder. Faced with overwhelming evidence, he pleaded guilty. The prosecutor, Paul Rofe, QC, said MacRae should die in jail, and asked for a non-parole period of 40 to 50 years.

'This case comes into the worst category for several reasons,' Rofe said. 'On each occasion he has come before sentencing court, the words "cold-blooded", "planned" and "execution" have been used. At the end of the day the public are certainly entitled to think this man should die in prison.'

When he was about to be sentenced MacRae addressed the judge, asking to be allowed to die in jail.

'To allow me leniency is a luxury I did not extend to my victims. The only way to show my remorse is to ask the court to show the same leniency that I showed my victims — absolutely none. 'I would ask the court to give me no possible chance of release before my death in custody.'

Justice Willams of the South Australian Supreme Court gave him two life sentences and extended his non-parole period to 36 years.

The earliest he could be released is in 2023, aged 74.

Born bad

'I'm a serial killer, I've got a problem'

AN observant postal worker, an unexplained hand wound and a small crucifix combined to snare serial killer Paul Charles Denyer, who could spend the rest of his life in jail for the random killings of three women around the Melbourne bayside suburb of Frankston.

Early on Friday, 30 July, 1993, about ten key investigators met at the Frankston police station to review information they had gathered since the killings had begun seven weeks earlier. The murderer had struck twice and the nature of the wounds and the timing led police to conclude the killer would murder until he was caught.

Nothing affects a community like a serial killer. The random nature of the attacks and the lack of any logical reasons why victims are picked spawns fear, bordering on panic.

There is a psychological tendency for people to 'blame' murder victims. If a victim is a criminal, a prostitute or a brawler the public attitude is that they in some way contributed to the crime. This is a defensive mechanism, in that it moves it away from the general public. But when a serial killer is on the loose then 'good' people are at risk. The next victim could be anyone.

The nature of homicide investigations is that police must try to get a breakthrough early or the case gets harder. Police say the first 24 hours are crucial.

In this case the pressure was intense. It was not so much that a killer could get away with murder but that one mistake, an unnecessary delay, a wrong conclusion, a false lead, could cost lives.

The Chief Commissioner, Neil Comrie, made it clear. Everything takes a back seat to the investigation into a serial killer. The cases could not go unsolved.

Police had to go through thousands of pieces of information from the public. Well-meaning people provide little snippets of information which are nearly always rubbish. For the police it was like mining for gold. They had to be prepared to sift tonnes of slag to find a nugget.

Although more than 200 police had been involved in the seven-week hunt, detectives knew they were no closer to finding the killer of Elizabeth Stevens, 18, a student, on 11 June, and Debra Fream, 22, a young mother, on 8 July.

They checked criminal profiles and detailed forensic evidence which was all logged on computer together with the tips and information provided by the community. They knew that the killer would strike again — soon. The head of the investigation, Detective Senior Sergeant Rod Wilson, then of the Homicide Squad, says: 'In a case like that you are always aware that time is the enemy, but you have to try to remain objective and use the methods which have proven successful in the past.'

The detectives' fear was well founded: the killer was meticulously preparing to kill again that very day. Around the time police were meeting, 21-year-old Denyer drove a short distance from his Frankston home to Skye Road and cut three holes in a cyclone fence near a bike track near John Paul College, a local secondary school. His aim was to ambush his victim and drag her into thick scrub away from potential witnesses.

Just after midday, he drove his yellow 1974 Toyota Corona to the Langwarrin Flora and Fauna Reserve. Police noticed the car in the reserve while they were on routine patrol at 12.10 pm. He later told detectives he had stopped to top up his leaking radiator but police had seen no signs of him near the vehicle.

They later established that Denyer had drawn detailed maps of tracks of the reserve, as part of his plan to abduct a young victim. They now believe he had been stalking a school group on an excursion in the park at the time, and would have abducted and killed one of the group if he'd had the opportunity. He waited for a straggler to drop behind, but the children stayed in a bunch. Denyer had to move on. After leaving the park, he drove back to Skye Road and sat in his car.

About 2.30 pm, Vikki Collins, a postie, drove past Denyer on her motorbike. She had almost completed her daily round, when she saw a car parked in front of her that had no rear number plate.

'I went past it and, while I delivered the mail at a house, I adjusted my mirror and saw there was no front number-plate on the car,' Collins recalled. The driver appeared to be deliberately slumped down, so that he was partly concealed by the steering wheel. Collins noticed a student walking near the car towards a bike track. It has now been established that the girl was Natalie Russell, a John Paul student.

For a moment Collins considered warning the teenager about the man in the car, but she worried that she would be told to mind her own business.

Instead, she decided to ring the police. She continued on her round until she found an occupied house, from where she phoned police and gave a detailed description of the car.

Seconds after the alert postal worker had noticed the car, Denyer got out, walked to the bike track, and ambushed and killed Natalie Russell.

Within 15 minutes, two police units responded to the call. It proved the vital break in the investigation, even though it came too late to save the teenager.

When Denyer saw the 17-year-old heading to the track, which separates the Long Island Country Club from the Peninsula Country Golf Club, he positioned himself in one of his hiding spots, armed with a kitchen knife and a leather strap. As the girl passed by, he began to stalk her, ensuring he kept his 120-kilogram frame on the wet grass so his victim would not hear his footsteps.

In the attack, he accidentally hacked his own hands, slicing flesh from one finger. As he left the scene he saw police checking his car, so he left it there and returned home, keeping his blood-soaked hands in the pockets of his jeans.

When Russell's body was discovered, police computer checks showed that Denyer's car had been parked at the scene of the murder.

For the first time, police knew they had a strong lead. Further checks revealed that Denyer had been seen at the Kananook railway station car park a week earlier and that he used to live in Long Street, the street from which Elizabeth Stevens had been abducted.

Police could now place Denyer in the area where all three girls had disappeared. Investigators later learnt that, before the Russell murder, Denyer had rung Cranbourne police station, claiming to have been harassed by the Homicide Squad and wanting to know whether he was still a suspect.

At that time he had not been approached by Homicide Squad and was not on any short list. Looking back, it was the call of a worried man. Or a grossly disturbed one.

When police picked him up, at 5.28 pm, he remained cool and denied any knowledge of the killings. He gave plausible reasons for being in the areas where he had been sighted.

As question followed question, he stonewalled. Then Senior Sergeant Wilson asked him about the cuts on his hands, and he said he had hurt himself fixing the engine of his car.

The cut on his right thumb came from sharpening a knife in a scabbard, he said. He then acted out how he claimed to have done it. Both the police and Denyer seemed to realise at the same moment that the suspect had made a telling mistake.

He held the imaginary knife in his injured hand when he tried to show police how he had cut himself. It would have been impossible for him to have injured himself in the manner he claimed. He then tried to change hands to illustrate another version of how he got the injury.

It still wasn't possible.

It was then 10.19 pm. Denyer knew he had been caught. Police knew they had the right man, but they also needed more information to mount a case. Further questioning elicited further lies.

After 1511 questions, police called a halt to proceedings so they could get a pathologist to try linking Denyer's hand wounds with evidence found at the scene.

During the break, Denyer was guarded by Senior Detective Darren O'Loughlin, of Frankston. The policeman, who wore a crucifix under his business shirt, escorted Denyer to the toilet just after 12.45 Sunday morning.

Denyer professed belief in God. He had decided to confess — not to his interrogators but to the quiet policeman wearing the crucifix.

Denyer said to him: 'I see you are wearing a cross under your shirt. Are you a Christian?' O'Loughlin said he was, and Denyer said: 'Okay, I killed them, all three of them.' He was ready to tell all.

At 3.45 am he began to make a videotaped confession to homicide squad detectives, answering their questions in a matter-of-fact way. He showed little emotion or remorse as he detailed how he had abducted and killed women who were strangers to him. He said he had wanted to kill since he was 14. He had been following women since he was 17. He said he struck when it had rained or was wet, in the hope that the water would wash away blood and other evidence.

The warning signs that Denyer was evil had been present for years. His little sister's toy bear was found with its neck and torso repeatedly slashed, covered with cigarette burns and with the stuffing had been pulled out. Fangs had been scrawled on its face. At the time the little girl was five; Denyer was ten. It was just one of many examples of unexplained violence that always pointed to the overweight, brooding loner.

Two years later a little kitten was found, with its throat slashed, hanging in a tree. Again, the finger was pointed at Denyer. He denied any involvement, but a relative checked his pocket knife and found blood and flesh on the blade.

A local girl complained that she thought someone in the neighbourhood had been stalking her. Nothing came of that.

Denyer had few friends. He liked to frighten people. The psychologist would later say he had a personality disorder. In lay terms, he was a fat, apathetic, lazy bully — and increasingly weird.

He left school and had a series of jobs which he lost through disinterest or dishonesty. Being a lazy thief didn't help his employment record.

His last job was at the aluminium boat builders, Pro Marine, where his bosses found the same problem every other employer had found: he couldn't care less. He wouldn't finish even the most basic task. Asked to sweep the floors, he would wander off, leaving the job half finished. The only time he used energy was when he fashioned scrap metal into daggers. One of those was later used as a murder weapon.

Denyer taught himself how to be a killer. He struck after rain in the hope that evidence would be washed away and used his bar radiator to change the pattern on the soles of his runners so they would not match imprints left at the crime scenes.

He had loved a horror movie called *The Stepfather* and delighted in turning up the volume to frighten his sister. He later copied the murder method used in the movie.

For years he had stalked women, looking for the chance to kill. In 1992 he decided to murder the sister of a neighbour. He went to the woman's flat, but it was empty. He broke in and stabbed the woman's cat and drowned three kittens in the bath. He smeared blood on the walls and wrote 'Donna and Robin — You're dead.' The girls were shattered. A few days later Denyer turned up and commented that he would love the chance to deal with the intruder.

He told police he killed because he hated women. In his flat tones he explained how his last victim Natalie Stevens, obviously knowing from the moment she was grabbed that this man was the serial killer who had murdered two young woman, had begged and tried to negotiate for her life.

'She said disgusting things,' he told police. This from a man who delighted in humiliating, torturing and slaughtering young women.

The quirks of a random killer are hard to fathom. Denyer followed hundreds of girls for years, but left most untouched. On 8 July he attacked Roszsa Toth, 41, outside the Seaford railway station. He jumped out of the bushes and grabbed her, sticking a fake wooden gun into her side and warning her not to fight. He put his hand over her mouth and she responded by biting him and breaking free. She ran out onto the road and stopped a woman motorist for help. Denyer hid in a park, then boarded a train and returned to Kananook.

Denyer walked for hours looking for a victim. He saw Debbie Fream pull up at a Milk Bar to get some milk, eggs and a block of chocolate. She had given birth to her son, Jake, only twelve days earlier. She left the car unlocked and he slipped into the car and hid in the back seat, grabbing her she returned.

The day after his last murder police waited for him to return to his Dandenong-Frankston Road flat to question him, but at that moment he may have been preparing to grab another woman.

A group of four women had gone to the Langwarrin Shopping Centre but one, Vicki Cooper, was asleep in the car, so the other three left her snoozing in the car park. They left the car unlocked.

About 40 minutes later the group returned. Parked right next to their car was an unregistered yellow Toyota. It was Denyer's. The car park was almost empty, yet the cars were side by side.

Denyer had the bonnet of his car raised and was looking at the motor. Police said he had used that tactic when stalking a victim.

One of the women, Wendy Halemba, said she saw a man between

the two cars and recognised Denyer as a former neighbor. She greeted him, but noticed that he seemed to be behaving strangely.

One of the women on the shopping trip was Mrs Halemba's daughter, Tamara. Denyer had once asked her out and she had refused. A short time later the family disturbed a prowler in the back yard, near the bungalow where Tamara slept. They found a screwdriver near the sleepout. Then the family's chickens were found hacked to death.

Collins said that when she was dozing she felt there was someone else in the car, but assumed it was her friends returning from shopping.

Denyer, thwarted, drove home. The police were waiting. It was to be the beginning of the end.

After the long interview he was prepared to co-operate fully. He returned to the murder scenes and calmly acted out his crimes for the police video camera. He even tried to joke with stone faced detectives..

Later in a police cell he told his girlfriend, Sharon, that he was the killer. When she asked what evidence the police had to link him to the crimes, he replied: 'My hands.'

'I'm a serial killer, I've got a problem,' he said.

He was sentenced to life with no minimum, but on appeal was given a minimum of 30 years.

Denyer, the sadist, the stalker, the peeping tom, the cat killer, the man who wanted to humiliate his victims, was put in jail with hardened criminals. He spends his days in protective custody.

Mind games

'He was the complete Jekyll and Hyde character'

LATE in the afternoon of 29 June 1991, Margaret Hobbs was turning her car into Springvale Road from Burwood Highway in Melbourne's eastern suburbs when she heard the radio news: a little girl had been abducted at Rosebud.

She felt sick. 'I thought, 'It's Robert Lowe',' she recalls. 'I knew he had a unit at Rosebud. And I knew he'd been building up to it.'

Three-and-a-half years on, the shock of that moment still registered on her face as she talked about a crime that wrecked so many lives.

By the time Hobbs heard the news that day, Sheree Beasley, the six-year-old girl, was dead, her tiny body defiled and hidden in a concrete pipe. But Sheree Beasley, the case, was just beginning.

That case ended, legally, at the Supreme Court, when Robert Arthur Selby Lowe was sentenced to life in prison for kidnapping and murdering Sheree.

Margaret Hobbs had known killers, rapists and compulsive offenders of all sorts in the previous 25 years, first as a parole officer, later as a psychotherapist in private practice. But none affected her the same way as the mild-mannered, middle-aged, middle-class salesman who revealed himself to her as a secret monster.

The first time she saw Robert Lowe was in 1984, when he was 47. He had been referred by his lawyers, who wanted a report to present to Springvale Magistrate's Court. He had been charged with exposing himself to schoolgirls at Glen Waverley shopping centre.

At first, Lowe appeared to be just another client undergoing therapy for compulsive behaviour — in his case, exhibitionism.

He was placed on a good-behaviour bond for a year on the obscene exposure charge. A condition was that he go to Margaret Hobbs for therapy for that period. He did. It became another habit he found hard to break.

Lowe was always punctual, always polite. But, as Hobbs sensed, never genuine. She realised she was dealing with more than just another 'flasher'.

Lowe was, and is, a neat and well-spoken man. Tall, thin, with curling fair to grey hair (and, later, a beard), he wore fine-rimmed glasses that lent a prim, bookish look in keeping with his standing as a church elder and Sunday school teacher.

This mild exterior concealed a calculating, intelligent deviate who told Hobbs he often exposed himself to young girls, sometimes first placing pornography (invariably stolen) where they were likely to see it.

As she spoke, Hobbs sat uneasily in a blue easy chair in the pleasant room where she has heard so many unpleasant things.

'He was the complete Jekyll and Hyde character,' she begins. 'I knew the bad one, the Mr Hyde bit, that was hidden from his wife, family and friends.

'He would sit here very attentively and take copious notes but he wouldn't enter into any sort of meaningful therapy. He pretended to be in therapy but he wasn't trying. I told him it wasn't any good, that he had to be completely honest or I couldn't help him give up obsessive behaviours … but he enjoyed it too much to give it up.'

At first, Lowe admitted only one previous conviction for obscene exposure but later acknowledged being in trouble often. In fact, he had a record of sex offences spanning three decades but had dodged many convictions through his deceit. Hobbs describes him as a skilled and habitual liar who thought he could 'run rings around police'. Which he often did — until he came up against the homicide squad.

'He is clever and enjoys the excitement of jousting with police,' she said. 'He is a sophist — that is, he is a skilful arguer who will mount a clever but fallacious argument to rationalise his behaviour.

And he is a specific liar. If you ask him if he has a blue car he will say, "Certainly not". If you change the question slightly and ask him if he drives a blue car, he will say, "Yes", but point out that he doesn't own it.'

Lowe saw Hobbs intermittently after his bond expired in 1985, and often called her. He was still offending, and appeared in court for wilful and obscene exposure, offensive behaviour and theft.

It was a disturbing pattern, although not yet sinister. According to Hobbs, that changed in April, 1990, when Lowe complained to her that police had spoken to his then employer after questioning him about approaching a girl in Yarraville. Although nothing came of the incident, it rang warning bells for Hobbs because it meant he was willing to accost a child rather than just expose himself.

'When he told me he'd been spoken to by the police about the incident with the young girl at Yarraville, I got very worried,' she was to recall. 'It was an escalation. He was getting bolder and the targets were getting younger.'

Soon afterwards, he approached some girls on Flinders Street station. 'They were holding some balloons. He said something like one of the balloons looked like 'a big dick' and made a sexual suggestion.

'The girls were frightened and ran out and spoke to a traffic policeman, who tackled him. He got charged and pleaded not guilty.'

By this time, Lowe had upset Hobbs' professional detachment. 'He came and told me all this very blandly, as if it was the most natural thing in the world. I told him to leave my rooms. I opened my door and ordered him out. I refused to support a not-guilty plea.

'He said, "You can't do this to me." But he went. I was worried about this escalation.'

Lowe brought his wife Lorraine with him to see Hobbs soon after the Flinders Street incident. Lorraine Lowe was distraught and at one point demanded of her husband, 'Why don't you just stop it?' To which he had replied coolly, 'Because it gives me too much pleasure.'

At that moment, Hobbs judged, he unmasked himself. 'Lorraine went pale. She realised her husband had built a cardboard cutout life for her.'

Lowe's solicitor asked Hobbs to write a court report to verify that he had been seeking therapy. She felt the first pangs of a looming crisis. Trapped between professional obligations to a client and personal feelings about his actions, she feared what he might do.

She wrote a court report which, she says, was a warning. 'I said this man had to be shown he couldn't do this sort of thing without being punished. I meant that he should be locked up.'

But the court judged otherwise. 'He was only fined $750,' Hobbs said bleakly. 'Six months later, Sheree Beasley disappears.'

On 25 July, 26 days after Sheree's abduction, Lowe came to Hobbs's office in Fitzroy. He was, ostensibly, querying an account but was agitated and refused to leave for hours. Hobbs said: 'At 5pm I walked downstairs to my (barrister) son-in-law's office and said, "I reckon Robert Lowe took Sheree Beasley. I wonder what sort of car he's driving." There'd been publicity about the suspect driving a blue hatchback.

'I asked the office girls if they'd noticed his car. None of them had. But next day one of them told me she'd seen him drive past later ... in a blue hatchback.'

Meanwhile, the police had reached the same conclusion. The same week, Detective Senior Constable Andrew Gustke, of the Zenith taskforce set up to investigate the abduction, identified Lowe as the driver of a blue Corolla similar to the car at the crime scene. He made a routine call to Lowe — and was immediately suspicious because Lowe conjured up an instant alibi and vehemently denied being near Rosebud on 29 June.

The hunt was on. The police brought Lowe in for questioning on 13 August, and did their homework, discovering his long history of sex offences.

On 26 September, Sheree's remains were found in a pipe near the Mornington-Flinders Road at Red Hill. Soon afterwards, the homicide squad secretly approached Hobbs and placed intercepts in her rooms without her knowledge to tape Lowe's conversations with her.

It was then that a homicide sergeant, Alex Bartsch, struck up a rapport with Hobbs vital to the ultimate success of the case.

In the following months, she was to have more than 100 contacts with Lowe, in person or on the telephone. Each word was taped and transcribed into thousands of pages of what became known as the 'Fitzroy tapes'.

It was a cruel experience for the psychotherapist. A mother and grandmother herself, she had to make the crucial decision that her commitment to the community was more important than confidentiality to a client.

Lowe, by this time rejected by his wife and two sons, used his interviews with her to start a bizarre ritual of dropping clues that he was the killer. It was an extension, she said, of his exhibitionism.

'He would come in here and say, "Margaret, would you tell my wife that I didn't put this girl in the car for sexual purposes". He was an arch-teaser. A shocker. He has absolutely no remorse, no sense of culpability. It was like *Silence of the Lambs*.' The reference to the film is not fanciful. Hobbs shuddered as she relived a scene she could never blot from her mind.

'One day, after the body was found, he brought in a rucksack and a plastic bag and put them down each side of his chair. He looked at me and said, "Margaret, do you really think I could bury a child in a drain to be eaten by maggots?"

'His face was chilling. He was enjoying every minute of it. As he was speaking, I noticed something white on the back of his chair. I thought it was a piece of cotton. Then I saw it was crawling. I thought it was a caterpillar. I took a piece of paper and walked over It was a maggot. There were hundreds of them, crawling over the chair, across the floor, up the wall.

'I screamed at him, told him to get out, and to take his filthy bag with him. He took the rucksack but left the plastic bag, and that's where the maggots were coming from. I wrapped it up and ran downstairs and threw it in the bin. I didn't want to know what was in it.'

Other scenes from those nightmare months were branded into her memory. Once she steeled herself to drive around Red Hill (where Sheree's body was found) with Lowe on the pretext it would help him build a case for manslaughter rather than murder.

'As we drove, he's telling me this dreadful story of putting her in the drain face up ... I had to turn my face away so he couldn't see the tears on my cheeks.'

Then, in early May, 1992, Lowe handed Hobbs a written 'confession' admitting Sheree had died after he had abducted her, but claiming that she had accidentally choked. Shaken, she managed to copy the document and hand it to police a few days later — the same day Lowe was picked up shoplifting with the original confession in his bag.

He was finally arrested in March 1993, when police decided they had overwhelming evidence.

Afterwards, Margaret Hobbs stripped her consulting rooms to exorcise every trace of Robert Arthur Selby Lowe. She threw out the desk, couch and easy chairs, the carpet, even the pictures on the walls.

Everything but the clock. But could never rid herself of the memories. She took them to her grave. She died in a car accident in January 1996.

POLICE interest in Lowe didn't finish with his conviction. An unsolved murder, which had played on detectives' minds since 1984, had many disturbing similarities with the Beasley case.

Kylie Maybury was six when she was abducted, sexually assaulted and murdered on Melbourne Cup day, 1984. Like Sheree, Kylie was grabbed on her way to a shop. Her body was dumped in a drain in Preston.

Old murder cases are never closed, although the reality is that they are rarely solved. The Maybury case was destined to remain a tragic mystery. But during the investigation into Lowe over the Beasley case, police were able to track him back to Preston in 1984.

Shortly before Kylie Maybury was murdered, Lowe was interviewed by police over offensive behaviour involving three young girls in Preston, only one kilometre from where Kylie would later be kidnapped. He was a travelling salesman whose work often took him to the area.

He had made sexual suggestions to the girls, and a neighbour took the registration number of his car. Police did not prosecute him because of lack of corroboration. His name was not passed on to detectives working on the Maybury case.

Significantly, perhaps, Lowe first went to Margaret Hobbs weeks after the Maybury murder. Privately, she always suspected he could have been the killer of the young Preston girl. After some years he drifted away — but returned to therapy two weeks after the Beasley killing.

There were many similarities between the cases. The girls were the same age and were abducted while on errands for their mothers on a day when Lowe was not working.

Hobbs said Lowe was fascinated by pink. Kylie carried a pink strawberry shortcake bag and Sheree was dressed in pink. The bag was later recovered near Ferntree Gully Road. Lowe lived off the same main road.

More in hope than expectation, one of the original investigators, Glenn Woolfe, now a detective inspector, ordered that Kylie's clothes, which had been kept as a possible court exhibit since the murder, be tested to see if modern DNA technology could help identify the killer.

The answer came back. It could be done.

The Victorian Government had passed legislation to demand blood samples for a DNA bank from convicted sex criminals and murderers where the crime had a sexual motive. Lowe was an ideal example of the need for such legislation. This would prove, one way or the other, whether the former church elder was a double killer.

Lowe decided to fight the order. The man who said he would take a lie detector test to prove he was not a murderer became surprisingly coy about the DNA test. The Office of Public Prosecutions found a possible loophole in the law through which Lowe could wriggle. Lawyers withdrew the case.

So determined were the authorities to test Lowe's blood that the Government reworded the Act in late 1997, putting a retrospective clause in the legislation in the hope of getting the convicted killer to provide a sample.

Biding his time

Never trust a caged dingo

THE best welder in Pentridge's J-Division blotted his copybook in 1992. After six years of faultless behavior, Raymond 'Mr Stinky' Edmunds — rapist, murderer and model prisoner — made a break for it.

And the quiet man with the loud nickname came within a sniff of getting away. The official line was that he was foiled only by the keen nose of a prison dog which led officers to find him hidden in a metal cabinet on a truck moving goods from the prison industries yard where he voluntarily worked seven days a week. There were persistent rumours, however, that the authorities had information and knew exactly when and where to have a dog when Edmunds made his move.

After his attempted jailbreak Edmunds, then 48, was moved to maximum security to spend his days with a neo-Nazi, a mass killer and serial murderer. He fitted in well.

Unlike many notorious inmates, Edmunds was prepared to bide his time and wait, until his carefully-planned bid for freedom. But his aborted escape has added more headlines to one of Australia's most notorious and long-running crime stories, one that has inspired extraordinary public fascination, a best-selling book and film negotiations. For all his infamy, Edmunds is a nobody: an introspective, hard working man whose very 'ordinariness' let him get away with murder and serial rape for nearly twenty years. Profoundly average — although far from normal — the adopted farmer's son who became a peeping tom, child molester, killer and rapist is in himself of little more interest than the dingo in the Azaria Chamberlain saga.

But as with the dingo, Edmunds' acts of random violence have had a seismic effect: ruining many lives, affecting scores of others. To those people belongs the real story.

That story begins in February, 1966: the week decimal currency was introduced, Sir Robert Menzies announced his retirement from Parliament and a young batsman called Doug Walters was picked to play Test cricket.

Australia, already shocked by the Beaumont children's disappearance in Adelaide a few weeks before, was confronted by another chilling crime.

On Thursday, 10 February, two teenagers disappeared from a pop concert at Shepparton's new Civic Centre: Garry Heywood, 18, a gangly apprentice panel beater with a touch of the lair about him, and Abina Madill, 16, extroverted and only a few weeks out of school.

At first the police assumed the pair had run away, but when Garry's immaculate, dark green, FJ Holden was found in Shepparton's main street next morning, his family and friends feared the worst. They knew what the detectives didn't, that young Heywood would never willingly abandon his car. Later, police accounted for every fingerprint found on the vehicle except one found on the driver's door, a fact they kept secret for 16 years.

The Homicide Squad was called in, and the town turned out to search, but nothing was found until 16 days later, when two youths stumbled on the missing girl's half-naked body in a paddock at Murchison East, 37 kilometres south of Shepparton. Heywood's body was nearby, a bullet hole through his skull.

In the months that followed, Shepparton became a town of stares, whispers and ugly rumor. Hub of a giant orchard area, the district population swelled each summer with the annual invasion of itinerant fruit pickers.

Young, and free with their money and their fists, they flocked into town at night; looking for a good time, often finding trouble. Trouble, after the bodies were found, meant being questioned about the murders. But there were too many potential suspects, and so the investigation narrowed to a few — to Abina's former boyfriend, a young mechanic called Ian Urquhart, and his friends. Urquhart's movements on the night of the murder didn't really tally with his being the killer, but he was the only person with a motive, that of jealousy.

The investigation wrecked Urquhart's life. Bashed and hounded by a couple of rogue police, he left Shepparton and, eventually, Australia, only to be killed in a speeding sports car in Singapore on the sixth anniversary of the murders, a haunting postscript to the murder story.

Urquhart's best friend, Peter Hazelman, also left town, eventually moving to Darwin to escape gossip and unhappy memories.

Abina's friend Jan Frost and her boyfriend (later husband) Max Hart were questioned repeatedly and roughly because they had been among the last to see Abina and Garry alive. They, too, left Australia for several years and even now choose not to live in their hometown.

Inevitably, given the profusion of potential leads, police made other mistakes. Forensic experts quickly determined that a relatively rare Mossberg .22 rifle was the murder weapon. But despite a nationwide 'search', detectives failed to check all available gunshop records, which was why they did not find that a Myrtleford sports store had sold a Mossberg years before to a farmer called Edmunds, Raymond Edmunds' adoptive father.

A few months after the murder a policeman came to the Gawne family's dairy farm at Ardmona, near Shepparton. He asked to speak to a 'Raymond Edmunds'. Edmunds, who had been on the farm for two years had moved a few weeks earlier to Finley, near NSW. The policeman said he would follow it up.

He didn't. If he had, it would have saved a lot more suffering.

Meanwhile, the two faint prints from Garry Heywood's car were to sit in a drawer of the fingerprint bureau in Melbourne for 16 years.

For nearly a decade in the 1970s and early 1980s, Melbourne's eastern suburbs were terrorised by a callous attacker known to police as 'the Donvale rapist'. The man — pudgy but strong, with sandy hair, a pot belly and soft hands — preyed on shiftworkers' wives at home alone with small children. He often raped women with their children present. The most chilling thing about the rapist was that it was obvious he watched families for weeks before striking, once even hiding under the floor of a house so that he could hear their conversations.

He carried a knife, was usually barefoot and, according to a handful of his many victims, had a peculiar body odor, a fact which lead a Sunday Press sub-editor to dub him 'Mr Stinky'.

As in the Heywood-Madill case of the 1960s, police investigating the rapes got nowhere. The only clues were prints from some of the rape scenes, but these did not seem to match anything held on record … until the day in June, 1982, that a young fingerprint expert called Andy Wall recognised that the rapist's prints resembled the mystery print taken from Garry Heywood's car 16 years before.

It was a marvellous feat of forensic work. Police now knew that the Melbourne rapist was almost certainly the Shepparton killer of 1966, but they still had no idea who he was.

A taskforce was set up. Two years of painstaking detective work followed. Thousands of hours and millions of dollars later, hundreds of men had been eliminated from suspicion, but little else was achieved.

Eventually, in early 1985, the taskforce was wound up. Only then, after 19 years of evading detection, did the wanted man blunder into police hands. He was picked up for indecently exposing himself in Albury on 16 March, 1985.

Because of tougher fingerprint laws in NSW, Edmunds was routinely fingerprinted. From that moment it was only a matter of time.

When the fingerprint reached the central bureau in Sydney five days later it was instantly matched with the 'Mr Stinky' print at the top of the wanted list of unidentified prints. The case was all over bar a small formality: the arrest.

Shepparton detectives did that next day, 22 March, at the factory where Edmunds worked in the Melbourne suburb of Highett.

Edmunds was subsequently convicted of the Madill-Heywood murders and five sex attacks, but because of limits to questioning under the since-abandoned six-hour rule he was not interviewed about dozens more rapes. Tracing Edmunds's life, detectives uncovered the story of an outwardly ordinary working man who was a secret monster — a violent sexual deviant who had beaten and raped his first wife, molested his daughters, and once beat a cow with a shovel for minutes on end.

Some police still want to talk to Edmunds about unsolved crimes, but cannot while he is in jail unless he invites them to. At least, they believe, he owes it to his victims to confirm exactly which rapes he is responsible for.

It is true that Edmunds pleaded guilty to the crimes for which he was convicted. But the belief that he ever truly repented seems hollow after his escape attempt six year later.

Has the last chapter of the 'Mr Stinky' story been written?

Who knows? Edmunds has half a lifetime left to wait and watch for his next chance. Some day, when the events of 1992 are just a hazy memory and he returns to the mainstream prison on a lower security rating, he will make another move.

Never trust a caged dingo.

It's a living

*Even in jail, Lew manipulated
the system to suit himself*

NOBODY who knew Reuben Lew was surprised that when he went to jail he spent the bare minimum term there. Nor that Lew — jailed for his commanding role in the Estate Mortgage scandal — somehow inveigled his way into leaving Morwell River Prison several times in 1994 to visit relatives, a privilege that led to a prison governor being suspended.

The governor probably suffered more over the incident than Lew, which would be par for the course. For most of his 62 years, Reuben Albert Lew has left behind a trail of people who suffered because they trusted him. The list includes, by some accounts, family and friends.

Even in jail, Lew manipulated the system to suit himself, despite an incident when another prisoner hit him with an electric kettle, reputedly because Lew tried to borrow it without permission. But according to prison sources, he also put his fund-raising skills to work for a charity run by inmates for disadvantaged children.

One pleasure he missed while behind bars was seeing the Melbourne performance of Jackie Mason, the New York comedian whose appearance at the Arts Centre in 1994 pulled a capacity crowd.

The audience loved Mason's line of humour. Especially the joke where he insists that the Israeli Prime Minister really wants to give back the West Bank to the Palestinians, then shrugs and explains 'but right now he can't — it's in his wife's name.'

Had he been there that night, Reuben Lew might well have laughed long and loudly. But more than 50,000 investors — mostly retirees of modest means — who lost their money and their peace of mind in the Estate Mortgage disaster of 1990 might not see the joke.

And if they could see Reuben Lew now, they might be even less amused. Because while they got left with the mortgages, Reuben seems to have got the estate.

In his wife's name, of course. And a few others.

THE six Estate Mortgage trusts were said to have assets in 1990 worth $1 billion and its 52,400 investors, many of them elderly and using their retirement packages had deposited $640 million in the group.

Bricks and mortar has always been considered a sensible and conservative investment strategy and the Lew-controlled Estate Mortgage seemed to be the top of the pack during a booming property market.

But as the boom started to run out of steam, the repeated assurance from Estate Mortgages that was all was well began to sound a little shallow.

Over the next seven years, a story of greed, corruption and misman-agement emerged as wounded investors and angry regulators took their grievances to the courts. Reuben Lew and his son Richard were jailed in late 1993 and Burns Philp was forced to offer investors $116 million in settlement for what one legal counsel claimed was like sentries falling 'asleep while trust funds ... were spent on speculative, hazardous and imprudent property investments.' Lew was later to admit doing deals with developers that would net him a percentage of their projected profit in return for providing finance. It was discovered that a cash-strapped developer had received loans from one Estate Mortgage company to repay loans to other parts of the group.

Seven years after the funds were frozen, investors are still out of pocket and almost 1000 have died. Managers have recouped about $340 million for investors through property sales and damages claims but have had to pay $30 million in legal costs. Of the initial $640 million frozen in 1990, $300 million plus interest is still unrecovered.

A CYNIC might say Estate Mortgage's walking wounded are lucky compared with some victims of the 1980s financial orgy. At least they don't have to go to Majorca to see where the entrepreneur they trusted with their money washed up.

Reuben and Sandra Lew moved out of their luxury apartment in Maple Grove, Toorak (later occupied by Robert Sangster's son Adam), soon after the Estate Mortgage balloon went up in 1990.

After an eight-week trial in 1993, Reuben Lew and his son, Richard, were found guilty of using their positions as company officers to gain financial advantage.

After two years at Morwell River and Pentridge, Lew saw no need to do a Skase, and seek refuge overseas. He rejoined his wife at the country retreat bought partly in her name in 1989.

The Lew estate is secluded — but little more than an hour's drive from Toorak. To get there, a group of disgruntled investors, for instance, could pool their pensions, hire a coach, and head east from Melbourne.

They would pass through a succession of semi-suburban hamlets — Seville, Launching Place, Wesburn — and, finally, reach Warburton, sleepy-hollow home of the old Weetbix factory and Seventh Day Adventists.

There, just east of town at Big Pat's Creek, in a valley over-shadowed by Mount Donna Buang, the small holdings give way to a neat boundary fence lined with hundreds of young oak trees.

An avenue of 80 mature oaks stands guard over a broad, well-gravelled lane running down to a tree-lined creek. On each side are picture-postcard paddocks fenced with post and rail, against a backdrop of hills snuggled against a blue mountain range.

Hereford cattle graze in one paddock, a couple of thoroughbred weanlings in the other. It could be, bar the gum trees along the creek, a scene from a millionaire's stud farm anywhere from Kentucky to Kent. Or, to be technical, a stud farm occupied by someone who still seems to live like a millionaire.

The view across the Lew estate is stunning. The place looks a million dollars, and no wonder: it's cost that and more, so far. On a clear day you might imagine you can sue forever.

But anybody who did sue shouldn't count on winning. When Reuben Lew declared himself bankrupt in 1994, he listed his worldly assets as a watch and cufflinks worth $150. Jackie Mason would love that.

Fortunately, Lew married well. Just as Alan Bond's family has come into money just in time to succour him in troubled times, Lew has been blessed with a spouse and business associates who keep him in something like the style he became accustomed to as a high-flying financier.

Such as where he lives.

The house that Sandra Lew built can't be seen from the main road. Nor from the tree-lined drive, even if a curious traveller follows it all the way to the creek, where 'Private, keep out' signs are posted on an electric fence.

The house can only be reached from a double-gated entrance opening off a dead-end road that most people would mistake as a private driveway. Intentionally or not, as hideaways go, it's as shrewdly sited as any European hunting lodge for the seriously rich and famous, wary of the long lens and the possibility of assassination attempts.

But there's more to the Lew house than the difficulty of seeing it. There are, according to locals, four generous bedrooms, the main with an en suite bathroom and walk-in wardrobes. It is solid brick, probably 50 squares in size, has expensive timber floors and open fireplaces and is reputed by local tradesmen to have cost more than $1 million to build.

But the most interesting thing about the house is when it was built. Wreckers demolished the perfectly-sound homestead that was on the site in 1990, and a small army of tradesmen started work on the new one immediately ... just as the Estate Mortgage empire crashed, burning more than 50,000 investors and most of a billion dollars.

A title search reveals Sandra Lew's name on only one small 18-hectare lot, which is one of the front paddocks. Another 98 hectares is registered in the name of Pindanon Pty Ltd. But it is well known in the district that there are several other titles that add up to more than twice that amount of land.

One well-placed source says the titles to the property are 'like a doughnut', with Sandra Lew's small central holding surrounded by others, most of which are — or were — nominally owned by a Hong Kong-based accountant.

To this end, farm 'reports' have been regularly drafted by Lew's staff to send to Hong Kong, and cheques for work done have at times been routed from Hong Kong.

Once, when he was flying high, Lew impressed people as charismatic, clever, charming, confident and cool. But that was $600 million and almost a decade ago. These days he is uncharacteristically shy.

He seems to have tried hard to vanish from view. Not only is his telephone number unlisted, but his address is not listed on the electoral roll.

The Lews drive a standard Ford sedan and a four-wheel-drive that show little sign of conspicuous consumption while they are in public. Once off the estate, they keep a very low profile, indeed.

At his trial, Reuben Lew's lawyer told the court his client was deeply remorseful for his conduct. The son of a grocer, he had risen from being a dairy farmer to the heights of big business without the privileges of white-collar offenders who normally appeared before the court.

John Walker, QC, told the judge that Lew's only remaining asset then was a mortgaged dairy farm and he and his wife were 'virtually destitute'.

Four years later, behind the tall iron gates and stone fence surrounding their estate, life goes on, and in some style.

Last week, balloons were tied to the gatepost after a family party.

This is one sign that a handful of friends and relatives are regular visitors. Some are known to share the Lews's enthusiasm for breeding and racing thoroughbred horses, and several have been regular faces at yearling and broodmare sales.

But the inner circle is small, these days. Not everyone who knew the Lews still associates with them.

One former business associate says Estate Mortgage hurt more than the small unit-holders who invested with it. Reuben Lew persuaded several people who considered themselves to be his friends to invest heavily in his companies. More than one family lost millions, and they have not forgiven him. Apart from personal losses they are also angry that he has brought disrepute to the overwhelmingly law-abiding Jewish business community.

Another associate describes Lew as 'the most charismatic person I ever met. I watched him dealing with (a bank) and it was mesmerising. He was a beautiful con man.'

These days, says the former associate bitterly, Lew's closest friends are probably his guard dogs, a pair of savage german shepherds he calls Topaz and Brahms. 'He calls them his children.'